Reaching the Goal
How Managers Improve a Services Business Using Goldratt's Theory of Constraints

by John Arthur Ricketts

ISBN: 0-13-233312-0

"Excellent writing…a beautiful piece of work. I consider it one of the best books on TOC to have emerged from outside my organization. In fact, I am so impressed that I've asked John Ricketts to be my coauthor for a series of books I plan to write on the concept of ever-flourishing companies."
—Eliyahu M. Goldratt, author of *The Goal* and founder of the Theory of Constraints (TOC)

Ricketts draws on Eli Goldratt's Theory of Constraints (TOC), one of this generation's most successful management methodologies…thoroughly adapting it to the needs of today's professional, scientific, and technical services businesses. He reveals how to identify the surprising constraints that limit your organization's performance, execute more effectively within those constraints, and then loosen or even eliminate them.

Eating the IT Elephant
Moving from Greenfield Development to Brownfield

by Richard Hopkins and Kevin Jenkins

ISBN: 0-13-713012-0

Most conventional approaches to IT development assume you're building entirely new systems. Today, Greenfield development is a rarity. Nearly every project exists in the context of existing, complex system landscapes—often poorly documented and poorly understood. Now, two of IBM's most experienced senior architects offer a new approach that is fully optimized for the unique realities of Brownfield development.

Richard Hopkins and Kevin Jenkins explain why accumulated business and IT complexity is the root cause of large-scale project failure and show how to overcome that complexity "one bite of the elephant at a time." You'll learn how to manage every phase of the Brownfield project, leveraging breakthrough collaboration, communication, and visualization tools—including Web 2.0, semantic software engineering, model-driven development and architecture, and even virtual worlds.

 Listen to the author's podcast at: ibmpressbooks.com/podcasts

Related Books of Interest

The Greening of IT
How Companies Can Make a Difference for the Environment

By John Lamb
ISBN: 0-13-715083-0

Drawing on leading-edge experience, John Lamb helps you realistically assess the business case for green IT, set priorities, and overcome internal and external challenges to make it work. He offers proven solutions for issues ranging from organization obstacles to executive motivation and discusses crucial issues ranging from utility rate incentives to metrics. Along the way, you'll discover energy-saving opportunities—from virtualization and consolidation to cloud and grid computing—and solutions that will improve business flexibility as they reduce environmental impact.

Lamb presents case studies, checklists, and more—all the practical guidance you need to drive maximum bottom-line value from your green IT initiative.

Implementing ITIL Change and Release Management

by Larry Klosterboer
ISBN: 0-13-815041-9

For the first time, there's a comprehensive best-practice guide to succeeding with two of the most crucial and challenging parts of ITIL: change and release management.

Leading IBM ITIL expert and author Larry Klosterboer shares solid expertise gained from real implementations across multiple industries. He helps you decide where to invest, avoid ITIL pitfalls, and build successful, long-term processes that deliver real return on investment. You'll find detailed guidance on each process, integrated into a comprehensive roadmap for planning, implementation, and operation—a roadmap available nowhere else.

Listen to the author's podcast at:
ibmpressbooks.com/podcasts

Related Books of Interest

Intelligent Mentoring
How IBM Creates Value through People, Knowledge, and Relationships

by Audrey J. Murrell, Sheila Forte-Trammell, and Diana A. Bing

ISBN: 0-13-713084-8

For today's enterprises, few challenges are as daunting as preparing tomorrow's leaders. Mentoring is one of the most powerful tools at their disposal. But not all mentoring programs are equally effective, and not all companies have learned how to sustain mentoring. One company has: IBM. *Intelligent Mentoring* reveals how IBM has done it—and offers specific guidance and best practices you can use to achieve equally powerful results. *Intelligent Mentoring* shows how IBM has fully integrated a diverse portfolio of formal mentoring initiatives into both talent development and innovation promotion. Whether you're a business leader, strategist, Chief Learning Officer, training specialist, coach, or consultant, this book presents a state-of-the-art framework for making mentoring work. Drawing on IBM's experience, the authors demonstrate how to build a diverse portfolio of effective mentoring programs... use mentoring to strengthen organizational intelligence...build sustainable communities of mentors and mentees...promote collaboration across differences... and above all, link mentoring to strategy and use it to sustain competitive advantage.

The Social Factor
Azua
ISBN: 0-13-701890-8

Can Two Rights Make a Wrong?
Reger
ISBN: 0-13-173294-3

RFID Sourcebook
Lahiri
ISBN: 0-13-185137-3

Mining the Talk
Spangler, Kreulen
ISBN: 0-13-233953-6

The New Language of Business
Carter
ISBN: 0-13-195654-X

SOA Governance
Brown, Laird, Gee, Mitra
ISBN: 0-13-714746-5

Service-Oriented Architecture (SOA) Compass
Bieberstein, Bose, Fiammante, Jones, Shah
ISBN: 0-13-187002-5

The Business of IT

The Business of IT
How to Improve Service and Lower Costs

Robert Ryan and
Tim Raducha-Grace

IBM Press
Pearson plc

Upper Saddle River, NJ • Boston • Indianapolis • San Francisco
New York • Toronto • Montreal • London • Munich • Paris • Madrid
Cape Town • Sydney • Tokyo • Singapore • Mexico City

ibmpressbooks.com

IBM Press Program Managers: Steven M. Stansel, Ellice Uffer

Cover design: IBM Corporation

Associate Publisher: Greg Wiegand

Marketing Manager: Kourtnaye Sturgeon

Acquisitions Editor: Katherine Bull

Publicist: Heather Fox

Development Editor: Ginny Bess Munroe

Managing Editor: Kristy Hart

Designer: Alan Clements

Project Editors: Jovana San Nicolas-Shirley and Julie Anderson

Copy Editor: Keith Cline

Indexer: Lisa Stumpf

Compositor: Jake McFarland

Proofreader: Williams Woods Publishing Services

Manufacturing Buyer: Dan Uhrig

Published by Pearson plc

Publishing as IBM Press

Library of Congress Cataloging-in-Publication Data
Ryan, Robert.
  The business of IT : how to improve service and lower costs / Robert Ryan and Tim Raducha-Grace.
      p. cm.
  ISBN 978-0-13-700061-6 (pbk. : alk. paper) 1. High technology industries—Management. 2. Success in business. I. Raducha-Grace, Tim. II. Title.
  HD62.37.R928 2009
  004.068—dc22

                          2009020220

           Pearson Education, Inc.
           Rights and Contracts Department
           501 Boylston Street, Suite 900
           Boston, MA 02116
           Fax (617) 671-3447

ISBN-13: 978-0-13-700061-6
ISBN-10: 0-13-700061-8
Text printed in the United States on recycled paper at R.R. Donnelley in Crawfordsville, Indiana.
First printing September 2009

To Caren, the love of my life

—Robert Ryan

To Kate and Elsa

—Tim Raducha-Grace

Contents

Preface

The Information Technology (IT) industry has undergone an amazing transformation from the introduction of mainframe computers to the current networked, high-speed IT environment. Technology has provided, and continues to provide, tremendous innovation that has enabled breakthrough changes in multiple industries over the past 30 years. However, while IT has evolved to a high level of technological maturity, IT organizations have been slower to adopt business practices, such as customer-aligned organizational designs, standardized business processes, systemic financial management, meaningful performance measures, and effective and continuous improvement initiatives.

A cause of this lack of business focus is that most resources in IT organizations are devoted to maintaining a technical environment, without sufficient customer or business focus. A number of recent industry studies, and our interviews with chief information officers (CIOs), indicate that a majority of IT resources go to maintaining existing IT infrastructure, and only a small portion of IT resources are committed to improving business practices and developing new IT services that align with the customer. Our work with a number of clients also indicates a focus for IT organizations on maintaining the existing infrastructure and a lack of focus on new, emerging technologies and solutions for their customers.

This book provides a practical guide on how IT organizations can filter through the vast array of competing alternatives to adopt, mature, and institutionalize standard business practices in their daily operations. Through these business practices, organizations can move to a greater focus on the customer while maintaining an effective IT infrastructure.

These practices enable a higher quality of service at lower costs. Implementation of standard business practices also helps reduce the frustrations of the customer, the operational and business units, and the IT organization. The application of standards results in realistic expectations for IT products and services. This book helps both internal customers and IT organizations understand the challenges the other group faces by showing how those groups can work together in a collaborative, effective model to enable the desired outcomes needed to achieve strategic goals.

We recognize the challenge of developing a practical guide that can help IT organizations more rigorously adopt standard business practices. We acknowledge that government, business, and nonprofit organizations come in a vast array of sizes, shapes, missions, values, and geographic alignments that impact how each individual organization will adopt standardized business practices. To address this challenge, this book culls lessons learned from management efforts across a number of organizations to help you achieve four primary goals:

- Apply business practices in IT organizations to optimize an IT budget and improve return on investment (ROI) from IT spending
- Improve customer satisfaction in operational and business units with the IT products and services available and provided to them
- Address the frustrations of IT organizations that result from numerous customer requests that are often outside of the scope of standard IT products and services
- Create more realistic expectations in the operational and business units in order to answer the following:
  - What IT products and services can be provided?
  - How are IT products and services priced and charged?
  - What are the expected performance levels?
  - What are the timelines and budgets?

With these goals in mind, this book is written primarily for three groups:

- The IT executives and managers in government, business, and nonprofit organizations who provide IT products and services to the operational and business units within their organizations

- The operational, or business, unit executives and managers in government, business, and nonprofit organizations who need quality IT products and services to run their operations, and primarily rely on their organization's internal IT organization to obtain these products and services

- Senior executives and board of directors in government, business, and nonprofit organizations who need an IT operation that enables operational and business units to work together to execute the strategy of the organization

IT organizations have been perceived as being focused on technology development and evolution, rather than being aligned to the business or operational units that they support. Although this perception may be unfair, IT organizations must continue to develop in their staff, from the CIO to the help desk employee, a full set of business skills. Culture is one of the hardest elements of an IT organization to change, and this type of change requires a committed, supported change management framework to be successful and sustainable.

This book is divided into nine chapters. It begins with the areas receiving the greatest current focus—best practice process frameworks, ITIL® adoptions, financial management, improved use of business cases—and then covers topics that will become focus areas in the future, including IT performance management and IT organizational alignment to their business users.

Chapter 1: Introduction: Improving Service and Lowering Costs IT organizations today must provide high-quality innovative products and services, maintain the existing IT infrastructure, *and* lower costs. This chapter introduces the four specific areas of business practices that can help organizations achieve this goal—defining IT services, managing their cost and value, and measuring their performance with a goal of improving service and lowering cost. Through these business practices, IT organizations can transform from cost centers that focus their resources on maintaining existing infrastructure to business partners that contribute to the organization's mission by aligning their investments in IT services.

Chapter 2: IT Service Lifecycle: Improving Business Performance The IT industry seeks to improve service while lowering costs. To do so, many IT organizations have adopted industry-accepted best practice frameworks to improve performance using IT service management (ITSM), including ITIL, the de facto ITSM best practice. Although improving business practices is important through the IT service lifecycle, this chapter focuses on identifying a number of specific ITIL practices, specifically elements of Service Strategy, Service Design, and Continual Service Improvement, which are critical to business management. We focus on these components of ITIL because they have the strongest ties to business discipline as opposed to technological enhancements or refinement within Service Transition and Service Operation.

Chapter 3: Adopting IT Service Management Using ITIL   Many IT organizations struggle with how to adopt all, or a part, of the ITIL framework. This chapter provides a planned and systematic change management approach to implementing ITIL based on real-world experience.

Chapter 4: IT Financial Management: The Business of IT Financial management of IT resources is vital to improving service while lowering costs. As this chapter explains, IT financial management includes overseeing and assessing the efficacy of current IT expenditures and planning for future investments based on the services your IT organization provides. After reviewing the foundational financial management activities of budgeting, accounting, and charging, this chapter then discusses some of the more advanced—and effective—financial management activities to improve service and lower costs.

Chapter 5: IT Business Cases: Realizing IT Value   IT organizations must determine whether investments in IT projects/services are paying off. If they are, these projects/services will clearly support the overall strategy and mission of the organization and be aligned with its services. IT organizations should use a standardized business case to determine the overall benefit of investments. A business case is a rigorous, standardized method to capture the benefits, costs, and risks associated with IT investments.

Chapter 6: IT Performance Management: Defining Success More and more IT organizations are developing performance management frameworks. However, not all those frameworks align IT performance measurements to organizational strategy and related metrics. This chapter explains what performance management is and why it should be a critical, ongoing activity for your IT organization.

Chapter 7: IT Business Skills: Enabling Customer Outcomes Effective IT business skills are critical to helping an organization achieve its goals and maximize the return from IT investments. This chapter explains how IT business skills contribute to these goals. The chapter then discusses how you can determine whether your IT organization has these required business skills. Then, the chapter covers how to address any gaps that may exist in your existing business skill sets.

Chapter 8: Success Stories: Improving Service and Lowering Costs IT organizations exist in a wide array of sizes, shapes, and focus areas. Several IT organizations, across the commercial, government, and nonprofit sectors, are successfully executing a number of the concepts in this book to improve their services while lowering costs. This chapter shares a few of these success stories.

Chapter 9: Going Forward Executing the concepts presented in this book will result in improved service and lower costs for your IT organization. Business discipline infused into IT organizations will result in IT organizations being able to move from the current daily focus of maintaining current applications and infrastructure to high-value activities. As your IT organization continues to evolve, it will drive top-line revenue growth, look forward and implement emerging technology, and better align IT operations to your organization's overall strategy and mission.

Acknowledgments

We want to thank the community of professionals who supported the writing of this book. Collectively, you gave freely of your time and expertise to make this a truly useful guide for companies, government agencies, and nonprofit organizations.

We especially want to thank Tim Blythe and Kevin Creed, who reviewed our initial book proposal and provided a wealth of feedback and encouragement throughout this project. We also want to thank the subject matter experts who reviewed our chapters and provided invaluable feedback. Linda Boyd, IBM® Global Technology Services; John Kamensky, IBM Center for the Business of Government; Bill Powell, IBM Global Technology Services; Sharon Taylor, ITIL V3 chief architect and president, the Aspect Group; Lynne Johnson and Ryan Smalley, IBM Global Business Services; Shari Hower, IBM Global Business Services; and Ian M. Swift of Qinetiq North America for their time and dedication to this project.

We are grateful to those who were interviewed for this book. We would like to thank Rob Carey, Department of the Navy CIO; Mykolas Rambus, Forbes Media CIO; Jim Haughwout, Neighborhood America CIO; Neil Miller, director, NETWARCOM CARS TF, and Charlie Kiriakou, CARS deputy director and security chief, NETWARCOM CARS TF; Greg Smith, World Wildlife Fund CIO and author of *Straight to the Top: Becoming a World Class CIO* (John Wiley & Sons, April 2006). The IBM Navy Account Team: Bob Reeve; Bill Timme, Rear Admiral, USN Ret; Jimmy Norcross, Chuck Dixon, Jim Garban, and Chris Lyons, who enabled the tremendous access to the U.S. Navy IT community, and for their overall support of this effort.

We also want to thank the leadership of our respective practices at IBM: Global Business Services (GBS), Strategy & Change (S&C) Public Sector practice, and the System and Technology Group (STG) Lab Services and Training. Toni Yowell, Quimby Kaizer, Emily Grogan-Craig, and Diane Knaut provided a wealth of support for this project from inception to production. We are indebted to the STG Lab Services and Training for their thought leadership, support, and encouragement, which was critical to making this book happen. We especially want to thank Tim Blythe, Leah Ann Seifert and Mike Kuhn for their support and thought leadership.

Bob would like to thank his beloved wife, Caren, who sacrificed during the many months that went into the creation of this book. And he wants to tell her that she is the most compelling woman it has been his great fortune to love. A woman who is a successful entrepreneur, businessperson, and is a beautiful, smart, fun, and generous spirit who has always been there for him. Thank you is not nearly enough.

Bob also wants to thank his children—Kelly, Robert, and Faith. Thank you for being such a never-ending source of joy in my life. I cannot imagine having ever having lived without each of you. I would also like to thank my parents, Robert and Eleanor, for having been so patient with helping me grow over the years. Mom, I am sorry you are not here to see this. Your son may have turned out just fine with your and Dad's enduring support.

Tim would like to thank Kate, for listening to countless ideas, frustrations, and challenges, and for her encouragement and feedback throughout this process. Kate's ideas, encouragement, and occasional smart aleck remark not only improved the quality of this book, but also made Tim's day countless times.

Tim would also like to thank his parents, John Grace and Joan Raducha, for their encouragement to start, continue, and complete this book. He would also like to thank Professor Emil Kreider, whose teachings in economics and business started me down this path, and to whom I will always be grateful.

Finally, an extra special thanks to our development editor Ginny Munroe, acquisitions editor Katherine Bull, and project editor Julie Anderson. Ginny's support, feedback, and guidance were invaluable to continuously improving the text. Katherine's direction and oversight made the entire road smooth to completion. Julie's efforts to bring this project to completion were also most helpful.

About the Authors

Robert Ryan is a senior practitioner in the IBM Global Business Services, Strategy & Change consulting practice. He has spent the past 25 years consulting to government and commercial organizations supporting change initiatives. He advises clients on strategic planning, culture transformation, balanced scorecard development and implementation, program/project management, process reengineering and process improvement, performance management communications/outreach, and facilitation. He is ITIL certified, and is focused on applying business discipline through practical solutions in IT organizations.

Mr. Ryan has provided services to the Department of Defense; the United States Navy, Marine Corps, Air Force, and the Defense Logistics Agency; a mix of federal civilian agencies; state governments; electric utilities, oil, nuclear power, coal mining; and financial institutions. He has supported all aspects of large-scale change initiatives, and has managed consulting engagements ranging from large-scale change initiatives, to small, limited-scope engagements. He has a Master of Business Administration (MBA) degree in finance from the University of Maryland, and a Bachelor of Accountancy (B.A.) degree from George Washington University. He is also a Certified Public Accountant (inactive license), and has spoken at a number of professional conferences on a range of consulting topics.

Tim Raducha-Grace is a managing consultant within IBM Systems and Technology Group's Lab Services and Training Consulting Practice. He advises government, commercial, and nonprofit organizations on the business value of IT investments and how to leverage these investments to achieve business objectives. He is ITIL certified and helps clients to improve service levels through following ITSM best practices, including ITIL. He also helps clients improve their financial performance through business cases, IT charging processes, and other financial tools to measure the business value of IT.

Mr. Raducha-Grace previously served as associate director of New York University's Center for Catastrophe Preparedness, where he led interdisciplinary research efforts on crisis management and disaster recovery. He also served as a policy advisor to Senator Susan M. Collins, the chairwoman of the Senate Governmental Affairs and Homeland Security Committee, for a range of issues, including science and technology programs, first responders, and government efficiency. He has an MBA degree in finance and marketing from the New York University (NYU) Stern School of Business and a Bachelor degree in Asian studies and political science from Beloit College. He also studied at Waseda University in Tokyo, Japan.

I

Introduction: Improving Service and Lowering Costs

Customers are increasingly demanding that their IT service providers, whether internal or external, demonstrate measurable value for the amount invested in IT. IT provides customers with many innovative technologies, but the benefits from IT spending have been difficult to quantify. Indeed, several studies have shown that these investments in new IT infrastructure and technology have not provided benefits commensurate with their costs. To demonstrate the value IT spending, IT customers want spending to target specific business needs at lower costs.[1]

For some business, government, and non-profit organizations, the perceived lack of measurable value from IT investments results from the IT service provider's ineffective business practices. Business practices include the methods, processes, procedures, and rules followed by an organization to achieve its objectives. Many IT organizations have developed, defined, and implemented operational business practices, such as change management, configuration management, and availability management, to support management of their IT technical infrastructure. By adopting business practices that enforce business discipline, IT organizations can improve service levels through more efficient use of resources.

This book focuses on four specific areas of business practices related to defining IT services, managing their cost and value, and measuring their performance with a goal of improving service and lowering cost:

- **IT service management (ITSM):** IT organizations need to further adopt and refine their business practices to align with their customers and contribute to business objectives. IT organizations have increasingly adopted a number of leading industry frameworks and best practices to improve service management across the lifecycle of a given service. Chapter 2, "IT Service Lifecycle: Improving Business Performance," introduces the ITIL framework, which is a leading practice framework that adopts a service lifecycle view toward ITSM. We focus on how to use elements ITIL's of Service Strategy, Service Design, and Continual Service Improvement to realize benefits from your IT investments by improving service and lowering costs. While ITSM must be looked at as a full lifecycle of support to customers, we concentrate on these stages of the ITSM lifecycle because they have the strongest ties to business discipline, as opposed to the technological business practices within the Service Transition and Service Operation stages. Chapter 3, "Adopting IT Service Management Using ITIL," then focuses on a change management approach to implementing ITIL.

- **IT financial management:** IT organizations need to measure their spending and how it aligns to customer needs, IT services, and business objectives. This financial management helps IT organizations provide services that meet customer expectations, on time, on budget, and at a perceived reasonable cost. Chapter 4, "IT Financial Management: The Business of IT," broadly discusses some of the critical building blocks of IT financial management (accounting, budgeting, and cost) and some more advanced topics (such as service valuation and demand modeling). Chapter 5, "IT Business Cases: Realizing IT Value," builds on this foundation and reviews business case analysis (BCA) and portfolio management, which are powerful tools, when properly developed and applied, to help IT organizations make better financial decisions.

- **IT performance management:** IT organizations need to develop, implement, and use on a continuous basis performance measures for their business practices. Many IT organizations have well-defined performance measures that relate to execution of the technical infrastructure (i.e., system uptime) and application development (i.e., lines of code), but they need to evolve their measurement of business practices to align with key business objectives. As discussed in detail in Chapter 6, "IT Performance Management: Defining Success," a rigorous, targeted set of performance measures will provide an IT organization the information needed to make better business decisions.

- **Customer alignment and enablement:** Customers want their IT service providers to enable outcomes that facilitate their business or operational solutions. Chapter 7, "IT Business Skills: Enabling Customer Outcomes," discusses IT alignment to customers via the leveraging of critical knowledge, skills, and abilities (either in-house or via partners and suppliers).

Although these four specific areas are listed here separately, substantial overlap exists among them. For example, ITSM is driven by available funding and organizational resources. ITSM is continually improved through the ongoing use of a defined performance management framework adhered to by skilled managers and staff who are creating outcomes desired by customers.

To optimize IT spending and improve customer focus, organizations are increasingly trying to make sure that IT services and technologies are on time, within budget, and of measurable value to the business unit. To generate a higher return on investment from IT investments, many organizations are seeking improved service at a lower cost.

IT organizations have available a range of tools and techniques to realize value from IT investments. Hardware and software vendors make available multiple alternative solutions, and rapidly evolve new solutions to automate strategic and operational IT functions. Many IT organizations undertake one-time projects, such as server or application consolidation, to both lower costs and speed up the provisioning of a given service. IT organizations are also increasingly focused on developing or acquiring new skills and abilities needed to deliver current and evolving solutions.

Many IT organizations are implementing elements of one or more ITSM frameworks. The de facto international ITSM best practice framework is ITIL, which is a nonproprietary U.K. government framework. It provides a framework for managing IT services and focuses on the continual measurement and improvement of the quality of IT service delivered from both a business and a customer perspective. Two major revisions to

ITIL have occurred over its 20-year history, the most recent in 2007, which introduced the ITIL service lifecycle (contained in five core books, an introduction, and related complementary guidance).[2]

Although ITIL is deservedly getting much of the attention for ITSM best practices to improve service and lower cost, it is only part of the solution to improve IT business practices. The development of IT business skills, the creation and use of business cases, and the implementation of rigorous performance management frameworks also help to deliver benefits from IT investments as measured by improved service and lower cost.

This book explores how you can integrate these business practices with ITSM best practices such as ITIL to realize value from your IT investments. By improving these business practices, IT organizations can improve service (by focusing on the customer) and can minimize costs (and thus direct resources to where they can generate a higher return).

How Business Practices Improve Service and Lower Cost

All organizations face a common challenge when attempting to improve IT business practices: where to start. All organizations are different, and these differences influence how each organization should adopt standard business practices. IT organizations have limited resources. Therefore, improvement projects should not be undertaken unless they are projected to provide a measurable return (return on investment [ROI]) that exceeds a minimum rate defined by each IT organization.

DEFINITIONS

A discussion about how to improve your IT service levels, while containing and ultimately lowering costs, requires a common understanding of several critical terms. The following are some common definitions of key terms we use throughout this book:

Customer: The *customer* is any internal or external purchaser or user of IT services. For example, internal customers may include organizations that use IT services, such as business units or operating units. At the same time, they may be external customers, such as business partners or direct customers of services. For example, a financial services organization that sells products to other businesses may include those businesses as IT customers because the IT infrastructure is critical to selling these products.

Service: A means of delivering value to customers by facilitating outcomes customers want to achieve without the ownership of specific costs and risks. (ITIL)

IT processes: A process is a set of activities with defined inputs that produces a specific outcome to an IT organization.

This book focuses on these IT processes: defining customers, reassessing customers' desired outcomes, delivering outcomes considered valuable to the customer, and optimizing organizational resources in the delivery of services.

Business objectives: A strategic goal/direction that is critical to the overall success of your organization, such as increasing shareholder value, increasing sales, or reducing costs.

IT Organization: An IT organization is an IT service provider that may be internal to an organization or external entity.

For each of the four business practice focus areas of this book—ITSM, IT financial management, IT performance management, and customer alignment and enablement—we have selected specific methods, processes, procedures, and roles that an IT organization can adopt to quickly achieve measurable benefits. We also share a number of success stories in Chapter 8, "Success Stories: Improving Service and Lowering Costs," and discuss how these IT organizations are able to successfully execute the concepts presented in this book. In Chapter 9, "Going Forward," we also summarize an approach to identify key areas for improvement that are immediately available to many IT organizations, and how to align your business practice improvement initiative with these goals.

The following section summarizes common frustrations related to service and cost that many IT organizations and their customers face. We then highlight key focus areas that we will revisit in Chapter 9 to help you develop your improvement initiative.

Improve Service

For an IT organization to provide the outcomes desired by its customers, it must align its products and services to the business, organization, or government it serves. The ultimate measure of the success and viability of any IT organization is the ability to optimally align to customer needs and expectations, and deliver a customer outcome at a price, time, and quality that satisfies, and eventually delights, the customers.

IT organizations with few standard business practices create challenges for both customers and themselves. Standard business practices provide a basis for repeatable, measurable processes that highlight opportunities for further efficiencies and improvements. High-performance IT organizations use standard practices to help stabilize, predict, and manage the development, delivery, and ongoing support for IT products and services. A consistent, high-quality customer experience results in loyal customers who will continue to select an IT organization as a preferred service provider.

IT organizations must continue to adopt, mature, and institutionalize leading business practices to address the following common complaints about IT products and services from the operational and business units. Table 1-1 lists common complaints about IT products and services from customers, mitigation techniques, and where in this book you can find more information about these practices.

Table 1-1   Common Customer Complaints About IT Service Levels and Mitigation Strategies

Complaint	How to Mitigate	For More Information, See
Reliability: Services are down frequently (e.g., email, hosting, application development, and network).	Specify and enforce service level agreements (SLAs) that define reliability/system uptime. Manage demand to minimize system demand. Create reliability performance measures for an IT scorecard and use that to manage.	Chapter 2 – IT Service Lifecycle Chapter 6 – IT Performance Management
Service level: The performance measures defined in our SLAs are not met.	Define service levels and expectations through SLAs. Measure service levels through performance management.	Chapter 2 – IT Service Lifecycle Chapter 6 – IT Performance Management

Table 1-1 Common Customer Complaints About IT Service Levels and Mitigation Strategies

Complaint	How to Mitigate	For More Information, See
Cost overruns: Development of new applications always runs over budget.	Cost infrastructure is in place to capture costs and avoid overruns. Business case defines planned costs and compares to actual results. New application development has defined performance measures.	Chapter 4 – IT Financial Management Chapter 5 – IT Business Cases Chapter 6 – IT Performance Management
Schedule overruns: Development of new applications always runs behind schedule.	Business case defines the schedule and key milestones, and measures achievement of milestones.	Chapter 5 – IT Business Cases
Incorrect functionality: My new application has functionality that does not solve a problem for my business unit.	Customer alignment prevents end users from receiving incorrect functionality for business use.	Chapter 3 – Adopting IT Service Management Using ITIL Chapter 6 – IT Performance Management

Many IT organizations without standard business practices have these common problems and suffer from poor customer perception. Customers view IT services as not delivering sufficient business value for the price. This book will help you improve business practices to run your IT organization in a way that meets customer demands and helps your customer understand what they receive and what they have to pay to get it.

IT organizations with effective business practices will be able to improve their delivery of services to their customers; those customers will experience a more meaningful service that is tied to the customer's sense of business value. This book covers topics that directly enable IT organizations to strengthen business practices to improve service and customer perception, including the following:

- IT service strategy
- IT service portfolio management
- Demand management
- IT service catalog management
- IT service level management

- Request fulfillment
- Continual service improvement
- ITSM improvement project
- IT performance management (IT scorecard)
- Skills alignment
- Financial management

When adopted, these specific areas will produce value for your IT organization, and ultimately additional value for your customers. This list of business practices is merely illustrative, however; it is not exhaustive.

By adopting these best practices, an organization can demonstrate the business value of IT. For example, by developing a service catalog, SLAs, financial management, and rigorous business cases, an organization can define the service, its cost, and its contribution to business objectives. At the same time, through effective portfolio management, an organization can determine the value this service provides to the organization based on a measure such as contribution to revenue. Based on this defined service, cost, and benefit, an IT organization and business unit can understand the value of the IT services and invest additional resources appropriately.

Lower Cost and Understanding the Value of IT Investments

IT organizations need to determine the costs and benefits of financial investments made in IT projects and services. Failing to understand these costs and benefits leads to a range of frustrations, such as a service's high cost, a lack of perceived benefit, or little perceived value. To be clear, these business practices are not only about lowering the cost, but also about finding the right cost—the appropriate cost given the benefit. Many organizations would gladly increase their cost by a dollar, pound, or yen if they could generate ten times the benefit.

COMMON QUESTIONS

1 Why focus on these business practices?

Because many IT organizations lack business practices, focusing on these areas can result in significant benefit. For example, an organization can better allocate resources to improve service and lower cost. According to a recent study, almost two-thirds of CFOs and CIOs do not know the size of their core IT assets, and one-third of organizations do not know what they spend on these assets each year. Without effective business practices, these numbers will continue to decline.

2 How does a focus on these business practices compare to a comprehensive ITSM approach?

Although a comprehensive ITIL implementation is best, this might not be a legitimate or achievable choice for many IT organizations. For example, many organizations do not have any existing business practices or do not have the resources to do a full implementation.

This book identifies high-value areas for improvement, such as financial management, performance management, and business case development, and explains how these activities

Many of the activities to control or lower costs can also generate benefits (e.g., improved service). For example, effective IT financial management helps to define the cost of a service. You can then determine whether this cost is too high relative to the service's value based on the service levels and the customer's satisfaction. Based on these and other measures, the IT organization can determine whether it should invest additional resources to improve service or reduce unnecessary resources to lower cost. These benefits should be kept in mind as we review opportunities to lower costs.

Without understanding the costs of a given service and the service's value, many IT organizations create a range of frustrations for their customers. Services are viewed as too expensive, not contributing to the business goals of the organization, or failing to provide the innovation that the customer requires. Table 1-2 lists some common complaints about IT services, mitigation techniques, and where in this book you can find more information about these practices.

Table 1-2   Common Customer Complaints About the Cost of IT Services and Mitigation Strategies

Complaint	How to Mitigate	For More Information, See
Cost overruns: IT projects and services always run over budget.	Create a business case that defines schedule and key milestones and measures achievement of milestones.	Chapter 4 - IT Financial Management Chapter 5 – IT Business Cases
No innovation: The IT budget is focused on maintaining infrastructure and not new services.	Prevent end users from receiving incorrect functionality for business use through customer alignment.	Chapter 2 – IT Service Lifecycle Chapter 3 – Adopting IT Service Management Using ITIL Chapter 4 – IT Financial Management Chapter 5 – IT Business Cases
Lack of business alignment: IT investments do not contribute to business objectives	Adopt business cases and services that link to business objectives.	Chapter 2 – IT Service Lifecycle Chapter 3 – Adopting IT Service Management Using ITIL Chapter 4 – IT Financial Management Chapter 6 – IT Performance Management Chapter 7 – IT Business Skills
Unclear benefits: The return on IT investments is unclear.	Adopt financial management to measure the cost and benefits of a service.	Chapter 4 – IT Financial Management Chapter 5 – IT Business Cases Chapter 6 – IT Performance Management
Lack of customer value: The IT organization and customer cannot establish the value of a given service or project.	Link financial management with the service strategy.	Chapter 2 – IT Service Lifecycle Chapter 7 – IT Business Skills

As IT organizations become customer-centric service providers, they require improved business practices to focus investments on areas that generate the highest return (as measured by the key business objectives). For example, as organizations face an increasing number of investment opportunities, they need a more rigorous process for understanding the costs and benefits of these investments.

Chapter 4 provides the framework, process, and tools to improve financial management of IT investments. Improved information about IT costs and value can also help organizations better budget for their annual IT expenditures. By establishing a clear process that links IT costs to the budgeting process, an organization can better forecast expenses and avoid shortfalls. It can also help to communicate the value of an IT service to its customers.

Chapter 4 also introduces basic ways to capture information related to IT resources. This chapter then discusses how to improve key IT financial management processes, including accounting, charging, and budgeting. In the context of these processes, we suggest ways to improve tools such as chargeback models and business cases. These tools help organizations execute these processes and provide a common basis for understanding between IT departments and business units.

Chapter 5 explains how to develop and use business cases to justify investments and how to decide which IT projects to fund. These business cases should be used throughout every project's lifecycle to measure the benefits generated by the project.

A business case captures a range of financial and organizational benefits from each potential IT investment. Some organizations wrongly believe the sole rationale for development and documentation of a business case is to have a project approved for funding. This shortsighted approach ignores the many benefits of a rigorous analysis of any potential IT investment, including the opportunity to measure and improve the ROI of your IT investments throughout a project's lifecycle.[3]

Finally, in Chapter 6, we define a detailed process for the development and selection of an initial set of performance measures to determine efficiency and effectiveness. These performance measures will help track the progress toward key business objectives.

Realizing Business Objectives for an IT Organization

IT organizations often attempt to implement ITSM improvement projects in the wrong way (attempting to change numerous elements simultaneously and with limited planning, focus, and organizational resourcing). To counter this, we outline a holistic, incremental approach. Our approach combines business practice initial adoption or improvements (using industry frameworks such as ITIL), enhanced financial management, the use of standardized business cases, the implementation and use of IT performance management, and proper alignment of the IT organization to the business customers to improve service at lower costs.

Each IT organization is unique, so key challenges differ for each IT organization: selecting the target areas for improvement, determining the optimal way to improve target areas, developing an organizational resourcing plan to support a change initiative, and chartering and measuring each change initiative with a fixed timeline and performance objectives that determine success or failure.

The business case for improved IT business practices is simple: enable IT organizations to provide superior service at lower cost. Providing customers with higher-quality IT products and services will help further organizational goals. In Chapter 8, for example, we share success stories about how improved service has led both to higher revenue and lower business costs. Table 1-3 highlights some key focus areas for improving services and lowering costs.

Table 1-3 Focus Areas for Improving Services and Lowering Costs

Focus Area	Method/Approach	For More Information, See
Integrate and align IT and business goals.	Enhance your organization's IT business skills.	Chapter 7 – IT Business Skills
	Develop an effective service portfolio management process.	Chapter 3 – Adopting IT Service Management Using ITIL
	Implement performance management using cascading IT scorecards.	Chapter 6 – IT Performance Management
Optimize IT spending and achieve cost savings.	Implement a financial management framework.	Chapter 4 – IT Financial Management
	Evaluate the ROI of immediate cost-cutting initiatives.	Chapter 5 – IT Business Cases
	Financial management provides information needed to better manage the following: demand management, capacity management, and server and application consolidation.	

Table 1-3 Focus Areas for Improving Services and Lowering Costs

Focus Area	Method/Approach	For More Information, See
Improve the success rate of your IT projects.	Determine the financial performance of services.	Chapter 4 – IT Financial Management
	Use standardized business cases to determine which IT projects to fund and measure ongoing performance of funded projects.	Chapter 5 – IT Business Cases
		Chapter 6 – IT Performance Management
	Utilize a performance management framework to measure portfolio performance.	
Manage and lead ITSM initiatives.	Determine which industry best-practice framework to adopt.	Chapter 2 – IT Service Lifecycle
	Determine what components of the framework to implement, and plan and execute implementation.	Chapter 3 – Adopting IT Service Management Using ITIL
	Utilize organizational change management to support service management initiatives.	Chapter 7 – IT Business Skills
Change the culture of your IT organization.	Execute an ITSM improvement initiative to enhance service.	All Chapters
	Focus on the customer, beginning with a service catalog implementation or improvement.	
	Focus on the customer with refined SLAs and operational level agreements (OLAs) as part of service portfolio management.	
	Create a climate of accountability through financial tracking and measurement.	
	Change the balance of the commitment of your IT resources to revenue growth and innovation, and reduce the focus on infrastructure maintenance.	
	Measure, measure, measure to create data to enable better decision making to achieve your strategy.	
	Commit to developing your workforce.	
	Align the organizational structure of your IT organization to a process-based approach aligned to the business.	
	Reward success!	

Next Steps

The IT industry is relatively young, but the rapid pace of change makes IT a compelling driver of business innovation. Change is constant in the IT industry as new products and services rapidly come to market. The challenge for IT organizations is to understand their customers to determine what outcomes their customers desire from IT to enable their business objectives. By understanding customers, IT organizations can determine which outcomes are currently being met through existing IT products and services, which products and services are no longer useful (and so retire them), and what new technology can be offered using planned or existing IT organizational resources.

To deliver in this customer focused environment, IT organizations must optimize the use of organizational resources. IT organizations should adopt and evolve business practices to optimize their business, specifically by using business practices that improve service and lower costs. This chapter outlined selected business practices related to ITSM, IT financial management, IT performance management, and customer alignment and enablement. IT organizations can adopt these business practices incrementally to achieve their customer satisfaction goals and objectives. The next chapter examines the specific elements of ITSM that IT organizations can adopt incrementally across their service lifecycle, using specifically selected practices from the ITIL framework.

Endnotes

1. Bob Zukis, et al., *Why Isn't IT Spending Creating More Value?* (Los Angeles, CA: Price WaterhouseCoopers, 2008), 12.

2. "An Introductory Overview of ITIL V3," *The IT Service Management Forum* (2007).

3. Zukis, et al., *Why Isn't IT Spending Creating More Value?* 12.

Suggestions for Further Reading

Aral, Sinan, and Peter Weill. "IT Assets, Organizational Capabilities and Firm Performance: Do Resource Allocations and Organizational Differences Explain Performance Variation?" Center for Information Systems Research, Massachusetts Institute of Technology, August 2006.

Bureau of Economic Analysis, http://bea.gov/, Accessed April 10, 2009.

"An Introductory Overview of ITIL V3," The IT Service Management Forum, 2007.

Zukis, Bob, et al., *Why Isn't IT Spending Creating More Value?* (PriceWaterhouseCoopers: 2008), 12, www.pwc.com/Extweb/pwcpublications.nsf/docid/9E5FE9283CE22B87852574630070C 3B0/$file/it_spending_creating_value.pdf

2

IT Service Lifecycle: Improving Business Performance

The goal of IT Service Management (ITSM) is to align IT services with business objectives and customers' needs. To achieve this goal, IT organizations must effectively manage IT services across a service lifecycle. That lifecycle begins with creating a service strategy. Then the strategy is translated into a portfolio of products and services offered to customers through scoping and design in the service design phase of the lifecycle. These products and services require ongoing operational support and continual improvement to meet the evolving needs of IT customers. And eventually, services are phased out and retired. For an IT organization to improve service and lower costs, it must review its internal operations holistically and consider how to apply business practices to improve services throughout this IT service lifecycle.

This book does not attempt to cover every possible industry framework IT organizations can use to improve their services. Many industry frameworks are worthy of consideration, but this chapter focuses on the adoption of specific IT service management business practices based on ITIL, a leading ITSM best practice. We select business practices for adoption, refinement and improvement that will provide measurable improvement in IT organizations relative to the investment required to implement and institutionalize them.

This chapter introduces selected ITIL best practices of ITIL to improve your IT business management to help you develop your service strategy, design your services, and measure their performance regarding service levels and financial impact. ITIL is a comprehensive approach to improving service management across the lifecycle of a given service. Although improving business practices is important through the service lifecycle, a number of specific ITIL processes are critical to business management. In this chapter, we use core components of the ITIL framework to show you how they link together to create improved business performance for your IT organization.

We specifically focus on how to use elements of service strategy, service design, and continual service improvement, as defined in Table 2-1, to improve service and lower cost. We concentrate on these components of ITIL and their associated stages in the service lifecycle because they have the strongest ties to business discipline (as opposed to technological enhancements or refinement within service transition and service operation). We do not attempt to discuss all the elements of the ITIL framework. However, although much attention has been paid to these best practices, we attempt to add more detail to the key ITIL concepts to improve business performance.

Our intent is not to prescriptively define these elements of the ITIL framework. Rather, we want to use elements of the ITIL framework to show your IT organization how to improve service while lowering costs. Therefore, we focus on the following processes and elements of this ITIL service lifecycle:

- Service strategy
- Service portfolio management
- Demand management
- Service catalog management
- Service level management: service level agreements/operating level agreements/continuity agreements/supplier agreements
- Change management
- Request fulfillment
- Continual service improvement

Other elements of the ITIL framework are discussed throughout this book. For example, Chapter 4, "IT Financial Management: The Business of IT," focuses on using ITIL Financial Management best practices. Chapter 5, "IT Business Cases: Realizing IT Value," addresses a key component of Service Portfolio Management: the creation and use of business cases.

Overview of ITIL

ITIL is a best practice framework owned by the U.K. Office of Government Commerce. ITIL is published under contract by The Stationary Office (TSO). ITIL is a government owned, nonproprietary framework of industry-accepted best practices for service management. In May 2007, the third version of ITIL was released, consisting of five core books covering the service lifecycle (see Figure 2-1).

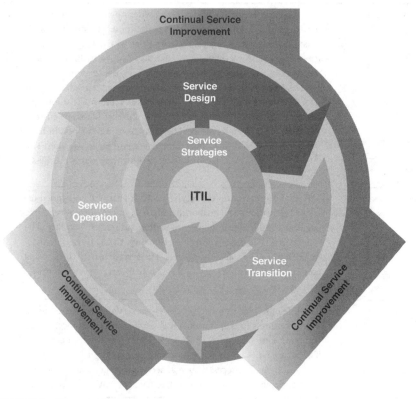

Figure 2-1   ITIL service lifecycle

The five core lifecycle elements of ITIL are as follows:

- Service strategy
- Service design
- Service transition
- Service operation
- Continual service improvement

These five core lifecycle elements of ITIL can be defined as shown in Table 2-1.

Table 2-1 ITIL V3 Lifecycle Components

Component	Description
Service strategy	The service strategy of any service provider must be grounded on a fundamental acknowledgment that its customers do not buy products; they buy the satisfaction of particular needs. The goal of service management is to transform existing assets—capabilities and resources—into value for its customers. The best service or set of services from a provider perspective is the service portfolio that produces the most value from the existing assets. From a customer perspective, the best service to be offered is one that helps the customer get more value from its assets. The purpose of the business unit and service management is to transform assets into business value. The service management capability itself becomes a valuable business asset.
Service design	Service design prepares the service package that will be handed to service transition. The goal of this phase is to provide a service package that includes both the service utility and service warranty. The service utility is the technical functionality; this is the aspect that most organizations already do well. The service utility is the associated service plans from service level, availability, capacity, continuity, finance, and security management.
Service transition	The role of service transition is to deliver services that are required by the business into operational use. Service transition focuses on implementing all aspects of the service, not just the application. This phase relies on an effective service management knowledge system and includes processes such as service configuration, change, release, deployment, and knowledge management.

Table 2-1   ITIL V3 Lifecycle Components

Component	Description
Service operation	The purpose of service operation is to deliver agreed levels of service to users and customers and to manage the infrastructure and applications that support delivery of the services. This phase includes processes such as service event management and monitoring, service request, identity and access management, and incident and problem management.
Continual service improvement	Continual service improvement (CSI) is concerned with maintaining value for customers through the continual evaluation and improvement of the cost, quality, and value of services and the overall maturity of the underlying processes.

Over its 20-year life, ITIL has moved with the direction of the IT industry from a function-based set of practices to a process-based set, and now to a service lifecycle management framework.

In the past, as IT organizations began to study how to adopt ITIL best practices, they often began by assessing the current level of organizational maturity around each ITIL process. In some IT organizations, this resulted in processes being established as new silos. The focus was on the maturity of individual processes rather than on the service or services that were to be managed. Some ITIL implementation projects would implement or improve processes (e.g., incident management) or a function (e.g., the service desk). This assessment was a relatively straightforward approach to ITIL at the time.

The current ITIL practices, which have evolved over time, incorporate current industry practices. These practices have also significantly expanded in scope and depth. The ITIL lifecycle approach builds on the earlier ITIL process focus areas. Although the ITIL lifecycle approach helps improve IT services' alignment with business needs, many IT organizations face challenges determining where to start their adoption of ITIL.

The shifting focus from process to lifecycle offers a greater insight into service value, performance, and cost. Many organizations that have used ITIL for years need to consider how the process-based approach they have adopted fits into the service lifecycle. The service lifecycle itself relies on processes to execute lifecycle activities. So, although the structure might seem quite different at first glance, each stage of the lifecycle is supported by the processes as in the past. This chapter helps you navigate the ITIL lifecycle approach using key lessons learned from ITIL implementations. We also call out the key processes of ITIL and suggest alternative approaches to beginning and sustaining your ITIL implementation. Chapter 3, "Adopting IT Service Management Using ITIL," further expands on this introduction by framing ITIL in an organizational change management framework to help you make your ITIL implementation a success.

IT Service Management

The key focus of the ITIL framework is IT service management (ITSM). ITIL defines *service* as:

...a means of delivering value to customers by facilitating outcomes customers want to achieve without the ownership of specific costs and risk.[1]

ITIL further defines *service management* as:

...a set of specialized organizational capabilities for providing value to customers in the form of services.[2]

ITIL defines *specialized organizational capabilities* as all the processes, methods, functions, roles, and activities that service providers use to enable them to deliver services to their customers.

The question IT organizations must answer is how IT organizations use the ITIL framework to develop, acquire, or improve their:

- Processes
- Methods
- Functions
- Roles
- Activities

The adoption of the ITIL framework must better enable your IT organization to deliver IT services to customers on a timely basis, within budget, with required customer functionality, and at an acceptable level of reliability (while allowing the organization to understand and mitigate risks).

WHERE TO LOCATE CURRENT ITSM AND ITIL INFORMATION

ITSM and ITIL are part of a rapidly evolving field that helps IT organizations better align services with their customer needs. There are a number of useful websites that provide current, updated information on ITIL and ITSM. The official websites for updated ITIL practices include:

- The UK Office of Government Commerce ITIL site: www.ogc.gov.uk
- The official ITIL site: www.itil-officialsite.com
- The OGC best practices site for ITIL practices: www.best-management-practice.com

In addition, there are a number of organizations that monitor ITIL and ITSM industry activity, including:

- Blogs, such as ITSMwatch www.itsmwatch.com
- Academic organizations, such as MIT, also provide podcasts and blogs www.sloanreview.mit.edu/blogs-and-podcasts
- The Stationary Office (TSO) provides low cost best practice templates, tools and resources to help you begin or improve your ITIL practices at ITIL Live: http://www.bestpracticelive.com/
- The IT Service Management Foundation provides a range of best practices and an on-line community: http://www.itsmfi.org/

The public website for a number of leading IT management consultancies will also contain ongoing, updated ITIL and ITSM information.

IT Service Strategy

A *strategy* is commonly defined as a specific course of action that utilizes resources to achieve a specific outcome or objective. Strategy was first used in military operations, but the term is commonly used in the business, nonprofit, and educational environments. Under ITIL and other ITSM best practices, the first stage of the service lifecycle is to develop a service strategy that helps move IT organizations away from a technology-centric strategy to a strategy aligned to customer needs and benefits. ITSM best practices then help an organization use their specialized organizational capabilities to provide value to customers in the form of these IT services. ITIL defines IT service strategy as how to design, develop, and implement service management not only as an organizational capability, but also as a strategic asset.

A primary goal of an IT service strategy is to create value for your customers. A well-defined, targeted business strategy (developed and adopted) will enable an IT organization to better serve its customers. ITIL segments value to customers into two categories, utility and warranty (see Figure 2-2).

Your customers must perceive the IT services provided by your organization as creating value. Both utility and warranty are critical concepts your IT organization needs to weave into your strategy approach and execution. Service Utility is the outcome that the customer receives from the services, whereas the Service Warranty is how the IT organization delivers the service. Everything your IT organization does must be focused on customer value creation. If your IT organization is considering any activities or processes that cannot be clearly tied to value creation for your customers, don't do it!

Value creation must be measurable to your customers. Ultimately, the value that your IT organization creates for your customers must be

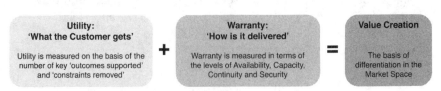

Figure 2-2   ITIL value-creation components

reflected in a defined return on investment (ROI), further discussed in Chapters 4 and 5, that exceeds the minimum ROI defined by each customer. Under ITIL, value creation is reflected to your customers as shown in Figure 2-3.

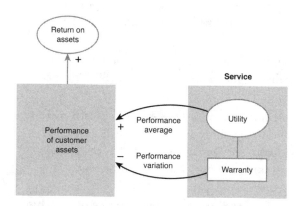

Figure 2-3 Helping customers achieve value using IT services

If you create sufficient business value in the eyes of your customers through a combination of utility and warranty, they will seek out and buy your services.

To develop your strategy and create sufficient value as measured by ROI, you should consider a number of issues:

- **Service provider:** Is the IT organization focused on delivering services to one business unit or the whole organization? Are you an external service provider dedicated to one customer or different customers? Although this decision might seem straightforward, you can use it to decide what your core services and core value proposition are to your customer.

- **Value proposition:** You should determine your position in the eyes of the customer. Is your IT organization a low-cost, no-frills service provider for basic commodity IT services? Is your IT organization a forward-looking, innovative organization that may charge premium prices for the IT services? Is your IT organization effectively a contract management organization, where you procure IT services from commercial service providers that are provided directly to your customers, with your IT organization only managing the contracting processes and oversight of the commercial IT providers?

- **External factors:** As you consider your value proposition, consider what external market factors may impact your ability to deliver this value. For example, if you are an internal service provider and seek to provide low-cost managed services, are your costs lower than the costs of external service providers?

- **Performance management:** ITIL also suggests that you identify critical success factors, which we discuss in detail in Chapter 6, "IT Performance Management: Defining Success."

- **Skills alignment:** Your organization must have employees with critical skills that enable alignment with your overall strategy. Chapter 7, "IT Business Skills: Enabling Customer Outcomes," will help you consider your current organizational skills and options for improvement.

You should be able to define and articulate your strategy at a high level to keep your IT organization focused on its implementation. Your IT line managers and staff should be able to articulate, if asked, what your strategy is in a concise manner that demonstrates their understanding of where you are trying to go strategically as an IT organization. According to Infosys CEO Nandan Nilekani, "It's really up to our ability to imagine what can be done that's limiting here, and it's important to imagine looking at the trends. It's to be able to say, the way technology is moving today, five years from now this will be so powerful or this will be so cheap or this will be so fast."[3]After you determine your value proposition and overall service strategy, you should leverage a number of processes, including financial management, IT service portfolio management, service catalog management, and others outlined in this chapter to develop a detailed plan to translate these goals into action and evaluate benchmarks for these goals.

This strategic positioning of your IT organization should also be periodically reviewed. For example, a number of IT organizations that started out providing almost exclusively mainframe services charged based on system utilization. Many of these types of IT organizations have struggled to evolve their strategy to adjust for the multitude of IT services their customers now expect them to provide and have begun to see a leveling of their top-line revenue growth. This leveling is often followed by eventual erosion of their top-line revenue growth as customers outsource their IT needs to cheaper, more reliable commercial service providers.

The question becomes this: "How does your IT organization position itself with its existing customers to remain a viable, desired IT service provider, and potentially target and acquire new customers?"

WHERE TO LOCATE SERVICE STRATEGY INFORMATION

There is a range of free information and low cost best practices to develop or evaluate your service strategy.

- Dr. Peter Weil's Center for Information Systems Research (CISR) provides a wealth of information on how to develop or improve your IT service strategy. This information can be found at:

  http://mitsloan.mit.edu/cisr/

- The Stationary Office (TSO) provides examples and templates to help you develop your service strategy at a low cost. This information can be found at:

  http://www.bestpracticelive.com/

IT Service Portfolio Management

Service portfolio management is the process of helping your organization offer those services that best meet your customer needs. By offering services that provide outcomes valued by the customers, an IT organization will be more effective in serving the needs of its customers. The service portfolio summarizes the services from the customer and business needs and can be used to evaluate current and future services. This segmentation of the IT service portfolio is a major enhancement of ITIL. Customers can find IT services listed in your IT service catalog that include descriptions meaningful to the customer, not just a listing of services based on supporting technology and technical infrastructure. IT leaders need to understand that the collection of IT services their IT organization provides, has provided, and will provide in the future is a portfolio of assets that must be strategically managed.

IT organizations must choose IT services that demonstrate high value for the business, in the face of an almost unlimited array of IT services they can offer to their customers. Not all IT services will provide a return to the organization to justify the investment of organizational resources to provide these services. Looking at IT services as a portfolio of strategic assets, IT organizations need to make disciplined investment decisions regarding what IT services should be funded.

The service portfolio process consists of four steps: define, analyze, approve, and charter. You define your current projects, analyze your projects based on a given framework for evaluating their value, approve the projects that meet your criteria for funding them, and charter their beginning. A key tool throughout these four steps is the business case, which helps screen potential IT investments before making investment decisions. Chapter 5 presents a more detailed discussion of business case development and use for IT organizations. This business case process can be used throughout the four stages of a service portfolio process and the service lifecycle.

When an organization decides to implement a service portfolio management process, it often faces a variety of IT services in different stages of the IT lifecycle, as shown in Table 2-2.

IT organizations do not have unlimited funding. Increasingly, IT organizations are under pressure to reduce costs yet provide higher service levels. A key activity for IT organizations to achieve these seemingly competing objectives is to develop, support, and retire IT services that provide customer outcomes on time, on budget, and with the IT organization assuming the risk related to supporting these IT services.

Table 2-2 ITIL Components of an IT Service Portfolio

Stage of IT Lifecycle	Description
1. Service pipeline	New IT services either (1) currently being developed and tested or (2) transitioning into active service.
2. Service catalog	IT services currently being offered to customers.
3. Retirement	IT services have been provided, but are either retired and unavailable or are being phased out of service.

Effective portfolio planning can help you avoid challenges at each stage of the IT lifecycle. This requires a comprehensive view of the relationship. The IT service portfolio listed in Table 2-1 is shown in Figure 2-4 from the ITIL framework.

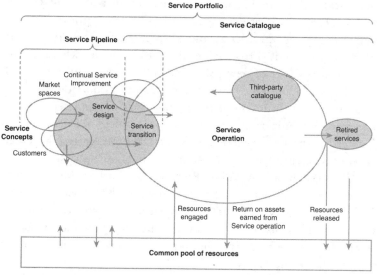

Figure 2-4 ITIL service portfolio components

A growing area of focus for IT organizations is in the service pipeline. The service pipeline includes new IT services being developed for customers. Historically, the push for new IT services in IT organizations has been driven by customer demands. A customer identifies the need for a new product or service to stay competitive in the marketplace and comes to the IT organization to determine how to create the enabling technology to support this new product or service. This push, however, from the customer into the IT organization for new products and services is beginning to change.

Portfolio management can be a powerful process to focus resources on those projects and services in the pipeline that most meet the needs of your customers and business objectives. For example, Mykolas Rambus, CIO of Forbes Media, uses a portfolio management process to put a structure on the IT project portfolio by creating an ideas funnel to identify the most valuable projects and services. The result: 75 percent of the organization's projects are now high value, up from 25 percent a year earlier. After developing this process to refocus on high-value projects, Mr. Rambus then worked to find ideas within IT and business units. These ideas identified a range of projects and services that increased top-line revenue.

The portfolio management process can also improve services in the service catalog, where IT organizations commit a majority of their resources. IT resources are engaged daily to keep applications running, respond to customer problems, and keep the infrastructure running to satisfy customer needs. Progressive CIOs at companies where technology is not only an enabler of new products and services, but where technology itself is a product or service sold to customers outside the organization, are increasingly involved in the new product and service pipeline for the whole organization, not just for internal IT services. According to Amsterdam-based Royal Ahold CIO Dave McNally, "Much of the focus, energy, creativity, and investment involve the customer."[4] U.S.-based CIOs such as Mykolas Rambus at Forbes Media and Jim Haughwout at social networking company Neighborhood America have worked successfully within their organizations to drive top-line revenue growth through the use of IT in new product development. You can read more about their efforts in Chapter 8, "Success Stories: Improving Service and Lowering Costs."

A glaring area of weakness for many IT organizations is the inability or unwillingness to retire IT services, especially specific applications. It is common to find a range of IT services being supported that have only one customer or that generate revenue that is easily exceeded by the commitment of resources to maintain these applications. At one client organization, retired IT staff were brought back on a limited basis weekly as consultants to support a specific application in use by one customer. The IT staff were brought back because the technology supporting the application was so outdated and current IT managers or staff were not willing to learn the application code because it was so arcane and outdated.

CASE STUDY: IT SERVICE PORTFOLIO MANAGEMENT

A large European client IT service provider to the banking industry was preparing for future positioning as a professional IT service provider. It needed to protect its competitive position, while expanding its role toward becoming a full-service competence center in IT service provision for banks. These goals required the client to identify cost drivers and inefficiencies in business processes, organizational units, and operations, and build a market orientated service portfolio based on demand pricing and service charging.

This effort began with creation of a strategic IT roadmap to move toward future growth and costs savings. The client was able to identify cost saving measures by recommending increased flexibility in the company's strategy and IT through componentization and reorganization across the enterprise. Several of the client locations were closed, and organizational functions redistributed. The company improved its IT services strategy by establishing a neutral platform based on business functions. This helped the company to generate strategic insights as a market-orientated IT service provider.

The outcomes of this alignment of strategy, organizational design, and supporting processes included the ability to create and evolve a business model, and portfolio of supporting services, to better serve all target markets.

There are many success stories in the IT industry of organizations that have taken a systemic, rigorous look at all of their supported applications and infrastructure and have executed planned consolidations and retirement of selected applications. We discuss in detail the successful efforts of the Department of the Navy CIO to execute systemic application and infrastructure consolidation in Chapter 8.

Service Portfolio Management is critical to improving service and lowering costs. To achieve this goal, we recommend that you leverage information from this book:

■ **Define existing services:** Create a formal service catalog process for establishing new services in your service pipeline, and retiring existing services. Use SLAs and other standard documents, also outlined later in this chapter, to work with your customer to establish their expectations. These activities help to establish your customer's expectations so you can continuously improve your services to meet them.

■ **Align financial management practices to lower cost and improve value of your services:** Develop financial management practices to determine the cost and value of each service using the practices outlined in Chapter 4. Then use a standard business case, as outlined in Chapter 5, to align investments with IT services. These practices will help you maximize your IT investments that improve the value of your service portfolio the most.

■ **Measure service performance:** Use the performance management practices, outlined in Chapter 6, to evaluate the performance of your service portfolio to ensure that you are meeting key service levels and optimizing your IT investments. These measures can also help you identify unmet customer needs that can be addressed through services in your service pipeline.

Demand Management

Demand management helps your organization understand and optimally meet customer demand for your services. This process helps you balance between two primary concerns: producing too much or having too little capacity. Maintaining excess capacity is a cost to an IT organization that will be absorbed by existing customers, and will result in increasing rather than decreasing costs. Too little capacity will result in customer frustration that their needs are not being met by an IT organization, and may result in the customer seeking out another IT service provider.

If you generate customer demand beyond what your IT applications and infrastructure can deliver, you will fail to provide effective customer service without increasing capacity to meet the demand. If you fail to generate sufficient customer demand to match what your IT applications and infrastructure can deliver, you have excess capacity that costs you funding to maintain.

You should attempt to understand customer demand. You first measure workload demands of one or more business activities and specific customers. You can then use this analysis to segment customers into different groups, such as core customers and heavy users. Using this information, you can provide key information to your capacity management process to determine what additional capacity is needed or what capacity should be retired. This understanding of customer demand then helps you to determine how you would like to influence their behavior.

You can balance customer demand against your IT capacity in a number of ways. You can provide financial incentives for customers that buy a large volume of IT services across a number of your service offerings. You can balance demand by encouraging your customers to use off-peak processing times, through offering financial incentives such as lower chargeback rates. You can also develop a service catalog to create an array of IT services to match varying customer needs. A common construct with certain IT products is to provide different levels of ongoing maintenance and support (e.g., gold, silver, and bronze). Customers can then make the trade-off internally to their organizational unit regarding what level of support they will pay for.

Your IT services can also be combined in a variety of creative approaches. You may reward a large, high-volume customer with free or highly discounted applications. For example, an organization may reward core customers with knowledge management tools, such as SharePoint, to meet their need for dedicated sites for knowledge sharing (for specific activities or initiatives). You may provide a basic service offering and enhanced service offerings around a basic service such as email. Many customers desire larger storage capacity for their email folders and are often willing to pay a premium price for it. These services help you segment your customers to better manage demand.

The criticality of your demand management process to generate information that feeds into the service catalog and demonstrates sufficient value to draw in customers makes this a logical, high-yield process for an incremental ITIL adoption. Your IT organization should recognize the costs of maintaining excess, unused capacity and recognize the risk of a lack of capacity on customer satisfaction.

IT Service Catalog Management

As your organization moves from service strategy to service design, a key focus should be on development and execution of service catalog management (SCM). A service catalog is critical for an IT organization to develop and maintain because it provides existing and potential customers a clear list of available IT products and services, which is vital to attracting and retaining customers. A service catalog is the starting point for many ITIL implementations because IT organizations recognize that at the most fundamental level they have not provided their existing and potential customers a comprehensive list of IT services that are currently available for purchase. For IT organizations that have never had a meaningful service catalog, the effort to create one is a difficult task.

As previously mentioned, a service catalog is one of the three components of your service portfolio, and this relationship is defined in ITIL (see Figure 2-5).

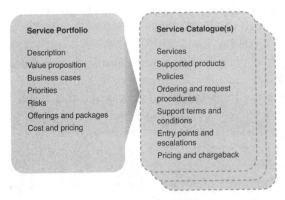

Figure 2-5   ITIL service portfolio relationship to service catalog

CASE STUDY: DEMAND MANAGEMENT

A global energy and petrochemical client company composed of multiple, geographically-dispersed business units wanted to achieve significant IT structural cost reductions while improving service across: 1) Applications, 2) Infrastructure, and 3) Demand Management. With cost being the initial key imperative, the use of a centralized, consolidated location was the primary driver of change, supported by a refined support model and processes.

The client organization consolidated 800 plus applications for support at the new, centralized location. Once support of the applications had been stabilized, the client refined the operating model, introducing a shared support model moving away from the silo application and geographical teams creating skill pools across applications. Together the teams began providing a service which included incident tickets, application monitoring, small enhancements and minor projects. This resulted in an increase in throughput and an improvement in operational excellence. With the benefits from these applications being transitioned, it was determined further service benefits could be realized if time-zone dependent applications could also be transitioned to a second delivery center.

Underlying the operating model are ITIL processes and procedures, including centralization of the global demand management processes. Implementing ITIL processes, and supporting software tools, is enabling the client to better manage demand across other divisions of its global business.

The service catalog must clearly define what service is being offered, its price, and key terms of the agreement. Although this task would appear to be straightforward, defining a service in a nontechnical manner that is meaningful to potential customers can prove difficult. Also, there is the question of bundling services and which types of services should be offered. Many services can be provided by combining or bundling different discrete IT services into an integrated service package, as shown in Figure 2-6.

Many IT organizations struggle to define a meaningful bundle of services that would produce a desirable outcome or level of value for their customers.

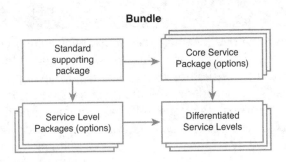

Figure 2-6 ITIL service bundles

A common mistake is to develop an initial service catalog that lists hundreds of discrete IT services on an Excel spreadsheet that customers find nearly unusable. Assuming a customer is willing and able to work through your Excel spreadsheet and locate an IT service he wants to purchase, this Excel spreadsheet cannot provide a mechanism to request a desired service. The initial challenge is creating a list of services that tie to customer needs, not technology or architectural platforms. A service catalog should not be a list of technologies. Instead, a service catalog should be a set of discrete or bundled IT services that the customers will find meaningful. To avoid this mistake, identify a customer benefit along with each service or bundle of services. If the customer does not receive a benefit, you probably should not include this service in your service catalog.

Your service catalog should be an interactive, searchable site that provides a well-constructed and priced set of IT services meaningful to the customer. Each IT service offered should provide supporting pricing, terms and conditions of use, offered service levels that can be quantified after purchase into a service level agreement (SLA), and an easy way to order each IT service. ITIL has decomposed the incident management process into three subprocesses, including request fulfillment.

An *incident* is a call to the service desk, indicating a disruption in service that prevents normal operations from occurring. Service requests flow through the request fulfillment subprocess. Your request fulfillment subprocess should include contact procedures (without having to contact your service desk) for current and potential customers who may order your IT services directly from your service catalog.

Your IT organization must commit sufficient resources to the critical effort of creating or evolving an IT service catalog. This effort requires a

CASE STUDY: IT SERVICE CATALOG IMPLEMENTATION

A European producer of milk and dairy products, with a presence in twelve core countries, initiated a process aimed at optimizing and improving management for both its human and technological IT resources. The company wanted to improve IT service response times, increase service level guarantees, and drive quality for business line requests, which would ultimately reduce costs, improve service quality and service perception, and increase IT department visibility. The IT department wanted to work internally to move toward a service-orientated model by creating and defining its IT Service Catalog by adopting ITIL best practices.

The company implemented their IT Service Catalog in three phases:

1. Assessed the company's IT environment to identify the services that the IT department delivered to customers and users. Using interviews and document analysis, the team formally and systemically inventoried and described services, providing consistent and homogeneous service definitions.

2. Next, the team designed the IT Service Catalog process, ensuring that the catalog is continuously updated and that catalog information remains consistent as the IT department and IT resources change. The process was developed in conformance with ITIL standards.

3. Finally, the team presented the company's IT leadership with an overview of available tools and technologies used to publish and automate the IT Service Catalog.

The new IT Service Catalog is now a central source of information on the IT services provided by the IT department, simplifying service management and creating a unique and more accessible view of IT services. The IT Service Catalog better aligns the services that users want with the services that company's IT department can provide; consequently, the solution helps the company to manage user expectations more effectively.

cross-functional team from across your IT organization to attempt to define, capture, and categorize your list of IT services. Among the measures of success for your service catalog is that the services offered are at a common level of detail and complexity. Having a service catalog that has both (1) buying and provisioning one server and (2) developing and implementing a large application as common services is a mistake and indicates your IT organization has not spent sufficient time and effort to create a common level of complexity across your IT service offerings.

Be patient. Creating a service catalog is not an easy effort. It requires a tremendous level of thinking, trial and error, and debate until your IT professionals can arrive at an initial, thoughtful service catalog to draw customers to your IT organization.

WHERE TO LOCATE IT SERVICE CATALOG INFORMATION

The official ITIL book on Service Design is published by the TSO and available from:

- www.tsoshop.co.uk

Appendix G: Example Service Catalogue provides an example of an IT Service Catalog.

There are a number of industry websites that track developments in IT Service Catalogs including:

- www.servicecatalogs.com
- www.itsmwatch.com

Also, a number of large and specialized consultancies provide IT Service Catalog information including:

- www.newscale.com
- http://www-01.ibm.com/software/info/ecatalog/servicemgt/index.jsp?tactic=sysmgmt

IT Service Level Management

ITIL defines IT service level management (SLM) as a function that "negotiates, agrees, and documents appropriate IT service targets with representatives of the business, and then monitors and produces reports on the service provider's ability to deliver the agreed level of service." SLM's goal is to document, define, and measure the level of service provided to the customer and ensure that this level of service meets the needs of the customer. The IT SLM process includes three key components: service level agreements (SLAs), operational level agreements (OLAs), and planning documents to improve quality of services provided (including continuity agreements and supplier agreements).

Service Level Agreements

Before an IT organization begins to provide services to a customer, a formal agreement should be negotiated and created to define all aspects of the services provided and the responsibilities of both the IT organization and the customer. This understanding between your IT organization and your customers is an SLA. SLAs are among the most misunderstood and misused documents in use in the IT industry.

While intended to be a governing agreement to define service agreements between IT organizations and customers, SLAs have been a source of frustration for IT organizations and customers for many years. To avoid this challenge, both your customer and your IT organization should agree that the purpose of the SLA is to create a framework where you and the customer—together—create target service levels and identify the responsibilities of both the service provider and the customer. ITIL suggests the following required elements for a standard SLA:

- Service description
- Scope of the agreement
- Service hours
- Service availability
- Reliability
- Customer support
- Contact points and escalation
- Service performance
- Batch turnaround times
- Functionality (if appropriate)
- Change management
- Service continuity
- Security
- Printing
- Responsibilities
- Charging (if applicable)
- Service reporting and reviewing
- Amendment sheet
- Glossary

The first challenge that must be addressed in working with SLAs is determining when the creation and enforcement of SLAs is warranted. Back to our discussion of a service catalog. There are differing levels of complexity to what can be defined or bundled as a "service." Although few, if any, services should be provided by your IT organization without an SLA, they should not be used to enforce minor technicalities and jeopardize the client relationship. You want to establish and maintain a positive, trusting, and ongoing relationship with your customers. To do this, you must ensure that the IT organization is consistent in scoping and using SLAs, and the IT organization should consult the customer about the scope and detail contained in each SLA. Collaboration and consistency help to clearly set expectations about the level of service.

A second related challenge in the creation and use of SLAs is the definition and enforcement of performance measures throughout the SLA. Your SLAs should define the specific expected performance levels for IT operations such as availability, reliability, performance, and continuity. These specific performance levels should be agreed to between the IT organization and the customer before the SLA is signed. However, much tension exists between IT organizations and customers in first defining performance level and, more important, what happens when the IT organization fails to achieve performance levels. (See Chapter 6 for an in-depth discussion of IT performance management and measurement.) One approach to ease this tension is for your IT organization to agree to provide high levels of service but clearly communicate to your customers that providing these high levels of service will come at a financial cost. This allows the customers to decide what is an acceptable trade-off between high service levels and related increased costs.

The charging section of each SLA should contain penalty clauses that result in reduced payments by the customer to the IT organization when any of the defined performance measures are not achieved for a specified period of time. Although invoking penalty clauses is a contractual right under the SLA, IT organizations have experienced situations in which customers appear to invoke penalty clauses for punitive purposes, which damages the ongoing relationship between the IT organization and the customer. Although such clauses are recommended in the ITIL framework, many IT organizations elect to not include penalty clauses in their standard SLA agreements.

The invoking of penalty clauses is part of the third challenge of SLAs, which is how to charge to IT services. The development of pricing for IT services, commonly referred to as *chargebacks,* is often a point of great contention between IT organizations and their customers. Although complex chargeback pricing models do exist, the capture, definition, and pricing of IT services still remains a relatively embryonic field. If you want to avoid this challenge, pricing should be clear, transparent, and well understood by both the customer and IT service provider.

Another approach to managing discussions with your customers about charging is the concept of *showbacks.* A showback is similar to a chargeback, except no money is paid by the customer to the IT organization. A showback is an educational tool for your IT organization to show its customers what they potentially would have been charged under alternative chargeback methods. This education process helps business unit managers and staff to understand how their demand for IT services is a driver of pricing.

A fourth challenge with SLAs is in the section titled "Contact Points and Escalation." This seemingly innocuous section of an SLA has created more problems than almost any other section. Some IT organizations create relationship manager (RM) positions to coordinate with individual customers. An RM acts as a focal point to make sure customer needs are met. The RM helps customers work with the IT organization across the range of IT support services needed to address IT issues. For example, if a customer has a service need that initially involves the IT application development unit, the service need moves to the IT networking unit and eventually the IT infrastructure unit; the RM is supposed to work across the IT organization to coordinate this cross-functional support.

The reality is that without collaboration between IT and RM, this support throughout the lifecycle is difficult to execute. Without this collaboration, customers reach out to multiple contact points in the IT organization to obtain service, which constrains the value RMs provide (to merely an oversight role). To address this challenge, your IT business organization and IT operational organization must be effectively aligned with each other and the business.

The outcome of IT service requests from operational and business unit customers is that multiple managers and staff from both the IT organization and the customer become involved in service resolution. To effectively define these contact points in an SLA, you should ask the following questions:

- Who should be listed as the initial contact points?
- How many secondary contact points should be listed?
- What are the true escalation points of contact for complex decisions?
- What is the timeline required for a response to a service request from the listed points of contact?
- Who serves as backup contact points when the primary contact point is either traveling or on vacation?

Managers and staff leave the organization periodically, are promoted into new organizational units and responsibilities, and move geographically in large organizations. As a result, you should update your SLA contact on a periodic, usually semiannual, basis. Within the SLA, also state that the operational or business units should have the responsibility to proactively contact the SLM function in your IT organization each time a change in a point of contact occurs.

A fifth challenge of SLAs is in the amendment sheet. Some IT organizations create a standard SLA template that is similar to a generic contracting document; basic terms and conditions, operating procedures, and required service activities are defined in the main body of the SLA. The amendment sheet should be periodically reviewed and updated. It is an important tool to reflect that changes to services being provided occur, adjustments to required performance measures are made, and pricing is adjusted. This amendment sheet should *not* become the SLA because an extensive number of amendment sheets can become nearly incomprehensible to understand and enforce.

Even defining service hours can be a source of friction between your IT organization and customers. For a large, geographically dispersed organization, how can the IT organization provide support to multiple time zones without staffing for 24×7 support services? A key challenge in determining levels of customer IT support is the trade-off between costs and benefits. Although it would be convenient for customers to have 24×7 support services, this can be cost-prohibitive for many organizations. Each SLA must define how customer support outside of the defined service hours, other than 24×7 support, will be addressed.

Operational Level Agreements

To support the goals within an SLA, IT organizations also make common use of internal agreements called *operational level agreements.* An OLA is an agreement between an IT service provider and another part of the same organization that assists with the provision of services. The primary goal of an OLA is to make sure that the internal organization's goals are aligned with those included in an SLA.

ITIL suggests the following required elements for a standard OLA:

- Details of previous amendments
- Support service description
- Scope of the agreement
- Service hours
- Service targets
- Contact points and escalation
- Service desk and incident response times and responsibilities
- Problem response times and responsibilities
- Change management
- Release management
- Configuration management
- Information security management
- Availability management
- Service continuity management
- Capacity management
- Service level management
- Supplier management
- Provision of information
- Glossary
- Amendment sheet

One of the elements not present in the standard ITIL OLA compared to the standard ITIL SLA is charging. OLAs are used as service support agreements within organizational units in your IT organization, so they often do not define intra-IT organizational charging. For example, we supported a client where multiple customers and IT organizational units make use of the centralized data center. The data center manager develops and enforces OLAs to try to keep control over what hardware and software is going in and out of the data center. He uses the OLAs to try to document required data center operations. This particular data center is reaching capacity on power and cooling, and the data manager center is frustrated by the constant turmoil in the data center. The OLAs are not accustomed to charging for data center infrastructure support, but rather to control required levels of racks, power, cooling, and cabling. OLAs are an excellent organizational tool to avoid conflict within your organization. Even when you recognize OLAs are not a perfect tool, the use of OLAs will be one more step your IT organization can take to improve internal operations.

Continuity Agreements

One of the key components of a standard SLA is service continuity. *Service continuity* (SC) is defined under ITIL as IT service continuity management (ITSCM). The goal of any service continuity agreement is for IT customers to have a process in place to ensure critical IT support for their business operations can be resumed within a defined period of time when a significant failure, or disaster, occurs that reduces or temporarily eliminates IT support. A significant failure, or disaster, is an event that causes a reduction in IT support at a level that impacts the ability of the IT customer's business to operate. Failures in IT support can and will occur. SC is focused on ongoing issue and risk identification and mitigation to reduce the possibility of a failure, and on maintaining operational plans and resources to recover from a failure as quickly as possible.

IT customers need to work with their IT providers to determine what the impact will be to their business from various levels of failure of IT support, referred to as business impact analysis (BIA). One of the more famous examples of BIA planning was nearly a decade ago, around the changeover from 1999 to the year 2000, referred to at the time as Y2K. The international business community was concerned about a potential failure of IT systems as the changeover from calendar year 1999 to calendar year 2000 occurred. Businesses did extensive planning with their IT providers to determine a range of potential failures from Y2K, and did extensive continuity planning to determine how to react to, and mitigate, any Y2K failures. This planning involved identification of issues and potential risks from Y2K failures, and continuity planning to mitigate various failure scenarios. Fortunately, the Y2K changeover did not result in significant IT or infrastructure failure.

There are a number of approaches to recovery from a failure of IT operations. Many IT organizations have a planned recovery site, typically some physical distance away from their primary IT physical operations, that can used on a fee basis for use to support IT operations during a gradual, intermediate, or fast recovery to normal operations. A planned recovery site, or backup site, can also be used for immediate recovery of normal operations. SC planning is more extensive than just recovery, but recovery of normal IT operations is typically the primary focus of SC planning.

ITIL suggests the following required elements for a typical recovery plan:

- Introduction
- Recovery strategy
- Invocation
- Interfaces and dependencies on other plans
- General guidance

- Dependencies
- Contact lists
- Recovery team
- Recovery team checklist
- Recovery procedure

A key element in determining the extent of SC planning and implementation is the cost of the SC planning and implementation balanced against the costs to the customers of an extended IT failure. While having a failure of IT support can significantly impact a business, the cost of continuity planning and implementation must not be prohibitive to the IT provider. SC planning must balance costs against realistic recovery times of IT operations.

Supplier Agreements

To provide IT products and services, every IT organization requires the use of external partners and suppliers to provide critical elements of supporting products and services for use by the IT organization. IT organizations buy hardware and software through a mix of providers, via a mix of purchasing channels. IT organizations also rely on external providers for ongoing support. This support can be technical expertise in specific areas, such as cybersecurity, that may not be a core competency of the IT organization, or for ongoing use of IT infrastructure, such as use of a hosting facility for data center demands that may exceed the capacity of an in-house data center.

The ability of an IT organization to obtain the most value from spending on external partners and suppliers is a critical success factor for an IT organization to provide IT products and services to its customers at competitive prices. Many IT organizations have contracts in place with external partners and suppliers that account for a significant portion of their budget and spending, and significantly impact the value of an IT organization as perceived by its customers.

Because IT organizations spend a significant amount of money on external partners, and suppliers, some tracking tool should be used, even a tool as basic as an Excel spreadsheet, to determine what type of spending is occurring (i.e., hardware, software, services, and so on), who is receiving the spending on an aggregate basis, the length and terms of current planned spending under either existing contracts or agreements or planned acquisitions that will occur, and the performance levels of external partners and suppliers.

The purchasing and acquisition of external products and services is a complex effort (and beyond the scope of this book). The critical activity IT organizations need to undertake is ongoing tracking and analysis of their external spending with a focus on value received for the IT organization versus the total cost of external purchasing and acquisitions. ITIL provides guidance in their service design, Appendix I, "Example contents of a Statement of Requirements (SoR) and/or Invitation to Tender (ITT)" on typical elements of a solicitation for products or services from external partners or suppliers.

Change Management

Change management is a critical area for process improvement and innovation in IT organizations. Many ITIL V2 implementations focused on improving the change management and related configuration management processes and subprocesses. ITIL defines *service changes* as "the addition, modification, or removal of authorized, planned, or supported service or service component and its associated documentation." Under ITIL, improving the change management processes, procedures, and activities remains a critical success factor for IT organizations to improve service and lower costs.

Customers of IT organizations are in a constant state of change. A changing marketplace, competing internal demands for organizational resources, global economic changes, and risk result in customers making continual changes to their supporting IT services. IT organizations need orderly, consistent, proven processes to manage this ongoing change. Customers can submit requests for change (RFCs) that can be processed in a structured manner through internal review and approval, before implementation. Other customer requests are emergency requests that must be addressed outside the structured internal review and approval process.

To effectively manage the change management process, you should create a transparent process where both the IT organization and its customers agree on how to document change requests and acknowledge, document, and act upon change requests (even if the action is deferment of the requested change until a later date, or rejection of the request because it is not necessary or because it is addressed in another RFC). Most important, ongoing communication must be provided to customers to provide a status on each request. This communication helps avoid a high number of emergency requests or poorly executed requests, which plague unsuccessful IT organizations. With change management processes and strong communication, your organization can prevent customer frustration and achieve their desired outcomes. However, these outcomes can be achieved only if your IT organization is responsive and effective in implementing change.

Because of the criticality specifically of change management for successful IT operations, whole books examine in depth how to develop, implement, and maintain effective change management processes. In most of these texts, a key focus is on the development of a service strategy to align your IT organization to your customers, develop and execute a service portfolio management approach (including service pipeline, service catalog, and retirements), and define customer services in SLAs. You must effectively transition IT services into operation and maintain these IT services in operation to satisfy the needs of your customers.

When you are targeting specific processes for improvement or reengineering under your potential ITIL implementation, change management is an area that warrants significant examination as a high-yield focus area.

Much confusion exists in IT organizations as to the difference between *change management* (CM), which is the formal processes and procedures for executing service changes just discussed, and *organizational change management* (OCM), which are the processes, tools, and techniques utilized in IT organizations to manage change in your IT organization. These are two completely distinct, different focus areas in the ITIL framework, and they should be addressed as separate focus areas in an ITIL adoption.

Much of our discussion in Chapter 3 will be how to implement an ITIL adoption focused on OCM techniques, which, at their ultimate, result in culture change within your IT organization. We recognize the underlying driver of organizational and corporate culture to any type of organizational change. Edgar Schein, an MIT School of Management professor, defines *organizational culture* as:

> *A pattern of shared basic assumptions that the group learned as it solved its problems of external adaption and internal integration, that has worked well enough to be considered valid and, therefore, to be taught to new members as the correct way you perceive, think, and feel in relation to those problems.*[5]

According to Schein, culture is the most difficult organizational attribute to change, outlasting organizational products, services, founders and leadership, and all other physical attributes of the organization.

Request Fulfillment

Request fulfillment is a critical enabler of customer service. Customers may want to use an IT organization's products and services, but if a process is not in place for customers to communicate their desired products and services, the IT organization will fail to provide customer outcomes. ITIL places a greater emphasis on request fulfillment, the process whereby customers and users can request services or information about current or future services and can respond to general questions. When existing and potential customers go to your service catalog, they should be able to utilize your request fulfillment process to enable the purchase of your published IT services directly from your service catalog. Your IT organization should develop and execute standard fulfillment procedures for each service offered in your service catalog. Included in your standard fulfillment procedures should be the ability to generate work or purchase orders for your services directly from your service catalog using your request fulfillment process.

A number of considerations exist in the ordering of your services, through your request fulfillment process, from your service catalog. The customer placing the order from your service catalog must have the authority to make a purchase. We have encountered a number of situations in which the manager or staff person from the operational or business unit making an order from a service catalog did not have authority to make the purchase. This disconnect should be identified when your SLM function attempts to define and complete a supporting SLA for the new service, but you can build activities into your fulfillment process by service to verify authority when the initial order is placed.

Another key consideration for your request fulfillment process is that your service catalog should have a self-service tool that provides a front-end interface to your IT organization. We live in an age in which we are all used to searching to fulfill our needs using common Internet search tools. The same thinking applies to your service catalog, and the next step in the customer purchase process for your IT services: Your service catalog should provide a searchable front end that enables your customers to quickly locate services they potentially will purchase from your IT organization.

One easy way to provide this functionality for your service catalog is to put it on an intranet site with the supporting functionality. Globally, a number of governments have led the way in development and use of online service catalogs for use by their customers.

The service catalog is only a portion of your IT organization's service portfolio, but the only portion of your service catalog customers are able to view (see Figure 2-7).

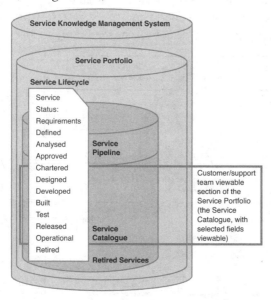

Figure 2-7   ITIL service knowledge management system

Ultimately, the request fulfillment process should connect your service catalog with your back-end processes, including incident and change management. These links will speed the purchase or acquisition process for your customers from their initial search of your service catalog to the order for service being implemented through an RFC in your change management process.

Continual Service Improvement

In Chapter 3, we will define the Continual Service Improvement (CSI) concept and present a high-level organizational and staff model for you to use to develop a CSI function. The critical driver of a successful CSI function for your IT organization is the ability of your IT organization to adopt, implement, and embrace a culture of continual service improvement.

A number of the required activities your IT organization will need to continually execute typically reside in your CSI function. Much of the monitoring, analyzing, and reporting on IT operations is consolidated in your CSI function. Although we discuss IT performance management in detail in Chapter 6, rigorous performance monitoring and reporting can be centralized in your CSI function. In addition, much of your SLM activities are also typically located in your CSI function.

The method that ITIL recommends to use to execute CSI projects is defined in a seven-step improvement approach (see Figure 2-8).

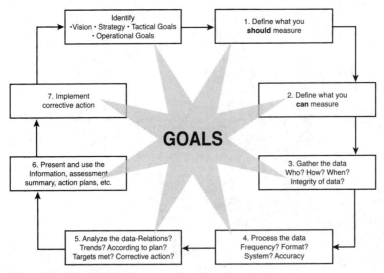

Figure 2-8 ITIL seven-step improvement process

Our clients typically have a large amount of data they can utilize to track performance in their IT organization. Unfortunately, this data is dispersed across a number of systems, platforms, and applications, each with a unique automated monitoring system that is not interconnected. Therefore, the CSI process helps to gather the *data,* convert it to *information,* and eventually evolve it into *knowledge,* and ultimately into *wisdom.*

A common way to translate data into information and knowledge is to package information into presentations, reports, and electronic

CASE STUDY: CUSTOMER FEEDBACK LOOP

A client organization executed a long-term project to consolidate multiple legacy application systems into one new integrated system designed to reduce processing time for end users while enhancing functionality. A number of end users starting registering complaints with the consolidated help desk; they said that they had asked repeatedly for changes in specific features of the multiple screens in use with the new system. When probing end users on how they were going about making requests for changes in the functionality of these screens, the end users indicated they had clicked on a feedback icon prominent on the initial screen of the new system and entered and submitted their requests using this feedback button.

The client CSI function scoped a small project to review how the requests and suggestions for change submitted through the system feedback button were being addressed. After an initial review of the feedback process and supporting system log, the CSI function determined that the feedback button submittals were not being reviewed by anyone in the client organization. Eventually, the feedback icon was eliminated from the initial system screen, and the end users were directed to submit requests or suggestions on system functionality through help desk tickets.

The success of your CSI function is driven by the capability of the CSI function to align all its improvement activities directly to goals and objectives of the organization. The relentless drive for improvement across your organization must be focused on better enabling the execution of your organization's strategy.

reporting tools (often referred to as *digital dashboards*) that provide meaningful information that your organization's senior leadership can effectively use to make decisions. We have worked with a number of clients who continue to struggle with performance reporting. With the rapidly changing external environment in which your organization operates, useful performance reporting can evolve rapidly. What was a critical performance measure one quarter can be rendered obsolete in the same fiscal year. Macro events like the September 11 tragedy and the 2008 economic collapse can quickly refocus organizational thinking regarding what are critical performance measures.

After September 11, 2001, many organizations examined their performance measurement systems and determined they had limited or no measures around disaster preparedness or reaction to terrorist attacks, so they increased their focus on risk mitigation. The 2008 economic collapse refocused many organizations on financial measures, including cash flow, accounts receivable collection rates, and other financial liquidity measures.

To effectively implement CSI functions, you must also engage appropriate line managers and staff. CSI managers and staff are experts in techniques such as Six Sigma, business process reengineering, and Total Quality Management (TQM), not technical experts in an area of your organization—for example, hosting services, targeted for a CSI improvement project. Gaining that organizational commitment of resources to CSI projects often requires a significant change in the culture of the organization.

Next Steps

In this chapter, we focused on the development and enhancement of the customer outcomes enabled by leading IT organizations. Beginning with a basic IT service catalog, moving through service portfolio management, and eventually into demand management, the ITIL framework provides a set of methods, tools, and processes IT organizations need. ITIL provides a level of detail for specific activities, such as the development and use of SLAs and OLAs, that, when adopted, enable IT organizations to improve service while lowering costs. This focus on improvement can be accepted into your IT organization by development and execution of a CSI function. In the next chapter, we move our focus to implementation of IT service management, focused on ITIL.

Endnotes

1. ITIL Service Design, Office of Government Commerce, 2007, Glossary, p. 309.

2. ITIL Service Design, Office of Government Commerce, 2007, Glossary, p. 310.

3. "India's Promise – Imagining the Future with Nandan Nilekani of Infosys," Transcript, *The Nightly Business Report*, May 28, 2007.

4. "The Right Timing," Retail Info Systems News, February 7, 2008, p. 3.

5. E. H. Schein, *Organizational Culture and Leadership*, 3rd ed. (San Francisco, CA: Jossey-Bass, 1985–2005).

3

Adopting IT Service Management Using ITIL

The goal of IT service management (ITSM) is to produce outcomes that customers consider valuable at the quality and cost levels desired by the customers. To optimize these service outcomes in an increasingly competitive, service-oriented world, IT organizations need to drive efficiencies into the business and operational practices used to execute the development, delivery, and ongoing support of IT products and services. These ITSM best practices must be part of the IT organization, not simply documents on a shelf or software applications that are rarely used.

To help you make these ITSM practices part of your organization, this chapter focuses on how to implement key elements of the ITIL framework using Organizational Change Management (OCM) best practices. These practices will help you develop service management capabilities more effectively and efficiently. We use an example of adopting components of the ITIL framework as an ongoing case study throughout this chapter to illustrate a practical example of an ITSM implementation project. However, ITIL is not the only industry framework that an IT organization can use to improve service while lowering cost, but is the example we use to demonstrate many of the elements of OCM common to many ITSM projects.

Adopting and adapting ITIL and ITSM best practices for your organization are fundamental changes in organizational and corporate culture. Incorporating best practices is a change in mindset more than a set of business practices outlined in Chapter 2, "IT Service Lifecycle: Improving Business Performance." Your ITIL implementation should focus on the practices most meaningful to your organization. By combining proven organizational change management approaches with ITIL, you can manage your ITIL implementation while avoiding key risks.

There are two aspects to the organizational and cultural changes needed to adopt ITSM best practices. You need to develop an organizational structure with supporting roles, teams, and functions required by service management and embedded into your IT organizational structure. You also need cultural change in your IT organization, with a focus on the changes needed in human behavior and decision making to improve your service while lowering costs.

This organizational change management approach will encourage your organization to embrace the need for standardization of business and IT operational practices. Adopting standards-based management practices is a step along the path to better service management. Repeatable, measurable processes are an essential element of a quality management system. Based on a review of successful and failed ITIL implementations, the approach also integrates key organizational change management techniques to avoid risks related to project sponsorship and a disengaged staff.

The role of IT is to support, enable, and automate business activities so that the organization can achieve its strategy and goals. Most organizations disproportionately invest in IT projects that simply maintain existing infrastructure, rather than services that meet customer needs. IT organizations should not only be focused on development of technology, but should instead focus also on a business-centric, service- and value-oriented approach to the management of IT. This OCM approach to helping your organization embrace ITSM and ITIL will help shift these priorities to the services that your customers value the most.

Managing Change

The first step for IT organizations to adopt leading ITSM business practices such as ITIL is to understand that applying business practices will involve a change in the culture of the organization. According to Greg Smith, CIO at the World Wildlife Fund, "Many technology professionals merely look to the capabilities of a product or solution, hardware or software, to maintain and grow the IT infrastructure."[1] Cultural change is difficult to achieve and requires a structured, measurable approach to transform organizational culture. There are a number of approaches to organizational change.

In 2008, IBM Global Business Services completed the "Making Change Work" study,[2] which explored differences in how change was implemented by more than 1,500 practitioners worldwide in organizations of varying size and cultures. One of the key findings of this comprehensive study was that only 41 percent of change initiatives in organizations were considered successful. The most significant challenges when implementing change projects are people oriented—including *changing mindsets* and *corporate culture.* Figure 3-1 shows some of the key barriers to successful change.

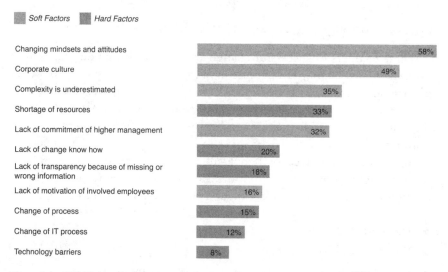

Figure 3-1   IBM "Making Change Work" study: Barriers to change

These findings demonstrate the criticality of nontechnical factors in helping IT organizations begin and institutionalize change, such as an ITIL implementation. So what are the factors that must be present for successful change and ITIL implementation? According to the IBM study, the factors shown in Figure 3-2 are critical for making change successful.

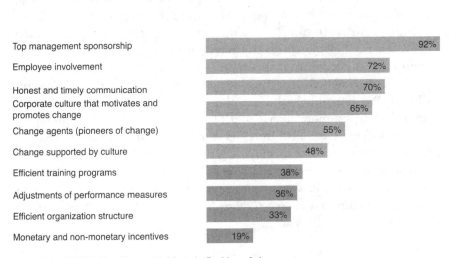

■ Soft Factors   ■ Hard Factors

Top management sponsorship	92%
Employee involvement	72%
Honest and timely communication	70%
Corporate culture that motivates and promotes change	65%
Change agents (pioneers of change)	55%
Change supported by culture	48%
Efficient training programs	38%
Adjustments of performance measures	36%
Efficient organization structure	33%
Monetary and non-monetary incentives	19%

Figure 3-2   IBM "Making Change Work" study: Enablers of change

These enablers of successful change are clearly focused on nontechnical issues. Change may fail because of hard factors, such as a lack of organizational commitment to training programs, adequate performance measures, or monetary incentives. However, the most frequent reasons for failure are soft factors, such as when managers and staff perceive that senior leadership in their organization is not committed to making change occur. Employees will not engage in change initiatives unless there is clear, consistent communication from the leadership of their organization. That communication and the initiatives should address:

- The need for change
- The commitment to change
- The change process, which involves *all* levels of employees

In many organizations, a core group of managers and staff will have established their credibility within the organization for being high performers who embrace change that is beneficial to the organization. This core group consists of leaders within the organization, and their actions and focus often signal to other members of the organization the important activities to support. Being able to identify, engage, and reward this core group of managers and staff as visible change agents implementing the clear, committed direction of organizational leadership toward successful change implementation is a critical (nontechnical) success factor for any change initiative.

Existing Skills in Your Organization to Enable ITIL Adoption

This section helps organizations identify the staff that may have the required skills to support an ITIL implementation. It further suggests that, as an organization focuses on improving its business and IT operational practices, it needs to broaden its staff skill set to include IT business skills.

In many IT organizations, the culture focuses on technology skills. Given the continuing, rapid changes in all aspects of technology, IT managers and staff focus on maintaining existing IT systems and applications through ongoing, incremental upgrades and patching. The focus in IT organizations on keeping the existing systems and applications running requires technical skills for this existing technology. However, given customer demand for new systems and applications, IT managers and staff also require ongoing training in new, emerging technology to continue to evolve their IT products and services.

In the past, many IT managers and staff did not focus on developing business skills. In many IT organizations, technologists were rewarded with career advancement, rather than those IT managers and staff who broaden their skill sets beyond a traditional technology focus. However, this need to develop cross-skills in the IT community has started to emerge as a trend.

Increasingly, the path to the CIO role requires individuals who can master both the technology and business elements of running a complex IT organization. According to Greg Smith, CIO at World Wildlife Fund, IT managers and staff should augment "existing skills by encouraging IT staff to expand their business knowledge by enrolling in outside educational programs such as project management certificate courses, MBA programs, or other educational certificates and curriculum that will build and strengthen effective IT-to-business skills."[3]

Leading IT as a service business, to help the business itself succeed, is not only a technical skill set. It also requires business skills that include organizational, technical, service, and process skills. As IT evolves into a critical, nonoptional business asset, IT leadership must also evolve. It is no longer sufficient for the CIO to be the chief infrastructure officer, chief information officer, or chief technologist. In reality, the role of CIO needs to evolve to be the chief governance officer within IT. The CIO must represent the business and ensure that IT services are well governed and well managed to produce the outcomes required by the business. This is more than a technology skill set.

IT organizations should also look within and outside the IT organizations for individuals who have MBAs or skills outside specific technologies. Although a multiyear MBA program is often not a realistic consideration for all IT professionals, the field of program and project management has grown in importance in the IT community. While IT organizations are often managing the development and operation and maintenance (O&M) of multiple applications, the development of a few large-scale applications can often consume the majority of IT spending for organizations. This focus on a few large-scale applications has brought increased management focus on tight management of these application developments and implementations, usually under some type of system development lifecycle (SDLC).

IT staff who have Project Management Professional (PMP) certification may also have insight to contribute to the service improvement initiatives. Although developing project management skills is not a path for technologists to develop the full range of business skills that will be needed in the next decade to fully optimize IT operations, PM skills have proven to be an effective initial step to integration of business and technology skills. The focus of PM on the following skills has been critical in integrating business practices into ongoing IT operations:

- Developing and enforcing timelines
- Developing and enforcing budgets
- Measuring the projected and actual financial returns from IT projects
- Integrating gate reviews into project timelines
- Tracking of plans versus completion through various techniques, including earned value management (EVM)
- Putting increased focus on developing and integrating end-user requirements as demonstrated by end-user accepted functionality

- Developing and using feedback loops throughout development and implementation

The push for identifying core business skills needed for IT organizations is still developing. The field of human capital management (HCM), and specifically the identification of core competencies for IT professionals, is just now beginning to be a focus area for IT organizations of the future. We discuss the emerging needs for identification of core competencies for IT professionals throughout this book, and specifically in Chapter 7, "IT Business Skills: Enabling Customer Outcomes," and link this key enabler to the maturation of business practices for IT organizations.

Managing Your ITSM Change Initiative

This section summarizes the key steps for managing your ITSM change initiative. To begin your initiatives, you should secure executive sponsorship, assess your readiness for change, charter your project, and adopt an implementation approach based on your organization's current capability compared with your stakeholder and customer requirements. We then suggest that you actively engage key stakeholders to sustain your momentum to change.

If your IT organization is even considering implementation of ITIL, someone in your organization recognizes the need for change in your current level of service management capability.

The first critical question you need to address as an organization is whether you have meaningful sponsorship in your organization for an ITIL change initiative. Although this seems like a simple question, your ITIL implementation will fail if you do not properly address this question before starting any type of ITIL implementation.

A successful ITIL change initiative requires sponsorship from a person high enough in your organization with formal authority to sponsor a meaningful change initiative that requires operational resources for a sustained period of time. This person must have clearly established:

- The need for change
- The business case that commitment of organizational resources to an ITIL change initiative will result in a net gain to the organization using an accepted measure of gain

- A compelling short, concise story supporting the need for change and related business case that can be communicated to multiple internal and external stakeholders to help drive the change process
- A willingness to communicate the compelling change story throughout the ITIL implementation, even when resistance to change occurs
- The internal and external credibility to be seen as a credible sponsor of a significant change initiative

If the ITIL initiative sponsor is the CIO, the CIO must demonstrate to the line managers and staff in the organization that he or she is serious about implementing ITIL and is willing to invest personal credibility to the change process. Sponsorship for the daily activities of an ITIL implementation will likely occur at the manager and staff level in most organizations, but clear, directly committed sponsorship must be present at all phases of the change initiative to be successful.

This commitment is demonstrated in its most basic way in the funding and staffing of a service improvement. If there is no funded and staffed project, nothing will happen. If a project is funded and not staffed, nothing will happen. If the people assigned to the project do not have a separation of project workload and business-as-usual workload, the project will not work.

If your ITIL initiative sponsor is below the CIO in the formal hierarchy of your organization, the sponsor must have visible, public support from the CIO that the planned ITIL implementation for your organization has CIO support. The heads of the organizational units that compose the IT organization typically have the daily, hands-on responsibility for an ITIL implementation. These tactical leaders of your ITIL implementation will often be the make-or-break factor for the ultimate success of your ITIL change initiative.

Readiness for Change

You secured internal, meaningful sponsorship for your ITIL implementation. The next critical question you need to ask is this: Is your IT organization ready to change? Again, this question seems relatively simple. It is not.

An ITIL implementation must be communicated to line managers and staff to show the compelling need for change. The need for an ITIL implementation does not mean that your IT organization is failing today. The risk is that as the IT marketplace continues to change and evolve, your IT organization begins to fail to keep up with this continual change, and eventually becomes

ITIL IMPLEMENTATION CASE STUDY

A CIO was conducting an internal videoconference to announce the pending ITIL implementation in the organization. While the CIO was talking through the timeline and milestones for this change initiative, a majority of the line managers and staff were not paying attention to the telecast; instead, they were visibly working on daily "crisis" issues throughout the telecast. When asked about this behavior after the videoconference, a number of managers and staff expressed common concerns about the ITIL implementation, including

- What is ITIL, and why should I care about it?
- This is another headquarters initiative that will not impact what I do on a daily basis.
- Why do we need to do this when our daily workload is already backing up and I have five other meetings today before I go home?
- Is this going to make my work any easier to complete?
- Who has time?
- This is another one of these "business school" ideas when I have five servers to provision before I go home.
- Why are we spending money on this stuff? I really need money to finish our virtualization implementation, not work on ITIL.

Continued on page 65.

overwhelmed by trying to create customized solutions to meet customer demands. The failure point is not necessarily today, but will occur in the future if you do not move your organization toward some level of process standardization to contain costs and enable meaningful outcomes to your customers.

The mindset should never be on "implementing ITIL." It should always go back to issues addressed by the three questions: Does the customer or do the stakeholders need an improvement to service quality, cost, or value? Is the quality, cost, or value problem occurring in the design, transition, or operational phases? How will you improve our service management capability to meet the stakeholder and customer requirements? The focus needs to always be on the service that provides the needed value.

Making this case for change requires ongoing communication throughout the change initiative. Although many IT managers and staff might be initially skeptical of a service management program or project as "another headquarters change initiative," acceptance of the need for change can occur over the course of the change initiative, especially if your change initiative is incremental. One common approach to increase the rate of acceptance by line managers and staff is to demonstrate initial, measurable returns for your IT organization from the initial activities of an ITIL implementation. If your IT organization targets selected IT processes for improvement or reengineering, you can start planning with identifying both tactical and strategic objectives. There are always some "quick hits," and they will be needed to show some positive incremental outcomes as a result of your initial activities. This demonstrated improvement will increase the rate of acceptance of your service management program by line managers and staff.

Although initial and ongoing communication about a planned ITIL implementation is a key enabler of success, a common approach to assessing the readiness of your organization for change is through a change readiness survey. Although there is a whole industry of thought about how to conduct change readiness surveys, there are also free, Internet-based survey tools that allow you to develop a survey of any type, of up to ten questions, using a standard multiple-choice, or Likert, scale for measurement. Free sites also enable you to ask open-ended questions when you are seeking more detailed knowledge of the enablers and constraints in the environment of your IT organization toward a change initiative. A review of some of these will help you gather ideas for how you would conduct a survey and what you might need to do this depending on your needs.

A survey tool enables your IT line managers and staff to anonymously respond to the questionnaire, and only the members of your organization who are conducting the survey are allowed to review the results. This, ideally, will enable your IT managers and staff to respond to the survey frankly and honestly about their perceptions of the reality of conducting a service management improvement initiative successfully in your organization.

If your IT organization is currently showing a limited readiness for change, you should not abandon your potential effort. Rather, an environment for your IT organization that indicates a lack of readiness for change just indicates you will need to tailor your service management plan to include a more significant effort to develop and communicate the need for change in your organization. This is not necessarily bad that your IT organization is not ripe for change. It simply impacts your approach. You must be realistic when starting any change initiative about the current state of your organization in terms of readiness for change.

Chartering Your Project

Your organization is ready for change. Where do you begin? This question seems relatively simple. It is not.

ITIL IMPLEMENTATION CASE STUDY (CONT'D)

Several months after our client CIO conducted a videoconference to announce an ITIL implementation initiative and the initial steps involved in this initiative, no activity had occurred on the implementation. The CIO was frustrated at this lack of movement, but eventually realized that announcing any change initiative without first putting a detailed structure and resource plan in place would not result in a successful service management improvement.

The CIO assigned the task of chartering, resourcing, and executing the program to the deputy CIO. The deputy CIO conducted a meeting with the heads of the five divisions within the CIO organization to restart the effort. Among the activities the deputy CIO conducted was to

- Formally create a charter for the overall project, which defined the timeline for the project, planned activities, assigned responsibilities, a formal reporting structure for activities on a fixed calendar, and expected outcomes and "measures of success"

- Ask each of the division heads to identify a cross-segment of line managers and staff from across each division to assign to the project on a part-time basis

- Assign specific components of the project to subteams that would be created from a mix of managers and staff identified from across the various divisions

- Hire an external consultant to work with the deputy CIO's project team to develop a notional roadmap of how to implement the various components of ITIL that would be needed within the deputy CIO's organization

Continued on page 71.

There are several positive elements of this change in the approach to an ITIL implementation:

- The CIO remains the sponsor of the project but recognizes the need to delegate the activities supporting this change initiative to a tactical level.
- The CIO (or designee) engages a cross-segment of division heads, managers, and staff into project activities.
- The CIO (or designee) creates a charter for this effort, which defines the initial timeline, boundaries, and definition of success for this change initiative.
- The CIO (or designee) recognizes the lack of internal service management expertise within the IT organization and brings in outside expertise to help define the roadmap of how to incrementally implement ITIL V3 best practices over a defined period of time.
- The CIO puts organization resources behind this initiative, signifying the importance of this effort to the organization.

Although many IT organizations want to skip the process of creating a charter to define a service management program or project, the development of this relatively simple document begins the process of forcing your IT organization to think critically about what expected outcomes, or measures of success, must be present for your organization to succeed. The charter is a document that should be reviewed periodically throughout an ITIL implementation to verify that your current activities throughout a project remain consistent with the initial requirements and objectives. The charter also becomes a critical document at different stages of a long-term service management program because some ITIL projects begin to veer off course from their intended outcomes without a charter to keep them focused on the end state goal.

The process for selecting and structuring the teams is a critical success factor to a successful service management program or project. One common point of failure for any change initiative occurs during the selection of the line managers and staff to assign to the initiative. Unfortunately, the managers and staff often assigned to a change initiative can be the poor or low performers because they are not in demand within their organization for other projects, not because they have the knowledge, skills, and abilities needed to effectively implement change.

Your core team must be composed of managers and staff who have demonstrated in their careers an openness and willingness to embrace and execute new ideas for the organization. These managers and staff must have internal credibility with their peer group in the organization. Your organization must view these individuals as smart, committed professionals who would commit only to a complex, long-term change project such as this if they believed such an effort would have measurable and positive long-term benefits to your organization. Your credibility and success will rest heavily on the individuals you select to execute the program.

However, we have seen a number of change initiatives fail when the change initiative is staffed based on resource availability, rather than required skills and experience. Your team will signal to the organization how much value you place on your change initiative. Everyone wants to be assigned to projects where they can potentially advance their career through being identified with successful change that provides measurable benefits to their organization. The adage "success has many parents, but failure is an orphan" applies equally to service management projects.

There may also be a need to seek external expertise. There are three primary focus areas to hiring an external consultant to support your ITIL implementation:

- **ITIL training and certification:** Many external consultancies provide ITIL training services to begin to educate an IT organization on the components of the service lifecycle approach of ITIL, and the underlying processes, methods, functions, roles, and activities that compose ITIL. IT organizations can use this training for individual managers and staff to obtain ITIL certification, and as part of an effort to get an IT organization certified ISO IEC20000. Training can be purchased from an accredited training provider. A comprehensive list of ITIL certifications is located at www.apmgroup.co.uk/ITIL/Qualifications/ITILV3Qualifications.asp.

- **ITIL assessment, planning, design, and implementation:** Each IT organization differs in size, structure, mission, complexity, and resourcing. An external consultancy should have experience in assessment, planning, design, and implementation with IT organizations of similar size and scope, and be able to apply lessons learned from these prior engagements.

- **ITIL management tools (selection, integration, and customization of software tools):** Numerous software tools exist to support ITIL. An external consultancy should have experience supporting IT organizations in selecting, integrating, and customizing relevant ITIL software tools to fit the unique requirements of IT organizations.

Some practical advice on hiring an outside consultant: The ability of an outside consultancy to provide your organization quality consulting services in support of your ITIL V3 implementation and service management initiative is driven by the quality and experience of the specific staff the consultancy assigns to your project, the methods they will use, and the intellectual capital they can leverage in the project. When you are selecting an outside consulting firm, it is critical that the consultancy identify the key managers and staff they will assign to your project, and you must ensure that these managers and staff are the actual people who execute the work onsite at your organization. Consultancies have a number of ongoing projects at any point in time, and you do not want to end up effectively training the staff of your outside consultants by having the consulting firm provide junior, inexperienced staff to your organization.

Your internal expertise and openness to change, along with the results of your change readiness assessment, largely determine the level of external support you require. Many organizations elect to make a few key external hires of permanent managers and staff with ITIL expertise rather than invest in large-scale external consulting support. Lastly, the IT industry has generated a number of sophisticated software tools to support ITIL implementations. The leading software vendors and a number of small specialty software vendors have developed a range of software tools that have automated much of the ITIL framework in a manner that support ITIL practices. According to Gartner:

> *One of the major contributors to hype surrounding ITIL is the marketing strategies of systems management tools vendors. Although the lack of effective tools can certainly be an inhibitor to the full exploitation of IT service management principles, tools should not be the primary focus. Tools that support the integration of ITIL processes are beneficial, but most IT operations organizations are not fully using the systems management tools they already have licensed.*[4]

Software tools are enablers of ITIL, but they are not the only enabler. Your approach to acquisition, use, and integration of software tools must be consistent with your overall approach to service management. If you do not align tool selection decisions with your overall service management strategy, you risk wasting valuable IT resources. If your project is a limited, focused adoption designed to improve only selected processes, purchase and use of a full suite of software tools will not make sense for your organization. However, you should select tools knowing that ultimately you will need to integrate all your tools to achieve long-term service management results.

Selection of point solutions should be approached cautiously. One key aspect of service management is that optimizing subsystems at the expense of the whole system does not provide maximum results. Optimizing a server does not optimize an infrastructure. Optimizing technical subsystems, process subsystems, or organizational subsystems does not yield the service management result that is desired either. So when approaching how to best improve a subsystem—whether technical or process or organizational—you must keep in mind a holistic view of the desired service outcomes. We recommend you scale the level of your software tools to match both the scope of your current project but, more important, match to the expected outcome required by your organization.

Developing Your Initial Service Management Strategy

Your organization has committed resources to your project. What strategy do you select for your ITIL implementation?

You can employ two primary strategies to implement ITIL:

- **Phased comprehensive ITIL implementation:** Implement the ITIL framework in discrete, continual implementation phases over an extended period of time, which would require a significant commitment of organizational resources over an extended period of time but would minimize the disruption to current IT operations.

- **Phased selected ITIL V3 service management improvements based on current business requirements for IT:** Implement selected practices from ITIL as well as other frameworks in a discrete, outcome-oriented approach over an extended period of time.

The phased comprehensive approach should be applied in a situation in which your organization needs much of the best practice processes, tools, and techniques defined in the ITIL framework, or other industry frameworks, but because of funding and resource constraints can address only certain parts at a time. This strategy should be applied for organizations that are not experiencing drastic change in their operating environment, but where long term the need has been identified for a best practice IT organization. Not every organization will benefit from the investment in improving its IT organization to a best practice level. Not every organization will benefit from the investment in improving every process within IT to a best practice level. Service management planning should identify which processes are in need of improvement based on stakeholder and customer requirements and should phase the project based on business needs. Whereas the process, organization, and technology design can all be done at one time, the implementation will always need to be phased. There is always a limited ability of an organization to absorb change. The service management plan should clarify the approach to design and implementation given resource constraints and the organizational ability and readiness to absorb change. The process changes implemented under this strategy often involve extensive process improvement, rather than process reengineering.

A number of organizations have outsourced a significant portion of their IT operations to outside vendors and have retained in house only a limited number of IT resources. Often, these IT resources are committed to repetitive processing of selected operations, such as payroll, mainframe computers, and other low-risk, repetitive IT operations. These organizations rely on the vendors who perform their outsourced IT work to be best practice IT organizations and do not want to incur internal costs to upgrade their in-house IT operations. Best practices are always a desired outcome for organizations, but the cost of obtaining best practices versus the commitment of organizational resources (primarily financial resources) must be weighed carefully. The assumption with the phased comprehensive ITIL strategy is that the analysis has been performed to determine that the benefits of process reengineering outweigh the costs of implementation and that best practices do not need to be achieved internally against all elements of the ITIL or any other framework immediately.

The phased selected strategy should be applied in a situation in which your organization is continually working to improve IT operations but has achieved an acceptable level of performance internally against a number of the ITIL framework elements. These organizations select only a portion of the ITIL framework to implement and can implement the selected improvements over an extended period of time. The process changes implemented under this strategy often involve extensive process improvement.

The phased selected strategy is a common strategy for service management improvement. Unless an IT organization is failing to meet customer needs, or appears to be in the initial stages of failing to meet customer needs, this strategy is consistent with continual improvement for most IT organizations. The biggest challenge of this strategy is the service strategy defining the stakeholder and customer requirements and the service management plan describing the scope of the service management system that will be addressed.

The required determination of what elements of the ITIL framework to adopt and the timeline or sequencing for the planned adoption can be done effectively by use of an outside consultancy. As you form your ITIL implementation team and subteams and begin to assess the current maturity level of your processes versus ITIL best practices, you will find strong, divergent viewpoints within your IT organization about current process maturity levels. The outside consultancy can bring a structured methodology, intellectual capital, lessons learned, and experience from other situations that can provide the objective help needed to facilitate collaboration internally and keep the focus on the desired outcomes.

Selecting Specific ITIL Elements for Adoption

Your organization has selected an ITIL implementation strategy. What elements of the ITIL framework do you target for adoption in the short, medium, and then longer term?

ITIL IMPLEMENTATION CASE STUDY (CONT'D)

After the deputy CIO restarted the service management project, the IT organization brought in an external consultant who conducted a baseline assessment of the current state of the operations of the IT organization. The external consultant assessed current operations and provided a four-phase timeline and plan for a focused ITIL implementation targeted on select ITIL processes.

A leadership team was created to review the external consultant's proposed ITIL implementation roadmap, and subteams were assigned to implement various elements of the proposed roadmap. Included in this plan were activities to determine which of the five divisions in the IT organization had the most mature current practices in each ITIL process area identified for improvement, and determine whether internal best practices by division could be adopted across the IT organization. An immediate plan was put in place to develop an initial service catalog for the IT organization and develop a standardized service level agreement (SLA) template for use across the IT organization beginning in the next fiscal year for the overall organization.

Although this ITIL implementation plan appeared to be feasible, several implementation issues occurred in the six-month period after development of this plan:

- Many line managers and staff still did not see the value of the ITIL implementation for the IT organization and either failed to attend subteam meetings or began to send junior staff to "take notes" in their place at subteam meetings.
- The five divisions had tremendous disagreements in subteam meetings over which division currently had the most mature, in-house processes.
- The initial attempt at a service catalog resulted in widely varying levels of detail for potential IT products and services to be listed in the catalog.
- Many line managers and staff resisted the attempt to define and adhere to detailed performance measures they would be held accountable for in the new, standardized SLAs.

This study illustrates the need for a clear executive sponsorship a team that is open to change, and a war to demonstrate the benefits of ITSM initiatives.

Much of the problem here resulted from focusing on implementing ITIL rather than on improving service management based on business requirements. A better approach, and the approach recommended by ITIL, is to start with stakeholder and customer service requirements and define a service strategy. Then produce the service management improvement plan based on doing what is needed to deliver the service strategy.

The ongoing issue of line managers and staff not seeing the value of the ITIL implementation reflects the need for continual stakeholder communications throughout the duration of your ITIL implementation from your project sponsor, to the line managers and staff, about the need and value of the project. In this case study, the organization addressed the issue through communication from both the CIO and deputy CIO to the line managers and staff about the need for service management improvement.

The issues of disagreement about who within the IT organization currently has best practices around selected ITIL processes and the resistance to clearly defined performance measures in the SLAs are deeper issues related to culture change within this IT organization. This IT organization had a history of a high level of competition among the five divisions. These cultural issues created multiple problems for the ITIL implementation. Attempting to define internal best practices among five competing divisions was not a realistic plan.

This need for culture change also directly impacts the creation and enforcement of defined service performance and outcome measures within the new, standardized SLA template. This IT organization had a history of strong demand for its products and services from internal business and operational units, so it was focused on maintenance of the technology infrastructure. This focus on maintenance is consistent across the IT industry. This IT organization had not historically focused on customer needs, requirements, and in working to be responsive to customer outcomes. However, it had experienced a leveling out of demand for its products and services over the period of three fiscal years leading up to the beginning of its planned ITIL implementation. Senior leadership both within the IT organization and in the broader organization recognized the red flag of weakening demand for the products and services of the internal IT organization.

Risk Determination and Mitigation

How do you identify and mitigate *service management improvement* risks? Business and operational units within organizations often rely on their internal IT organizations for IT support because they do not want to accept the risks of IT operations, especially development and implementation of mission-critical applications. One of the benefits of a well-managed IT service provider is the expertise in service risk mitigation. The ITIL (and other available frameworks) provides guidance for risk identification and mitigation. ITIL focuses on risk that is present in all aspects of IT service management.

If you want to determine risks, the first critical step is to create an initial list of potential risks to the success of your service management project. You can accomplish this step as you are initially chartering your initiative. Several common risks to service management projects can be identified in your initial implementation planning, including:

- Loss of sponsorship due to competing organizational priorities or through change in senior leadership in your organization.
- Resource commitment that is not firm or reliable. This applies to project funding and human resources.
- Lack of sufficient expertise and intellectual capital to plan, design, and implement the needed service management improvements.

Although the list of potential risks to your ITIL implementation can be numerous, these three risks have derailed many implementations.

Risk mitigation is the development and execution of approaches to reduce these initial risks and potential risks that are identified during service management planning and throughout the program or project. As part of your planning, at least monthly you should schedule a risk review meeting with key members of your team to review your current list of identified risks, review the status of all risk mitigation efforts assigned to specific members of your team, identify any new risks to the project, and make new assignments of risk mitigation to members of your team.

The identification of new risks is the responsibility of the entire team, not just project leadership or outside consultants. The members of your team working on daily activities have the most direct insight into any new or emerging risk. It is critical that each member of your ITIL implementation team understand and take personal responsibility for the need to identify new risks as they emerge and communicate these new risks to their subteam or team leads. The monthly review of potential new risks should include these potential risks identified by all members of your ITIL implementation team.

You must be realistic in understanding that risks are inherent in any change initiative, and proactive identification and mitigation of risks will significantly increase the probability of a successful ITIL implementation for your organization. We discuss risk throughout this book, but risk mitigation is often overlooked as a critical success factor specifically for service management programs and projects.

Mapping Your Target Processes for Improvement/Reengineering

You have identified your service management processes or functions you plan to implement or improve in your IT organization. How do you document them?

A process is a:

[S]eries of logically related activities or tasks (such as planning, production, sales) performed together to produce a defined set of results.

The key elements of a process are those activities that result in fulfillment of a customer need. Processes should be designed with the desired outcome as the primary driver. After you have selected processes for improvement or implementation, you should document your current process by target area.

For example, assume you have selected IT financial management from the service strategy component of the ITIL lifecycle as a target improvement area under Phase 1 of your project based on the most pressing business needs you are facing. If you determined that your current IT financial management processes exist and are evolved enough to warrant a process improvement effort, rather than process reengineering, you should begin your improvement efforts by documenting the current IT financial management processes.

Begin with a graphical representation of the discrete activities that compose an individual process. A process should begin and end by capturing a discrete set of measurable activities that will be required to transform specific measurable inputs into specific measurable outputs that result in desired outcomes. Process diagrams can capture progressively more detailed views of activities as they are created. For IT financial management, a potential approach is to define three major processes for this focus area: 1) service accounting, 2) service budgeting, and 3) service charging. These three major IT financial management activities are not the only processes defined under IT financial management, but they do provide an example for a specific ITIL framework process that could be targeted for improvement.

For each of these three major IT financial management activities, your team should create an initial, high-level process diagram that captures the major end-to-end tasks in each focus area. Although a number of electronic tools are commonly used to develop process diagrams, Visio remains somewhat of a standard electronic tool for process map creation and evolution. However, increasingly the software industry has created process mapping tools with increased functionality, such as IBM WebSphere®, for more complex process map modeling, including advanced "what-if" scenario development. For basic process mapping, Visio remains in common use.

After developing your initial high-level process diagrams, you should develop subprocess maps. For example, your activity diagram for the budgeting area may include eight critical tasks. Each of these eight tasks could be further defined in eight specific task diagrams providing greater detail of the specific set of procedures that make up each of the eight critical activities. If you have resources for an outside consultant, we recommend that you use them at this time to bring in an outside perspective. An impartial perspective is helpful in facilitating process modeling workshops. For example, this outside perspective can help you determine the scope for each process mapping activity to produce meaningful current or "as-is" process maps of your current IT operations.

Many organizations select processes such as IT financial management for adoption under their ITIL implementation but realize that they have embryonic or nonexistent financial management processes. If this is the case, you should design your new, or "to-be," IT financial management processes under process reengineering. In this case, you would not attempt to develop process maps for your current IT financial management processes but would instead skip directly to the creation of future IT financial management processes.

The development of new processes is a more challenging effort than the baseline process mapping. Often, documenting current processes teaches your team members how to create process diagrams, teaches them how the diagrams translate into concrete activities within the real organization, and provides insights into how work can be done for the new processes to be adopted. Although the current process diagrams must be accurate, we encourage you to move relatively quickly through the diagramming of your current processes, instead of getting bogged down in overly precise attempts to capture every nuance. A skilled, experienced facilitator can enhance this effort greatly by applying practical experience to bound your process baseline effort.

The critical element of your process analysis is in the development of the new processes. The development of new processes is an opportunity for your line managers and staff to create processes exactly as they would like to see these processes executed. Based on years of experience working within your IT organization, line managers and staff have an unmatched view of both the positive activities they execute to ultimately satisfy customer needs and the frustrating flaws in current processes that can create unnecessary inefficiencies and delays in daily IT operations.

It is a critical success factor to engage your line managers and staff, in a meaningful way, to fully apply their years of expertise about the current state of your IT operations in the creation of new processes. Your line managers and staff have the microview into the reality of daily IT operations and should be willing to apply this knowledge to the development of new processes that will govern their work. Among the objectives of process diagrams is to:

- Eliminate unnecessary, non-value-added steps or activities in your current processes
- Eliminate waste of any kind of organizational resources used in your current processes
- Create new steps or activities that add value to each process and improve the outcomes from each process in a measurable manner
- Streamline current processes to create the maximum benefit to the customer for minimal commitment of resources, including time
- Document the measurable inputs and outputs, the end-to-end flow of activities, and the roles that will perform them and the enablers required for their execution

Although this list is not intended to be a comprehensive view of all the desired outcomes from the development of process diagrams, it provides focus to the broader concept of CSI.

The execution of process workshops to develop new processes requires skilled facilitators to both manage the workshops to draw out the required knowledge from participants to develop the future process diagrams and look for common elements in them. Developing future process diagrams can become challenging because workshop participants often have competing, strong viewpoints as to the future process diagram's activities. The facilitator must work to build consensus during these workshops so that all participants in each workshop feel that their viewpoints were heard, examined, and ultimately incorporated in some manner in the future process designs.

One of the challenges of process design workshops is the multiple integration points between processes. Future processes never stand alone when implemented. Rather, there are multiple integration points between the various processes and activity level designs. Your initial process documentation workshops will address current processes that may work in isolation; however, as your process design effort evolves, you will begin to design process interfaces between processes covered by different development teams or other processes that are not in the scope of your project but have critical interfaces. After you begin to integrate processes, you will gain a clearer picture of the potential future state of your service management capability. Linking the teams also brings into focus questions and concerns from line managers and staff about how the new processes will impact them individually.

During process mapping sessions for future processes, the realization often sets in that proposed changes to specific processes, although beneficial to the overall IT operations, might start to point to logical changes in the current organizational structure of your IT organization.

Institutionalizing Your ITSM Change Initiative

Your change initiative is now well underway. You have created the project team and subteams that are working to implement the elements of the ITIL framework you have targeted for adoption. You have gone back and reviewed your initial ITIL implementation charter, and you believe you are on track to achieve the desired outcomes meaningful to your organization from this change initiative. Now what?

A critical question you need to address as an organization is this: How do we make ITIL processes adopted by our organization a normal part of ongoing operations, rather than a "change initiative" requiring special resourcing, activities, and tracking separate from normal IT operations?

You will need to complete several steps to institutionalize your ITIL adoption, including the following:

- Continue proactive stakeholder management and communications.

- Conduct a second, in-progress survey of key internal managers and staff to assess the current acceptance and understanding of your ITIL implementation.

- Plan discrete activities to formally, publicly complete your ITIL implementation.

■ Create and resource a continual service improvement function to proactively continue to adopt the ITIL framework elements as needed.

Ongoing Stakeholder Management and Communication

You have secured support initially for your ITIL implementation project, and you have at least successfully completed several of your project milestones. How do you continue to engage your key stakeholders through completion?

During the first steps of any change initiative, there is often much enthusiasm and energy. The sponsors are visible, the line managers and staff are engaged in change subteams, the target is clear and defined, and the change initiative starts off crisply.

By at least the midpoint of your initial plan for your project, you should be able to determine whether:

■ The project is fundamentally on schedule.

■ The effort has broken down and requires a substantial effort to get back on schedule.

■ The effort needs to be refocused due to lack of commitment, or the change effort has been lowered in terms of the priorities of your IT organization by competing demands for internal resources.

Assuming your effort is on schedule, we recommend you take some time to engage your stakeholders in a meeting to celebrate success. For example, you might want to highlight that improved business or operational practices have enabled you to achieve the goals of your SLAs. Your team at all levels may be experiencing some level of stress by the midpoint of the project. It is a good idea to stop to celebrate at key milestones to recognize how much work your team has already completed. It can be easy to become frustrated and see only the problems. This obstacle can be overcome by taking the time to acknowledge past problems that were recognized and overcome, many activities have been completed, and progress is occurring. Sometimes just getting people together in an informal setting helps let off steam as a pressure release that can itself help the project immensely. Another aspect of this informal outing is that often new solutions are found and new problems or gaps are realized that could present a problem during implementation. You should not underestimate the importance of informal gatherings to celebrate.

One approach to celebrating success is to hold a project "open house." Specifically, set aside several hours during normal working hours to allow all the stakeholders of your ITIL implementation to come to a large meeting room, in the physical space where your team is conducting a majority of the work, to visually review the work products your ITIL implementation team has generated. This discussion may also help staff to share lessons learned regarding the implementation.

Invite all the critical stakeholders, both internal and external to your organization, to come to this open house to review the work of your team. The team members would be present to give a brief presentation on the focus areas for their work, ideally by subteam, to give the stakeholders a view of:

- Work completed to date
- Focus areas for adoption and related improvement in current IT operations
- Planned future activities to completion
- Expected outcomes and performance measures documented to date
- Any achievements, such as draft SLAs or improved service levels

The desired outcome of this open house is to keep your stakeholders involved in the project beyond the initial kickoff meeting and initial activities. The open house allows the stakeholders to see that tangible, real activities have occurred toward ITIL implementation, and it also reinforces to your ITIL implementation team members that senior leadership and key stakeholders are still visibly committed to the change effort.

In addition to some type of open house, the midpoint for your project is also an ideal time to develop and implement a "road show," or standard presentation, for external stakeholders not physically able to attend the open house. The standard presentation will summarize the ITIL implementation efforts completed to date and planned activities to completion, but most important, it will define and communicate the desired outcomes of the entire effort.

Road show presentations are a critical success factor for an IT organization conducting a large-scale program that has a large, physically dispersed customer base. For example, if you are a large IT organization providing IT products and services to business units inside a global corporation, taking a road show to multiple internal customer sites dispersed around the globe can be a powerful tool to communicate change to your customers. The customers will likely have only a limited interest in the mechanics of your project but will be interested in the outcomes to your IT organization that will result in improved IT products and services for your customers.

Customers want continually improving IT products and services at declining prices, and they also want access to emerging technology that has practical applications for their business activities. The open house is a powerful tool for communicating with your immediate stakeholders and senior leadership from your customer base; you can provide a focused, thoughtful summary that your IT organization has accomplished the following:

- Undertaken a serious change initiative focused on improved service management to improve customer service. A detailed description of the outcomes to be achieved through the project.

- Project performance—status of schedule, costs, functionality, and quality criteria.

- Project phases, milestones and time lines—where are you now and what is the schedule going forward. When they will be impacted by the outcomes.

- Commitment to adopting internally accepted best practices and standards for the management of IT services.

Proactive communication to your internal and external stakeholders will help with acceptance as a normal part of ongoing IT operations, rather than a one-time change initiative designed to only "check the box" that an ITIL implementation was conducted.

In-Progress Survey of ITIL Acceptance

You are at least 50 percent successfully complete in your ITIL project plan. How do you determine the status of acceptance of ITIL in your IT organization?

In every type of change initiative, people seem to react to change in three categories:

- **Early adopters:** These people embrace change, see the need for change, and act positively to enable change in their organization.
- **Resisters:** These people oppose any change to their work environment and will look for, and point out, any stumbles in the change process.
- **Messy middle:** These people have a profoundly mixed reaction to change and wait to see whether a fledgling change initiative is going to succeed before fully committing or fail before pulling back.

At the midpoint of your project, you should develop a rough allocation of the line managers and staff in your IT organization into the three primary categories listed here.

There are not inherent positive or negative connotations regarding the allocation of your IT organization in terms of stage of acceptance. Rather, the distribution of your line managers and staff into these categories indicates the following:

- The success of your ITIL implementation to date
- The level of corrective action, if any, you need to take to keep your project on schedule for successful completion
- The likelihood of the overall success of your service management program and achieving the desired outcomes.

We recommend the use of a second survey of your line managers and staff, to determine their level of acceptance of your ITIL implementation. Although it is typically ideal to quickly complete a survey, we recommend you allow for a longer period of time for your line managers and staff to complete this survey to get a high rate of response. Even if you have to email your line managers and staff to get them to respond to this survey, a high response rate will benefit you by giving you the clearest view possible of the current state of internal acceptance of your service management program or project.

If you receive a high level of negative feedback from your line managers and staff about their level of acceptance of your project, you will need to take a hard look at your activities to determine if you:

- Have the wrong team members for your team
- Under-resourced the project or applied resources with the wrong skill sets
- Were overly optimistic in the overall project timeline, not allowing for a period of acceptance internally
- Misunderstood that service management involves a change in culture, which is a long, sometimes difficult process

To successfully implement service management improvements, you might need to hire new managers and staff with skills needed by your improved organization, and you may need to let go of some of your current line managers and staff who cannot adapt to changing skill requirements. You do not necessarily have to go outside your current team to find new skill sets. Training of your existing IT managers and staff is an alternative to external hires to fill critical skill sets.

Planned Completion of Your Service Management Project

How do you know when your ITIL implementation is complete? Change initiatives do not always have a finite end. Initial enthusiasm for a change initiative, such as a service management project, can be overtaken by other priorities. Line managers and staff begin to have their time taken up by new and often competing priorities for your IT organization.

It is critical that you have a finite completion date and set of activities planned from the initial stages of your project to establish a clearly understood completion date and completion criteria. The risk of a lack of a finite end to your effort is that the project slowly loses momentum and can eventually stop before completion. How you complete a change initiative is often more critical than how you start or execute a change initiative. Line managers and staff can grow weary of a service management project that drags on for an extended period of time, with no finish in sight.

One potential approach to completing your project is to clearly define milestones, which will occur to define completion of your service management improvement program. You must be sure your project has truly completed all required activities successfully before reaching a specific, planned milestone. However, when you complete a milestone and achieve all related success measures, you should have clear communication to your ITIL implementation team, IT organization, and your critical stakeholders (including key customers) that a significant milestone has been achieved. Celebrate success. Make sure you communicate to all of your involved stakeholders that progress is being achieved, and more importantly, change is occurring in your IT organization that will produce meaningful benefits to your stakeholders.

Communicate achievement of milestones with your key customers. The primary driver of your undertaking the project was to improve service to your customers and provide outcomes desired by your customer base. The objective of a project is not to "check the box" that your IT organization has applied the latest industry fad to your organization. The objective of adoption of ITIL (or any other) framework is the production of increased value from existing capabilities and resources, which usually includes higher customer satisfaction, so the customer should be included in your critical, ongoing communications about the success of your project.

Early in your project, you will have developed a communication plan that defined the channels, or mechanisms, for you to communicate with each of your stakeholder groups. You will need to use the channels that have proved most effective from your initial plan to communicate the success and ultimate closure of your project.

Enable Continual Service Improvement

How do you continue to improve your IT services by adopting additional elements of the ITIL framework beyond your initial ITIL implementation?

Establish a continual service improvement (CSI) practice that will work to improve your IT operation, using some elements from quality systems and frameworks. Establishing repeatable measurable practices and services is the foundational activity required to enable continual improvement. A good first step is to be sure you capture all the documentation and work products produced during your project and store them in a knowledge system. Take the time to have the team meet and document lessons learned. Document who the participants were in the project and establish either a formal Center of Excellence for service management or a virtual and informal one.

A number of continual improvement quality systems and frameworks are in common use in the IT industry, including variations on the following:

- Lean and Six Sigma
- Control Objectives for Information and Related Technology (COBIT)
- Projects in Controlled Environments, V2 (PRINCE2)
- Capability Maturity Model Integration (CMMI) and CMMI for Services
- Project Management Body of Knowledge (PMBOK)
- ISO 9001. This is *the* quality management system for both products and services. Its supplement, ISO IEC 20000, describes how to apply ISO 9001 principles to an IT service management system
- ISO IEC 38500. This describes principles and practices for the corporate governance of IT services and service management processes

A CSI practice, when properly staffed, resourced, and executed, can provide measurable returns to your IT organization from ongoing improvement activities. You must also encourage a culture of your IT organization that moves toward a culture that values CSI efforts. This requires making the case to your line managers and staff that they will achieve real, measurable value from CSI efforts. Line managers and staff continue to reward "fighting fires," or addressing immediate issues, rather than taking the long view and understanding that a crisis environment does not need to pervade your IT organization. CSI efforts are designed to look objectively at your daily operations and identify systemic weaknesses in all elements of your IT organization that can be corrected to gain long-term efficiencies.

This focus on addressing systemic issues within your IT operations helps you overcome one of the key barriers to measurable returns from ongoing activities, which is a culture that does not embrace change. IT line managers and staff are focused on the daily activities needed to keep the existing IT infrastructure running. CSI efforts, although valuable, take a commitment of time from line managers and staff, and CSI efforts are often not considered mission critical to IT organizations. To make CSI efforts a critical, integrated part of your daily operations requires a change in culture.

However, convincing your line managers and staff that taking employee time and other organizational resources to commit to a CSI effort is the best use of these resources can be difficult. The approach we recommend to enable this understanding of the value of CSI efforts is to develop and execute a focused internal communication plan to spread the word to your line managers and staff that:

- Senior leadership across your organization is committed to CSI efforts.
- You will enhance your career by volunteering and driving CSI efforts.
- Measurable returns are obtained by your organization through CSI efforts, which ultimately benefit your customers.

The staffing of your CSI organization should be relatively small compared to your overall organizational staffing. CSI managers and staff work with your line managers and staff to identify opportunities for improvement across your IT organization. Your CSI function will be the central point in your IT organization for gathering, tracking, and acting on proposed CSI opportunities. Your CSI organization will not take action on all CSI opportunities identified across your IT organization.

Your CSI function will need to gather and create a tracking list of potential CSI opportunities. However, your CSI managers and staff will need to practices some initial analysis on potential CSI opportunities before chartering an internal CSI team and taking action on a potential improvement opportunity.

Next Steps

This chapter, using the ITIL framework as a case study, defined critical elements to successful implementation of an ITSM improvement project. However, these critical organizational change management principles also apply to other improvement projects for an IT organization. In the next chapter, we begin to define the financial management approach, practices, and systems that must be in place in an IT organization to successfully capture and analyze financial information needed for effective decision making.

Endnotes

1. Greg Smith, *Straight to the Top: Becoming a World Class CIO*, Hoboken, New Jersey: John Wiley, 2006, 83.

2. "Making Change Work," IBM Global Business Services, 2008.

3. Smith, *Straight to the Top*, 83.

4. "Best Practices," Gartner for IT Leaders.

Suggestions for Further Reading

"Best Practices to Successfully Implement ITIL," Gartner for IT Leaders, March 1, 2007, ID Number G00146542.

Broussard, Frederick. "IT Service Management Needs and Adoption Trends: An Analysis of a Global Survey of IT Executives," IDC, September 2008.

Custy, John. "Practical IT Service Management: Rapid ITIL Without Compromise," JPC Group, Numara Software, November 12, 2008.

DuMoulin, Troy, Pink Elephant, and Ken Turbitt. "Survey Results: ITIL Best Practices in SAP Environments," BMC Software, June 2007.

"How to Develop and Apply SLAs in Outsourcing," Gartner, February 7, 2007, ID Number G00143550.

"An Introductory Overview of ITIL V3," itSMF, The IT Service Management Forum, Version 1.0, 2007.

"Making Change Work," IBM Global Business Services, 2008.

Shallcross, Michael. "ITIL V3 and the Evolution of Service Management," IBM Global Services, 2007.

Smith, Greg, *Straight to the Top: Becoming a World Class CIO*, Hoboken, New Jersey: John Wiley, 2006.

4

IT Financial Management: The Business of IT

Financial management of Information Technology (IT) resources is a powerful process to improve service while lowering costs. Simply stated, IT financial management is the process of overseeing IT expenditures, with the goal of providing both business units and IT departments with a common framework to evaluate services and plan for future investments to optimize IT spending.

As technologies become more complex, the financial management of IT investments has proven challenging. Many IT organizations lack financial management experience. Similarly, business units often lack a clear understanding of the technology enabling a given IT service. As a result, many organizations find it challenging to develop a budget to expand a given service, account for key costs, or charge for services. Many organizations lose opportunities to maximize their return on investment (ROI) for IT resources as the management of budgets and tracking of IT utilization and costs fail to occur.

With worldwide IT spending estimated to exceed $3 trillion in 2009 according to the Gartner Group, the potential benefit of maximizing this spending is substantial.[1] Many governments, businesses, and nonprofit organizations have recognized the growing importance of IT financial management. In a recent Interactive Data Corporation (IDC) survey of 600 IT organizations worldwide, respondents cited "cost/budgets/financial concerns" as the top priority needs for IT supported businesses.[2]

This chapter provides a tactical roadmap illustrating how to improve specific IT financial management practices based on best practices, including Information Technology Infrastructure Library (ITIL)®. First, we summarize the need to structure financial management activities based on an organization's IT services. Aligning financial management activities with IT services helps IT organizations to account for charge, and budget for services based on customer demand.

We then summarize the three basic IT financial management activities—budgeting, accounting, and charging—an organization should have in place to cost-effectively deliver services that customers value. While ITIL now provides guidance on a range of effective and value added financial management activities to improve service and lower costs, we spend a significant amount of time on these basic activities because many IT organizations lack the ability to budget, account, or charge for the value of services. Without effective budgeting, accounting, and charging activities, an organization cannot effectively undertake these value added activities to improve service and lower cost.

After summarizing the activities and benefits of basic financial management activities, we discuss how the information can be used to improve service and lower cost through more advanced IT financial management activities, including service valuation, service provisioning, cost optimization, service investment analysis, and demand modeling. For example, by using accurate IT accounting information, an organization can effectively value the service to satisfy its customers, manage demand, and maximize the return of its IT investments through service portfolio management. This discussion of value added financial management activities also continues in Chapter 5, "IT Business Cases: Realizing IT Value."

Define Service-Based IT Financial Management Activities

IT financial management helps an IT organization determine the financial value of IT services provided to its customers. ITIL refers to this activity as service valuation, whereby each service is valued based on the cost of the service and value added by both the IT service provider and the customer's own assets.

Service-based IT financial management aligns the basic activities, accounting, charging, and budgeting, with other customer facing ITIL processes. For example, the IT organization tracks expenses against the services outlined in the service catalog on a continuous basis through the IT accounting. Similarly, IT budgeting generally consists of an annual or multiyear effort that measures existing financial commitments and estimates future expenses related to its services. Because most IT organizations need to recover costs or generate a profit, they implement a charging process, and customers are billed for the IT services that they consume.

Accounting, charging, and budgeting activities provide critical outputs and improve service through investing in the high-value services through rigorous service investment analysis, business cases, and portfolio management. Similarly, these outputs can lower costs through monitoring expenses related to a given service and determine whether it can be provided more effectively, referred to as service provisioning optimization in ITIL. We first define these basic financial management activities in the following subsections.

FINANCIAL MANAGEMENT INFORMATION CAN BE USED TO IMPROVE SERVICE AND LOWER COSTS

Effective financial management processes help an organization to improve service and lower costs. IT accounting helps an organization monitor IT expenses against budgeted goals and prevent budget deficits and losses. IT accounting also provides the information with data to value a given service, referred to as service valuation in ITIL. By identifying the true cost and benefit of services, an organization can conduct service valuation analysis and optimize its investments in the highest value services. Finally, IT accounting provides an organization with a standard language that internal and external customers business partners, and IT can use to evaluate the cost and benefits of IT services. This standard language includes a standard basis for estimating costs across services, standard rates, and standard approaches to measuring utilization or consumption of services. This common framework improves customer satisfaction.

An effective IT charging process improves customer satisfaction through transparent rates that demonstrate the value of the service. From the service provider's perspective, the IT charging process is a critical tool to influence customer behavior to improve utilization of IT resources. The charging process also helps the IT organization model, or forecast demand, and plan for appropriate levels of capacity in the capacity planning process, summarized in Chapter 3, "Adopting IT Service Management Using ITIL." This demand modeling also helps the customer plan and budget for future expenses. Finally, the charging process helps develop a common basis (rates) to discuss the value of IT with internal and external customers.

The IT budgeting process enables an organization to maximize IT investments by evaluating its portfolio of projects based on common financial methodology. This process is often linked closely with the service portfolio management process highlighted in Chapter 2, "IT Service Lifecycle: Improving Business Performance," to maximize IT investments. The IT budgeting process is also critical to any cost savings efforts because it helps identify areas of costs savings by comparing annual budgets.

IT Accounting

IT accounting is the process of collecting financial information—both costs and benefits—for IT services and organizations. IT accounting helps the organization determine the financial cost, benefits, and risks of an IT service. IT accounting differs from traditional financial accounting in that it collects information based on an IT customer or service.[3] IT accounting translates financial accounting information regarding assets, liabilities, revenue, and expenses in a framework that helps both the IT department and business units identify and track benefits and expenses related to specific IT services and customers. ITIL and other frameworks provide a range of guidance into grouping expenses; the three basic characteristics of an IT accounting framework are as follows:

- **Cost and benefit types:** The category of expenses (such as hardware, software, and staff) and benefits (such as contribution to net income)

- **Cost classification:** The end use or purpose of the expense, such as capital expense, direct or indirect cost

- **Customer/service recording:** The assignment of an expense or cost to a specific customer or service

Using these three characteristics, IT accounting assigns a cost type, cost classification, and service to each IT expense. Many different areas within the organization generate and consume IT financial information. For example, IT accounting for a particular IT service may draw information from a business unit, a project management organization, a corporate accounting department, and the IT department.[4] As the IT accounting process becomes more mature, it brings together expense information from a range of sources within the organization to capture the actual cost and benefits of a given IT service.

IT Charging

Charging is the activity of billing internal or external customers for IT services. In some cases, the business unit, government organization, or nonprofit absorbs these costs through the organization's overhead or as a line item in its budget. However, as organizations improve their IT accounting practices, they develop a range of methods to charge or bill for IT services to achieve priority goals and identify the costs of a specific service. The IT charging activity combines the service's rate and the measure of consumption or utilization to create a bill or charge for the internal or external customer.

Together, the rate and measure of consumption help the organization develop charges or assessments to recover total costs of providing a service or achieve target profit goals.

IT Budgeting

Effective IT budgeting identifies all future IT expenses related to a particular service, operation, or customer for a given period of time. Budgeting for IT expenses combines previous commitments, such as recurring hardware or software maintenance, and new expenses, such as additional staff to determine the resources for a given service or activity.

As with budgeting for any investment, IT budgeting is based on discounted cash flow methods. There is a time value to money. For an organization to make long-term investments using organizational resources, these investments must generate a positive financial return for the organization. Financial returns for investments are typically projected out for several years, and projected financial returns in future periods are discounted to current value using a discount rate determined by the organization. This results in IT expenditures being required to generate positive net present value (NPV), or positive value using other discounted cash flow methodology used by your organization. NPV and other discounted cash flow methodology are common methods for determining the financial value resulting from the investment of organizational resources.

Value Added Financial Management Activities

Accounting, budgeting, and charging are the basic IT financial management activities. Using the outputs from these activities, mature organizations can undertake a series of value-added activities to improve service and lower cost. We define these activities in this section.

As IT accounting and charging methods improve, the organization may use them to forecast demand for the services defined in the service catalog or in the underlying service pipeline. This information can then be used to develop appropriate capacity within the capacity management process. ITIL refers to this practice as demand modeling, which helps to ensure that an adequate level of service can be provided to customers. It also helps customers budget for specific services.

Demand modeling used in conjunction with charging can help the IT organization to influence customer behavior. For example, you can use lower "off-peak" billing rates to encourage customers to use IT services at specific times in the day. This influence can help IT service providers work with customers to avoid costly spikes in cost, for either the customer or the service provider. These practices are summarized in the charging discussion later in this chapter.

Mature IT financial organizations also use this financial management information to determine the benefits of financial investments made in IT projects through service portfolio management, service, and business cases. By understanding, tracking, and budgeting for sufficient resources, your organization can realize the level of value adequate to justify the use of organizational resources, time, and budget for the project. At the end of this chapter and continuing in Chapter 5, we discuss the use of business cases as a practice to best manage the service portfolio and invest in a given service.

Financial management information can also be used to improve the cost and service level through optimizing the costs related to the services in your service portfolio and evaluating alternatives based on these costs. This process, referred to as service provisioning optimization, can help organizations evaluate services that may generate revenue, but are exceeded by the commitment of resources to maintain these applications. We discuss these advanced activities at the end of this chapter.

Integrating Financial Management Activities

Effective accounting, charging, and budgeting practices are linked together through a continuous information flow. As shown in Figure 4-1, the IT budget predicts the budgeted amounts for the upcoming year, which the IT accounting process measures. The IT accounting process determines the cost of a given service, which provides critical information to the charging process. As an organization's financial management process matures, these practices will become increasingly linked.

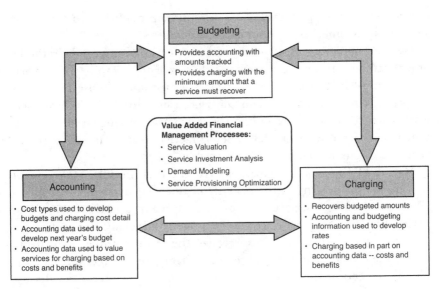

Figure 4-1   Importance of integration between IT accounting, charging, and budgeting

The method for grouping IT budgeting items should be closely tied to IT accounting and charging activities. For example, Organization ABC has determined that its IT accounting cost types will be hardware, software, personnel, and facilities. The organization should use these cost types to develop its IT budget and forecast future expenses. By linking IT costs to the budgeting process, businesses can forecast their IT expenses and more easily prevent IT budget shortfalls.

Identifying Your IT Resources and Services

An inventory of IT resources and linking them to your services is the foundation of financial management and its key practices—accounting, charging, and budgeting. Through an effective process for identifying your IT assets, you can determine your resources, their cost, the charge for their use, and the budget for maintenance or improvement. In their recent book, *The CMDB Imperative*, Glenn O'Donnell and Carlos Casanova highlight a number of practical steps to developing this inventory. The authors discuss these topics extensively in their book, and we strongly recommend you consider these approaches as you implement a method, such as a configuration management database (CMDB), to manage your IT resources.

This list of resources also provides a critical link between IT operations, business units, and IT services. Figure 4-2 highlights how this understanding of your IT resources is the foundation for your IT financial management process.

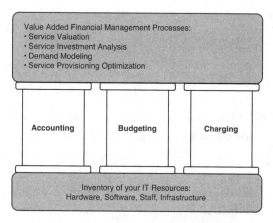

Figure 4-2 An accurate inventory of your IT resources is the foundation of the key IT financial management processes.

Few organizations can define accurate cost data for all software applications, hardware, and networking equipment that enable their core business practices. According to recent academic research, almost two-thirds of chief financial officers (CFOs) and chief information officers (CIOs) do not know the size of their core software assets. A third of organizations do not know what they spend on these assets each year.[5]

To develop this inventory of your IT resources, you should first link financial management activities and tools. Chapter 2 summarizes many of the ITIL best practices, including using service catalog management to create an organization's IT service catalog and configuration management to create a CMDB. In each of the following areas, we link these financial management practices to the ITIL best practices highlighted in Chapter 2. This shows a key benefit of ITIL, namely the linkages between IT service level management and financial management.

We also recommend that you develop a standard process that links data within your organization. Although ITIL best practices suggest using a CMDB as a central repository of the location of IT assets, many IT organizations capture IT assets in stand-alone spreadsheets and software applications that are maintained by both the operational and financial organizations. This approach makes finding a central location of all required information difficult, if not impossible, for many organizations.

To link these spreadsheets, we recommend that the IT organization utilize financial expertise within its own organization or reach out to the overall organization's accounting staff to develop an organization wide list of IT resources. Together, they should:

- Establish a common format for collecting information on IT resources
- Formalize information-sharing organizational structure (such as monthly meetings) between the business units, accounting department, and IT department
- Clarify roles and responsibilities for collecting and maintaining customer and service information
- Automate collection of IT resources (inputs into the spreadsheets) wherever possible

An additional best practice is integrating usage and accounting information through an application that combines information about assets, usage, and accounting. For example, IBM's Tivoli® Usage and Accounting Manager (TUAM) measures, analyzes, reports, and bills the utilization and costs of different IT resources. This tool can automate and consolidate your knowledge of both IT resources and their costs. These benefits are further discussed in the accounting and charging sections later in this chapter.

Implement the IT Financial Management Maturity Model

Government, commercial, and nonprofit organizations vary significantly in the maturity of their IT financial management practices. Some organizations have highly-evolved, mature IT financial management practices, whereas other organizations are just beginning to apply leading financial management practices to their IT organizations. Organizations can be divided into four levels of IT financial management practice maturity. The four levels are best described by the organization's view of IT: the reactive organization, the cost center, the profit center, and the business partner. Figure 4-3 summarizes these four phases and shows that improved accounting, charging, and budgeting are the foundation for more effective IT financial management.

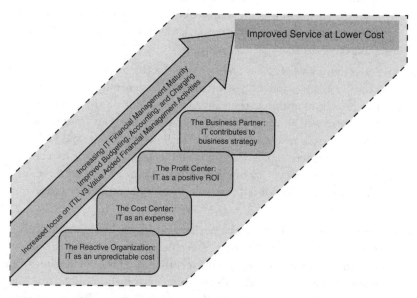

Improved Service at Lower Cost

Increasing IT Financial Management Maturity
Improved Budgeting, Accounting, and Charging
ITIL V3 Value Added Financial Management Activities

Increased focus on

The Business Partner:
IT contributes to
business strategy

The Profit Center:
IT as a positive ROI

The Cost Center:
IT as an expense

The Reactive Organization:
IT as an unpredictable cost

Figure 4-3   Increasing IT financial management maturity will improve service and lower costs.

The IT financial management maturity model identifies an organization's current IT financial management practices as one of these four maturity phases based on the current financial management practices and tools applied to IT resources. This IT financial management maturity model will help you to identify your current stage of maturity, establish a goal for improvement, and identify which practices to target for improvement activities. These decisions will help your organization develop a company-specific roadmap to develop your IT processes, focused on accounting, charging, and budgeting.

The four phases of the IT financial management maturity model reflect industry best practices, evidence from industry and academic research, and a range of industry case studies. The following list summarizes each of these four phases and the next section discusses each in detail:

- **The reactive organization** is the least mature IT financial management organization and views IT as an unpredictable cost. These reactive IT financial management organizations have little visibility or accountability for IT costs. These organizations lack effective accounting, charging, and budgeting for most IT expenditures.

- **The cost center** views IT as an expense. It is the most common maturity level for IT organizations. These organizations generally do not value services or seek to optimize their investments. Within these organizations, IT is viewed as a cost recovery organization, and its budget is designed to match revenue with costs, with no profit. Internal IT organizations recover these expenditures through charging a tax or fee across business units to recover IT funding. Most organizations that serve external customers do not fall into this category because they charge for a service.

- **The profit center**[6] views IT as a positive return on investment. Within these organizations, the IT budget is evaluated based on its business impact, similar to any other capital expenditure. This organization aligns its financial management activities with its customers and services. The IT department works closely with the business units to develop a transparent charging methodology, which may be based on actual utilization of IT resources.

- **The business partner** is the most mature IT financial management organization, viewing IT as a contributor to the achievement of the organization's strategy. These organizations use service investment analysis to evaluate alternatives for the IT budget. Service provisioning optimization is used to benchmark current services and determine alternatives. The IT organization charges internal or external customers through automated resource-based tools that identify the specific asset and services that use this asset. This organization can effectively value its services by considering a range of benefits related to the IT resources and significant risks.

Develop a Roadmap for Improving IT Financial Management Practices

One of the biggest challenges to improving an organization's IT financial management process is identifying a starting point. Before your organization invests significant resources or time in developing new tools, we have identified a process to identify your current IT financial management maturity level. An IT organization, with support where possible from the operational or business units, should conduct an initial assessment to determine the current maturity level of IT financial management practices and then establish a target and timeline for improvement.

Determining the Maturity of Your IT Financial Management Practices

To improve IT financial management, an organization must first identify the current level of maturity of its IT financial management practices against the IT financial management maturity model. This process, however, is not linear. Your organization may have the budgeting process of a cost center, but the accounting and charging processes of an organization that views IT as a profit center. To help you identify this level, you should assess yourself against three questions, summarized in Table 4-1. After you answer these questions, you should review the common financial management practices, benefits, and evidence relating to each stage.

Table 4-1 List of Three Questions to Determine your Organization's Maturity Model

Question	Guide to Determining State
Which financial management activities most reflect those in my organization?	Review the practices of each maturity stage to determine where your organization stands against each process.
Are my financial management practices generating costs or benefits?	Evaluate which benefits and costs summarized in this chapter best reflect your organization.

Table 4-1   List of Three Questions to Determine your Organization's Maturity Model

Question	Guide to Determining State
What evidence (financial and operational) best reflects my organization's financial management process?	Review the evidence for each maturity stage and determine which relates to your organization.

The Reactive Organization: IT as an Unpredictable Expense

The reactive IT financial management organization has the least sophisticated IT financial management maturity. It suffers significant costs from the lack of these practices and reactively responds to financial decisions.

- **Financial management activities:** The reactive IT financial management organization has limited, if any, formal IT accounting, charging, and budgeting activities. The organization spends IT resources with limited operational or financial planning. The organization also lacks IT accounting to determine whether the IT budget is spent to achieve intended service levels.

- **Impact on Cost and Service:** The lack of financial management creates significant costs, such as unpredictable IT expenditures that raise the cost of providing services. The lack of a structured IT budgeting results in unplanned IT expenditures that do not achieve desired service levels. The lack of an effective accounting process might cause resources to be spent on IT projects with lower ROI than targeted by your organization. For example, in purchasing a server, the organization does not consider its wider use and whether the equipment could be used to support other parts of the organization. There are also operational costs, such as wasting time or using it ineffectively to "fight fires" or develop workaround solutions as the organization tries to secure funding for needed equipment, software, or other IT resources.

The reactive IT finance organization often incurs cost overruns that make service unpredictable. For example, the development of new applications might seem to always run over budget and are delivered late to the customer. Business units are often at odds with the IT department due to unclear or inaccurate charging for IT services. The annual budget process likely seems rushed and out of sync with the larger organization's budget process.

The Cost Center: IT as an Expense

The cost center views IT as a cost recovery organization. The annual goal of a cost recovery organization is to exactly match operating costs to resources received through budget allocations and fees charged. In government, cost recovery organizations are often working capital funds:

- **Financial management practices:** The cost center only occasionally works with a central budget office or finance department on IT spending, maximize investments, or forecast demand. The cost center's IT budgeting is based on a break-even goal, with projected budgets for current and future years often based on the budgets of prior years and actual spending. However, a risk with developing current and future budgets based on the prior years' budget is that the organization assumes that the prior year's IT spending is appropriate based on current operational priorities. For example, a provider of email services purchased an expansion of its storage capabilities every other year. This expansion is included into its budget and charging rates. Little thought is given to maximizing this investment and whether virtualization of existing storage resources could save money. The cost center often uses a basic chargeback model that begins to link the IT budget with accounting costs and charges to internal customers, such as business units, or external customers. A chargeback model is a financial model developed to determine how to charge users of IT products and services for these services.

- **Impact on Cost and Service:** The cost center experiences fewer unpredictable IT expenditures than the reactive organization. As a result, its IT organization is more likely to recover all its costs. However, IT resources are not maximized and targeted to the highest value services. For example, because the chargeback rates are often on a flat fee or IT tax, it does not accurately reflect the utilization of key resources. As a result, underutilized IT assets may be perpetuated and demand cannot be forecasted.

FINANCIAL TERMS DEFINED

As IT financial management practices improve, they apply an increasing amount of financial rigor to make IT budgets, projects, and investment decisions. The following terms have a range of meanings and often differ within and between organizations. In most organizations they are simply financial methods to demonstrate a project's value, as measured by netting of potential benefits, against the potential costs incurred to achieve these benefits. In Chapter 5, we give alternatives to NPV, but we generally recommend using NPV as the best way to determine the value today of a given IT investment.

The following are key financial terms and how these terms are used:

- **Discounted cash flow:** A general approach to evaluate the value of new projects and investments. This approach includes NPV and other methods. This method enables IT departments to compare projects that generate costs and benefits from different periods of time.

- **Discount rate:** The finance organization of many organizations will establish a discount (or hurdle rate) for NPV. Then for each project, expense, or budget item under consideration, its calculated NPV value must be greater than the established hurdle rate for that calculation. A discount or hurdle rate is usually applied when the cost of funds or discount rate is included in the financial calculations. As you talk with your corporate finance department about the discount rate, you must include a risk premium on the discount rate for investments with a higher level of risk.

- **Net present value (NPV):** NPV takes future cash flows and discounts them to their present-day value using the discount rate. These future cash flows may be positive, such as revenue from an IT service, or negative, such as a server cost today.

  NPV = ($ in future) / (1 + Discount rate)

The Profit Center: IT as a Positive ROI

All organizations have limited resources to achieve their objectives. Resources must be utilized in a manner that generates a positive return for their use or investment. As an IT organization matures its financial management practices on the IT financial management maturity model, the IT organization is better able to generate a positive ROI:

- **Financial management practices:** The IT profit center uses actual accounting data to value its services. It uses this accurate data to develop clear rates in its charging process and uses these rates to model demand. It combines these rates with accurate usage information to help the customer meet its goals for IT services. The profit center also combines its IT budgeting process with its business case, portfolio management, and service investment analysis to generate a positive ROI, as measured by NPV, on its IT investments

- **Impact on Cost and Services:** The organization provides its customers with a clear value for its services. The value of a given IT service is defined for the customer and recovered through an effective charging process. Effective accounting provides the organization with a clear understanding of the cost of specific IT services. IT budgeting allows the IT department to integrate with the larger organization and ensure that its resources are allocated in the most effective manner.

In contrast with the cost center that only occasionally works with a budget or finance department, the profit center's financial management practices reflects a basic level of integration between IT operations and the finance teams. Costs might reflect rough total cost of ownership (TCO) estimates, although portions of these costs will be estimates and assumptions. For example, the organization might not be able to attribute power consumption of specific applications and might still provide estimated consumption levels.

The Business Partner: IT Contributes to Overall Strategy

The business partner is the most effective, optimized IT organization and viewed as a trusted business partner. A trusted IT business partner contributes to the organization's overall strategy and mission:

- **Financial management:** IT resources contribute to overall organizational strategy. Business cases determines the NPV for potential expenditures. Effective investment analysis determines that potential IT investments with either a negative NPV or NPV below a target minimum level established by the organization will be rejected, protecting the financial goals for the organization. The IT accounting reflects a high level of detail to provide the organization with a complete measure of IT costs related to each service. Also in this phase, an organization charges IT costs to its business units. These charges are based on total costs and actual utilization. These cost estimates are transparent, exact, and provided to the business unit on a periodic basis. The ability of an IT organization to provide customers transparent IT costs is a critical success factor in establishing trust with the IT provider.

- **Impact on Cost and Service:** An organization's IT services see a wide range of benefits from optimized IT financial practices. The managers and staff will spend less time responding to crises and requests from the operational and business units and instead allocate a predictable amount of time to these efforts, translating into more predictable service levels. The organization also achieves a range of financial benefits, including lower costs. For example, the organization is able to achieve a higher ROI on its IT investments, and a greater portion of its IT budget is devoted to high value services, as demonstrated by service investment analysis. The organization also maintains a focus on IT costs by understanding the true cost of provisioning a given service.

Organizations with optimized practices carefully plan and measure IT expenditures because operations can accurately forecast needs in capacity and the associated expenses. The organization knows the specific costs for each service because the costs are often linked to the IT service catalog and the service catalog management process outlined in Chapter 2. As a result, the pricing for service level agreements developed in the service level management process is transparent to the internal customers, IT department, and external customers.

DON'T LET THE PERFECT BE THE ENEMY OF THE GOOD!

Total cost of ownership (TCO) is a financial model developed primarily by Gartner that attempts to define the common cost, benefit, and risk elements of a well-developed IT cost baseline. Although trade publications recognize TCO as the industry best practice, it can be more than some organizations need (or can manage) for beginning to understand costs because of some limitations inherent in this model. For example, for many organizations simply improving business case may be able to immediately lower their costs. The bottom line is that although TCO studies can be very helpful, you do not necessarily need this level of detail to realize significant improvements.

Establishing Goals for Improving Your Financial Management Practices

After you assess your current maturity level in IT financial management, you then should determine the desired future state for your IT financial management practice. Determining the future state involves a trade-off of the benefits of a more fully matured state of IT financial management versus the cost of implementing new or improved processes for the organization.

The amount of improvement in an organization's financial management practices depends on the resources applied to the effort, the executive sponsorship, support from the IT organization, and other environmental factors. The following summarizes these key issues:

- **Executive sponsorship:** Executive sponsorship is critical to successfully improving financial management. Ideally, the chief executive officer (CEO) would be visibly supportive of this type of initiative. This support helps to encourage collaboration between the CFO (and other finance staff) and the CIO (or IT director and staff). Without this support, a change initiative to significantly improve IT financial management is unlikely to be successful or provide benefits to the organization.

- **Resources and staff:** The IT financial management improvement initiative should consist of motivated staff and resources that draw on a range of part-time staff from key departments such as business units/customers, finance, and other areas.

- **Culture and organizational preparedness:** Based on your organization's culture and structure, you should consider its overall preparedness for financial management process improvements. You should consider whether these improvements are understandable and relevant to the organization. If not, you should consider how these process improvements can be better framed to address challenges facing the organization.

- **Timing:** The ideal timing for undertaking an IT finance improvement initiative is a few months before the beginning of the annual budget planning process. This allows time to evaluate which phase of the maturity model applies to an organization and to establish the goals for improvement.

- **Information sharing:** Information sharing between finance and IT staff is critical to any IT finance improvement initiatives. On one hand, financial staff must distill and provide key information related to infrastructure costs. On the other hand, IT staff must provide accurate information about key IT assets.

- **Support from IT division, customers, and internal partners:** Communicating key benefits of an IT financial management improvement initiative to the IT division, customers, and internal partners is critical. First, many IT organizations have multiple continual improvement, or change, initiatives ongoing at any point in time. Underscoring these benefits to the IT staff will help them participate more actively in the initiative. Showing IT staff this type of information can help them understand that this IT financial management improvement initiative will provide them with significant benefits. Similarly, if your organization engages internal or external customers, you must demonstrate to them the value of this initiative: that it will improve service and lower cost. Finally, the finance department will be more likely to engage if it knows that it will receive fewer ad hoc requests for financial data and IT charging and budgeting will become more predictable.

Use ITIL's Continual Service Improvement Approach to Avoid Key Mistakes

Improvements should be based on a clearly identified target end state and a roadmap to get there. This process should be based on ITIL's continual service improvement (CSI) approach that will help you to identify key business objectives, evaluate where you are today, establish measurable targets, determine a path to reach your targets, and measure your outcome. We discuss this approach in detail in both Chapter 2 and Chapter 9, "Going Forward." Otherwise, significant time and resources can be wasted developing cost estimates based on inaccurate data or tools that are not supported by a robust IT financial management infrastructure.

Software tools, financial models, and studies are all tactical tools that can be applied to improve IT financial management operations, but should not be the starting point for an improvement effort. Table 4-2 highlights common mistakes IT organizations make when first attempting to develop and mature their IT financial management practices.

Table 4-2   Common Pitfalls on the Road to Improving IT Financial Management Practices

Common Pitfall	Result
Purchase expensive asset management software packages to identify all IT assets without developing an improved process	IT staff may resist implementing this software. Even if you know the asset, you will not know the cost, leaving you with only a piece of the puzzle.
Conduct extensive TCO study without collecting data or developing a process	The cost of doing this study can outweigh the benefits. Developing a one-time study will not provide an ongoing stream of data to improve the overall process.
Initiate a corporate finance task force review of IT spending	The corporate finance organizations may not have the required level of technical knowledge about the IT resources they are attempting to review.
Not establishing a process to eliminate failing projects	For many IT organizations, particularly application development organizations, a key problem is not having a process to eliminate failed projects. This process should be in place in conjunction with any financial management efforts.

Instead, to improve the maturity of an IT financial management organization, the organization should focus on improving specific practices. For example, if an organization wants to move from a reactionary organization to a cost center, it might decide to improve charging and budgeting. After you have decided to improve a given process, you can identify or develop supporting financial tools such as a basic chargeback model. A standardized business case methodology could become part of an IT financial management improvement plan.

Because relatively few organizations know the true costs and benefits of their IT resources, many organizations have an immediate opportunity to improve the return on their IT investments. Just determining the costs of each service is an effective starting point to make immediate, measurable improvements through the practices outlined in this chapter.

Improve IT Financial Management Practices to Improve Service and Lower Cost

The following sections focus on ways to improve the basic and value added IT financial management practices, and how this information can be used to improve service and lower costs. We discuss ways to improve these practices within each maturity phase. For example, the following section summarizes how to account for IT services, given the approximate IT costs and benefits available. By reviewing this information, an organization can develop a plan for improving these IT financial practices to improve your IT financial management maturity. Improving IT financial management requires change in a mix of IT organization, tools, and processes. As you develop your roadmap, you should use project management and change management best practices that have historically worked for your or other IT organizations. Using project organization charts, roles and responsibilities, and communication plans helps to make the implementation and development of financial management processes clear. You can start by reviewing the Organizational Change Management approaches to an ITIL implementation included in Chapter 3.

Improve IT Accounting to Value Services

We recommend that you align your IT accounting practices with the services in your service portfolio. This alignment will help you improve your IT accounting and provide you with a better understanding of the costs, benefits, and risks associated with each service. Determining the cost, benefit, and risks of each service can be complex. When an IT organization begins the process of identifying the costs associated with a service, it will need to consider alternative approaches to account for items other than the acquisition—costs such as power consumption, staff costs, and infrastructure. For example, with the rise of virtualization and enterprise servers, the process for establishing an service's share of the total server cost can prove difficult.

Because of these challenges, organizations face a choice about the degree of specificity regarding the cost of an IT asset. A simplistic cost estimate can focus on the initial acquisition cost and annual maintenance expense. A more inclusive cost estimate will use TCO, which we discussed earlier in this chapter.

To help you determine your approach to accounting for costs based on a service, we outline different options and provide an example of a simple hosting service. This example provides you with the context for our recommended approach.

Basic Approaches to Improve IT Accounting

In our IT financial management maturity model, the reactive organization, which reviews IT as an unpredictable cost, simply accounts for total IT costs. The reactive organization does not decompose expenses into cost types and linked with services. Any organization that is more mature than a reactive organization will have an IT accounting process that will:

1. Categorize expenses using cost types and cost classifications.
2. Assign costs to services through service recording.
3. Apply a consistent method for using actual costs, averages, or estimates.

Each of these steps is discussed in the following sections.

Categorize Expenses Using Cost Types and Cost Classifications

To develop cost types, we generally recommend that you develop basic types that can be applied consistently across your services. These costs will include hardware, software, maintenance, personnel (employee and contractor), miscellaneous personnel costs (training, awards, and so on), building and facilities costs, internal and external overheads, and supplies. These costs are decomposed into the following cost types:

- **Hardware:** This cost type includes the initial hardware purchase, depreciation, maintenance, installation, and any upgrades. This hardware includes servers, mainframes, storage (disk/tape), printers, load balancers, and other devices.

- **Software:** This cost type includes any software or application. It often includes the operating system, database and data management, messaging, middleware, ongoing patches, and upgrades.

- **Infrastructure and environmental costs (nonsoftware):** These cost types, including floor space at a data center, power, upkeep/maintenance, security, networking and Internet bandwidth, and supplies, can be substantial for an IT organization. As a result, many organizations develop average costs for a given asset, such as server racks, and distribute them across the data center.

■ **Staff costs:** Many organizations use estimates of staff time allocated to a specific activity, such as provisioning a server or patching an application, to develop the cost. These estimates are often developed through interviews with staff about time incurred for conducting specific activities. These estimates can be confirmed by reviewing overall staff costs and infrastructure supported to determine whether these estimates appear reasonable. Alternatively, other organizations simply allocate a percentage of staff costs to a particular service without conducting specific time estimates per service. Mature organizations should evaluate historical time tracking data.

■ **Overhead:** Organizations capture a number of operating cost types in the cost category of overhead. Included in overhead are a number of cost types, including management salaries and other expenses that are not specifically allocated to other cost categories. Many organizations group into the overhead cost category a number of unallocated costs that are not appropriate for infrastructure and environmental costs. Potential inaccurate cost allocations into overhead can cause significant confusion among the customers of IT organizations. Whenever possible, making specific cost allocations to cost types other than overhead is preferable to combining costs into overhead because it provides more transparent, actionable data to the customers.

Many organizations use several additional ways to group cost, which the ITIL refers to as cost classifications. These classifications depend on the organization's structure and IT accounting practices. These options include grouping costs by:

■ **Direct and indirect costs:** Direct costs are those attributed to a specific service. Indirect costs are those costs that relate to a number of different services that cannot be exactly allocated between services. In some cases, indirect costs are simply included in an organization's overhead.

■ **Fixed and variable costs:** Fixed costs are those that do not change based on the IT resource. For example, the maintenance cost or server cost would be a fixed cost. A variable cost example is staff costs, which might increase based on a given level of utilization.

■ **Capitalized costs:** Although capitalized costs may span multiple cost types as defined previously and may vary based on the organization, they are a widely used cost accounting method to spread IT costs over time. Although these costs may be excluded like data conversion and prototyping, they may be important to your organization. Tracking these costs requires additional tracking during implementation, and you should work closely with your finance or accounting department.

As the IT accounting matures, cost types are classified in ways that add value to the organization and are increasingly aligned with key business decisions.

Assign Costs to Services through Service Recording

After developing your organization's cost types, you will group these cost types by a given service. Many IT organizations are technology focused, and as a result, their IT accounting methods are focused on specific technology platforms. Best practices, such as ITIL, recommend that organizations develop service-oriented accounting, which aligns all costs with a particular service, not with a technology platform.

When an IT resource, such as a server or staff person, is dedicated to a given service, it is clear where you should account for the cost. However, a major challenge is the allocation of shared resources, such as a virtualized server, by many different IT services. A common method for allocating the cost of a shared resource, such as a pool of shared servers shared by a set of applications, is to first group these shared costs and allocate them proportionally based on a the respective service's share. For example, you may decide to allocate a shared pool of staff members based on the percent of time dedicated to a specific service. Similarly, the cost of a shared pool of servers may be allocated to a number of services based on utilization rates of a given set of applications. Network costs may be allocated by the percentage of networking costs used by a given service.

To break down the technology silos and account for IT costs based on a service, the organization can develop a simple IT accounting form, such as the sample shown in Table 4-3 for a Web service. The sample organization has grouped the cost types by hardware, software, staff, facility, and depreciation and recorded these costs to a web-hosting service.

Table 4-3   Sample IT Accounting Form for Web Service

Web Service

Cost Type	Amount	Date Purchased
Hardware Costs		
UNIX® Servers		
UNIX servers' maintenance		
Load balancer		
Load balance maintenance		
Storage		
Software Costs		
Operating system		
Web service software		
Staff		
Salaries and benefits		
Facility		
Space		
Power		
Networking (switches and routers)		
Depreciation		
Hardware depreciation		
Software depreciation		

Apply a Consistent Method for Using Actual Costs, Averages, or Estimates

To gather expense information for a given service or activity, you can use three industry-accepted methods: estimates, averages, and actual IT expenditures. Actual expense data should be used whenever possible. However, within many organizations, exact data might not be available, usable, or might be cost prohibitive to collect relative to the benefits.

A NOTE ON APPLICATION DEVELOPMENT, DEMAND MANAGEMENT, AND PORTFOLIO MANAGEMENT

In general, IT operations—including the data center, networking, and infrastructure groups—are more transactional (such as resolving a help desk ticket, resetting a password, adding memory to a server), whereas application development projects (such as building or improving a customized system) are more project focused. Although both IT operations and application development have several of the same budgeting challenges, there are key differences to keep in mind.

Although the preceding framework applies to all IT services, application development organizations may want to emphasize their focus on staff costs and software maintenance costs because they are often the highest line items.

Focusing on these costs helps predict usage of development resources. For example, one organization we interviewed established a goal to forecast 18 months forward the usage of project management, analysts, development, and quality assurance resources for specific services. As part of this goal, the organization linked its financial management, service level management, demand management, and portfolio management to deal with the inevitable changes in priorities and to ensure alignment with business objectives.

This connection with demand modeling and portfolio management allowed the application development group to think about the skills it will need in advance of project initiation and in many cases more accurately estimate project costs.

As your organization develops these cost types, you should utilize the service level management, demand modeling, and portfolio management information in Chapter 2 and Chapter 5, on IT business cases. This can help assure your IT accounting process is effective.

For example, if an organization has begun only to develop cost types and a basic accounting framework, it would be costly to collect retroactively the prior year's expenses and group them by service. Although sometimes necessary to use estimates, samples, or averages, you should try to use actual costs whenever possible. If you use estimates or averages, we also recommend you develop a plan or timeline to eventually capture actual costs:

- **Estimates or samples:** Based on a sample purchase order or industry averages, estimates are sometimes used to develop the cost of a specific service. A significant drawback of using estimated costs is that estimates are based on assumptions and do not reflect the true cost of service. As a result, estimates can create the risk of losses and inaccurate information being provided to customers when poorly applied. For example, if an organization prices its hosting services below its true costs, it might cause its business units to overuse these services. The IT organization will then lose money on each hosted server.

- **Averages:** Based on the average cost of a large sample of purchase orders, averages are sometimes used to develop the cost of a specific service. For example, an organization might estimate the cost of a UNIX server based on the average cost from multiple UNIX server invoices. These averages are more accurate than a single sample or industry estimate because they capture the information of your organization. Averages are less likely to understate of overstate the cost of a particular resource, as compared to an estimate or sample.

- **Actual costs:** Including actual costs is preferred whenever possible. The key to useful actual cost data is gathering IT expense information in a useful and agreed-upon format with your accounting or corporate finance department.

Table 4-4 summarizes how to develop a plan to improve your IT accounting information. Still if you cannot gather actual cost information, you can begin to better account for your IT costs using estimates or averages and tailor them to your environment.

Table 4-4 Developing a Plan to Improve Your IT Accounting Information

Instead of...	Try...	How...
No cost information	Estimates	Gather cost estimates that reflect your operational environment. For example, if you are trying to estimate the cost of the server and are using an online quote, use your typical server type, operating system, and amount of memory. Seek out industry averages and multiple estimates to determine whether your internal estimates are realistic. Collect past purchase orders so your estimates are based on your organization.
Estimates	Averages	Collect as many purchase orders as possible for a given item, such as a server, to determine the average cost. Use average payroll information to develop an average full-time equivalent (FTE) rate.
Averages	Actual costs	Assign service-based identification numbers to IT expenses. Require your staff to assign an ID based on the service to each IT expense. Develop a monthly process to receive accounting information. Facilitate a meeting with the IT, accounting, or corporate finance department to develop a framework for collecting IT costs. Time tracking for FTE costs, particularly for application development organizations.

Improving an IT Accounting Process to Become the Profit Center or Business Partner

As an IT organization matures its financial practices to become a profit center or business partner, customers begin to view IT as a positive ROI or business partner. The organization's cost types are closely linked to operational information. IT financial processes reflect actual accounting data instead of estimates. Its costs/expenses are more closely tied with the organization's IT service catalog. The organization also identifies the value of IT, including its intangible benefits.

Improve Your Accounting Framework by Linking Costs to Your Service Portfolio

While throughout this book we advocate a service-based approach to financial management, an IT organization seeks to mature its IT financial management practices to a profit center or business partner, it must link its costs to its service portfolio. This practice helps you understand the cost structure of a specific service, referred to as the service provisioning value by ITIL, and provides a range of benefits. It enables an organization to benchmark against another IT service provider, support the creation of standard chargeback rates, and compare actual expenditures against a specific budget.

To implement this method requires that all IT expenses be either coded against a specific IT product or service or allocated across several specific IT products and services. For example, a shared application server may be applied to three different services whose applications reside within the server. An effective way to code expenses is based on the organization's IT service catalog, which includes a list of IT products and services provided by an IT organization, a description of each product and service, and a cost to purchase each product and service.

In the example in Figure 4-4, this sample organization has developed a process for aligning its costs to its services and organization.

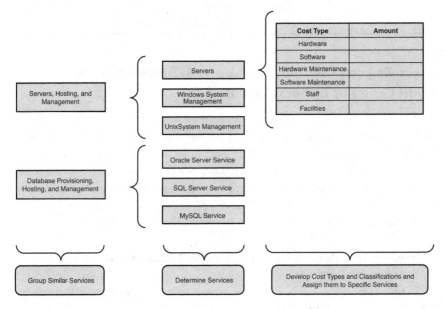

Figure 4-4 IT accounting assigns expenses to specific services through cost types and classifications.

This detailed cost information helps an organization to improve service by developing accurate pricing for IT services by gathering increasingly detailed accounting information. This allows the organization's larger financial processes to integrate with the organization's processes for charging internal or external customers for IT products and services, and ultimately budgeting for new and ongoing IT expenditures.

IT ACCOUNTING BASED ON SERVICE PORTFOLIO IMPROVES SERVICE AND LOWERS COSTS

An organization can use service-based IT accounting information to improve service and lower costs by feeding accurate cost and benefit information to the value added IT activities. For example, two organizations used this information as follows.

Use Service Investment Analysis to Improve Service: One organization used SIA to rank IT investments based on most value services as defined by service catalog. This practice helped the organization to optimize IT investments by improving the service levels of the most valued services.

Use Service Provisioning Optimization to Reduce Costs: An organization can use this accurate and service based financial data to compare the cost of providing specific services. For example, an internal service provider benchmarked the per GB charge of providing storage. After they determined that the value of the service was below the external provider, they developed a strategy to lower their costs.

Capture Actual Costs and Compare Against Your Budget to Prevent Cost Overruns

As your IT financial management processes improve, actual accounting data replaces industry averages and estimates. As noted previously, this actual data allows the accounting process to provide charging and budgeting processes with more accurate cost information. Using actual costs is often a significant change from the cost of service delivery currently used by the organization for ongoing IT financial management, chargebacks, and internal control functions.

For example, instead of average FTE estimates, the organization will use actual staff costs based on HR records and organizational charts. More accurate staff costs help identify hidden personnel costs. For example, while many staff include only those application developers or system administrators who work on a given service, they miss those administrative or other support staff whose costs must also be recovered. These actual costs can then be compared against a budgeted amount, thereby creating the ability to provide periodic (monthly, quarterly, and so on) financial reports to senior management and preventing cost overruns.

Improve Cost Type Links to Operational Information

As your IT financial management practices mature, IT cost types and service recording should be linked with the organization's inventory of IT assets. This inventory is often shared between the IT and financial organizations. In evolved IT financial management organizations, where its customers view IT as a business partner, the IT and financial organizations share a common set of information from a single database but just access different views. Table 4-5 summarizes some sample information you will gather for a server resource that links the server, software, application it supports, financial information, and the delivered and expected quality of service.[7]

As your organization's IT financial management matures, you may collect and link increasing amounts of operational information. For example, you may decide to collect additional data points on quality of service than those listed in Table 4-5. You may also want to collect similar information on networking, application development, and application maintenance.

Improving IT Charging Based on Services

IT charging is the process of billing for IT services rendered to internal or external customers. The charging process uses two key sets of information: 1) rates based on accounting information, forecasts of current and future customer demand, and other relevant information; and 2) usage information based on actual measures and estimates. Together, this information is used to create a price, or assessment, for a given service, as shown in Figure 4-5.

Table 4-5   Example of Linking Financial and Server Information

Server	Operating System Software Stack	Applications	Financial	Quality of Service
Server name	Operating system	Application name	Hardware depreciation	Server outage history
Primary function	Middleware	Application version	Hardware maintenance	Server utilization status
Installed location	Database	Registered users	Software depreciation	Business criticality
Vendor machine/ model	Application(s)	Concurrent users	Software maintenance	Service levels
Date installed	Monitoring and security tools/agents	Annual application growth rate	Facilities costs (power, floor space)	Backup
Operating system	Administrative tools/agents	Platform affinities	Staff	Disaster recovery (DR)
Memory and disk type and quantity	Tape backup agent	License type (named user, subscription, concurrent users) and expiration dates		

Charging Process Develops Rates, Captures Utilization, and Results in a Final Cost or Assessment

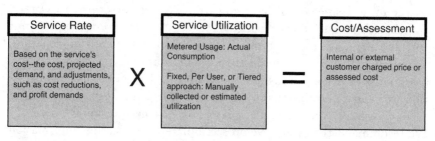

Figure 4-5   Charging process develops rates, captures utilization, and results in a price or assessment.

Determining Cost Center Charging Methods

As organizations mature from a reactive IT organization to an IT cost center, they develop a standardized charge or assessment framework using a chargeback (or IT costing) model to define available costs associated with its services. Through the development and population of a chargeback or IT costing model, you will determine your service rates. There are many different definitions of chargeback models, but they combine IT accounting data to determine a service's cost with usage data from capacity management and other processes to develop a price. In an article on CIO.com, titled "Chargeback Demonstrates IT Value in the Enterprise," Mark J. Denne discusses a number of approaches to developing chargeback methods.[10] They include subscription, peak level usage, user-based pricing, and ticket-based pricing.

Regardless of the pricing method you choose, cost centers, by definition, charge an appropriate level of fees for IT products and services to exactly equal the costs incurred by the IT organization to provide these IT products and services, which is considered "break even" from a financial perspective.

To help you develop your rate and a means for capturing utilization information, we have summarized a general method for developing a chargeback model. This method includes developing a chargeback model to determine the rate; populating the chargeback model with a mix of assumptions, averages, and actual costs; and determining utilization, or quantity of services. Developing measures of utilization is a key link to the demand management process.

Develop Chargeback Model to Determine Rate for Each Service

The cost center uses the chargeback rate and utilization method to develop a pricing or assessment method to recover these costs through a charge or assessment. To determine your service (or chargeback) rate, you should start by creating a chargeback template to determine your cost and populate the chargeback template with expense information. This will help you determine the cost of your specific service. Then, based on your pricing decisions and ability to determine service utilization, you can determine the rates you will charge for a given service.

To determine your chargeback rate, you first need to know your cost. We recommend that you develop a template for collecting information by service that allows you to provide a top-level summary sheet, while also providing significant detail on specific areas in the services inputs and buildup worksheet.

The top-level summary sheet can then be used as a common language between the business unit and IT unit regarding the cost of a specific service. Table 4-6 shows a simple framework to develop the top-level summary sheet. The top-level summary worksheet highlights the unloaded chargeback rate, applicable overhead rates, and published chargeback rate for your services. The unloaded chargeback rate, also often referred to as all direct costs, is the cost without any overhead applied.

Table 4-6 Top-Level Summary Sheet

Published Service	Unloaded Chargeback Rate	Administrative Overhead Rate	Published Rate (Rounded)
Hosting	$16,428	5%	$17,250
Batch processing	$2,857	5%	$3,000
Collaboration service	$3,809	5%	$4,000

This top-level summary sheet is useful to both the IT organization and the business group because it:

- Is simple to understand
- Demonstrates transparency of overhead costs, which can be a contentious issue between business units and IT organizations
- Provides detail to executives who might be reviewing their rates and budget

Next, the organization should develop a summary of key costs for each service, such as the service inputs and buildup worksheet in Table 4-7. These costs include hardware, software staff costs, and other cost types. If an organization has created cost types within its IT accounting practices, these costs should match these types within this sheet. This sheet is critical for transparency of IT costs and establishes a common understanding with the business unit. The business unit and the IT department can review the various inputs to a service to determine whether they are necessary.

Table 4-7   Services Inputs and Buildup Worksheet

Published Services	Hardware Cost (Purchase Price)	Operating System (One-Time Cost)	Staff Setup Cost	Annualized Amount (with 3-year Depreciation)	HW and SW Maintenance	Annual Staff Cost	Annual Cost
Hosting	$12,000	$2,000	$4,000	$10,000	$1,429	$5,000	$16,428
Development of enterprise resource planning (ERP) customized application	$12,000	$2,000	$4,000	$10,000	$1,429	$150,000	$166,428

As you will see from Table 4-7, the process can be used for transactional services, such as hosting, or project services, such as application development. These buildup worksheets are effective ways to account for the need to capture differences in types of services, infrastructure, networking, and application development. To provide additional detail, you should develop a service-specific worksheet that includes the detailed support for your service's inputs and buildup worksheet. Several options to develop these service-specific summary sheets follow:

- **Use worksheet from accounting process:** If your accounting process has grouped cost type information according to each service, this sheet can provide this role. For example, this accounting sheet can provide the detail you need regarding hardware, software, and personnel costs, which can be linked to the services inputs and buildup worksheet.

- **Create new worksheet that includes accounting data and assumptions:** Organizations must often make a number of assumptions related to key costs. You should consider developing a worksheet that includes both accounting data and key assumptions.

- **External contracted (base) costs:** The organization should then create a sheet that includes external costs, such as software licenses or vendor cost that are often external to the organization.

- **Internal costs (for example, salary, overhead, and financial information):** This sheet generally includes internal costs, such as overhead, staff time, and other inputs that are internal to the organization. These sheets also summarize service-specific assumptions, such as the staff time allocation cost estimates for staff activities discussed in the basic approaches in the earlier section "Basic Approaches to Improve IT Accounting."

The structure of these worksheets needs to be tailored to your organization. You should structure them based on the information you have available and the audience that will use this information.

Populate the Service Chargeback Model with a Mix of Assumptions, Averages, and Actual Costs

After the finance and IT organization complete the chargeback framework, they should then work together to insert costs into the model. We would like to reinforce our discussion in the accounting section on using estimates, averages, or actual IT expenditures to develop costs. Many cost centers use assumptions and averages, rather than cost accounting data. For example, instead of listing the exact price of a server, the IT organization might list an average rate, sometimes referred to as a blended rate. These blended rates are the average of a number of purchase orders to determine the typical cost. Also, instead of exact FTE estimates for system administrators, the organization might develop a blended rate that reflects the average cost of a system administrator.

In addition to the discussion of estimates, averages, and actual IT expenditure data in the accounting section, we provide key examples of benefits assumptions if actual data is not available:

- Estimates or averages provide a baseline set of data to continuously improve your chargeback or IT costing model each year. For example, the first year an organization develops a cost model, a large percentage of the data may be based on the best assumptions that can be made at the time using available source data. However, each year the organization can replace key data with actual data.

- Developing a mix of estimated and actual data creates a framework for enacting key process improvements. For example, it provides a common framework for the IT and finance departments to share information. This framework can help translate financial and operational information and help both the IT and business teams learn.

Determine Charge or Assessment Method through Standardized IT Pricing Framework

Reactive IT organizations charge their internal or external customers through corporate overhead allocations rather than direct invoicing. This lack of transparency in IT budgeting is often viewed as a tax on business units and creates resentment by the business units. As an IT organization matures to a cost center, it develops a method to estimate the service's cost and the customer's utilization. This standardized IT pricing framework captures a service's cost and utilization (where appropriate). This framework could also service as the customer invoice. A simple customer template could look like Table 4-8.

Table 4-8   IT Pricing Framework for Business Units

Published Service	Service Increment	Service (or Chargeback) Rate	Service Utilization	Total Chargeback Cost (or IT Price)
Hosting	Per server	$12,000	1	$12,000
Batch processing	CPU second	$0.3	10,000	$3,000
Collaboration service	Per site	$2,000	2	$4,000
Application development	Per statement of work (SOW)	$25,000	1	$25,000
Total				$44,000

The previous pricing framework highlights the difference between transactional services and services, such as application development, that may be based on a statement of work (SOW). The final item, application development, is an example of a project-based service that employs staff or contracts. Some organizations may take an SOW approach, in which a defined SOW summarizes that payment that will result from a given set of deliverables, such as the completed application or software package. Alternatively, you could develop a per-hour rate for application developers and charge the customer this hourly rate.

After the IT organization has developed a framework, it should use this as a tool to engage its customers in a discussion of the charging process. These initial discussions will foster acceptance of this framework within the organization. The organization can then develop the inputs to the framework including the service (or chargeback) rate and the service utilization.

Determine Utilization or Quantity of Services

Because the IT organization has established its costs, it now needs to work with its existing customers to project out the near term the expected demand for each IT product and service, measured in projected quantity of IT products and services; to establish the projected overall demand, and to develop pricing for each IT product and service offered using project demand as a key assumption.

To recover costs, you must develop an accurate measure of the quantity of services used by a customer or service. The cost center often uses actual measures and estimates to measure the quantity of resources used by each customer. As with expenditures, you should use automated tools to collect actual costs of service utilization data whenever possible. Following is a summary of three methods to measure utilization:

- **Metered usage:** When the utilization can be precisely measured, the organization generally uses metered usage. This method is based on actual utilization, whereby the organization automates the collection of quantity of resources used by each consumer based on the agreed-upon metric. For more service-based estimates, this may include a time tracking system to track the time of application developers.

- **Fixed- or user-cost approach:** Many cost centers may also decide to simply divide a service's cost by this forecasted quantity to develop a unit price. This process, referred to in ITIL as *fixed or user costs,* is one of the most simplistic methods for determining pricing. This fixed price could include a subscription to use a specific quantity of services. The more accurate the demand forecast, the fewer risks the IT organization will incur a budget shortfall. This fixed-cost approach can also be used if an SOW specifies a specific price for a specific output, such as the development of a new ERP system.

- **Tiered utilization:** A hybrid approach includes tiered utilization, whereby an organization measures utilization of a specific service and groups customers into tiers. This utilization data may be gathered through either a demand management or capacity management process under ITIL. The use of an automated tool often supports this effort because one method to stratify the pricing of multiple tiers of IT product and service offerings is based on utilization versus resources.

  Developing tiered utilization can be combined with tiered rates, in which the IT organization offers tiers of IT products and services, such as stratifying storage into managed and basic storage. In other cases, the organization will offer premium and standard levels of support. Accurately presenting the tiers of IT products and services will help to clarify the pricing for internal and external IT customers.

Improving Your Charging Process to Become a Profit Center or Business Partner

To improve the charging process as the organization views IT as a positive ROI or a business partner, the IT organization captures more accurate usage and cost information, often using automated tools that track IT resources and link them to their costs. The IT organization also develops linkages with other ITIL processes to considers as it develops rates. For example, it effectively values services and develops pricing in concert with the IT service catalog and aligns its expenditures to the service levels outlined in the service level agreements (SLAs) developed through the service level management process. This process is discussed later in this chapter.

Many IT organizations also use chargeback models to price selected IT products and services, typically limited to the IT products and services provided in their IT service catalog. The cost analysis supporting the development of a chargeback model also provides operational information that IT organizations can use to manage their resource consumption, resulting in continuous improvement in IT operations.

Improve Your Service or Chargeback Rate to Improve Service and Lower Costs

To improve service or chargeback rate, your organization should use only exact costs to develop its IT costing model. The IT accounting process should provide exact costs that can be leveraged in the IT costing model. For example, the service-specific sheets discussed in the previous section should just be outputs of the IT accounting process. This data provides the organization with a true understanding of the provisioning value (or the cost) of each service. As a result, the organization can conduct service provisioning optimization activities to benchmark its costs against competitors.

As your charging and pricing process becomes more advanced, your organization's price per billable unit recovers your full cost and a surplus amount that is the hurdle rate, which is discussed earlier in the chapter. For example, if your hurdle, or discount rate, was 5 percent, your IT price would be 5 percent above the cost of your service. This pricing method subjects your IT services to the same project standards commonly used in other financial initiatives.

To improve service, an organization should link charging to the various internal contracts between the IT organization and its customers (SLAs) and internal contracts between organizational units within the IT organization (operation level agreements, OLAs) discussed in Chapter 2. This linkage helps the IT organization to clearly establish the value of its services to its customers. For example, if a customer would like more backups or quicker response time than the organization typically offers, the organization may want to develop a pricing mechanism to recover these costs.

Implement Automated Tools to Monitor Resources, Costs, and Utilization

To improve service, the organization should also charge customers for usage, rather than approximate consumption. As an IT organization matures from a cost center to viewing IT as an ROI or business partner, the IT organization often implements an automated solution to identify and monitor IT customers' utilization. These high-performing organizations often move toward resource-based chargeback software. There are a number of automated financial management tools. For example, Figure 4-6 summarizes how the IBM Tivoli IT Usage and Accounting Manager (TUAM) provides an IT organization with the capability to automatically monitor a given IT asset and attribute this asset to a given business unit.

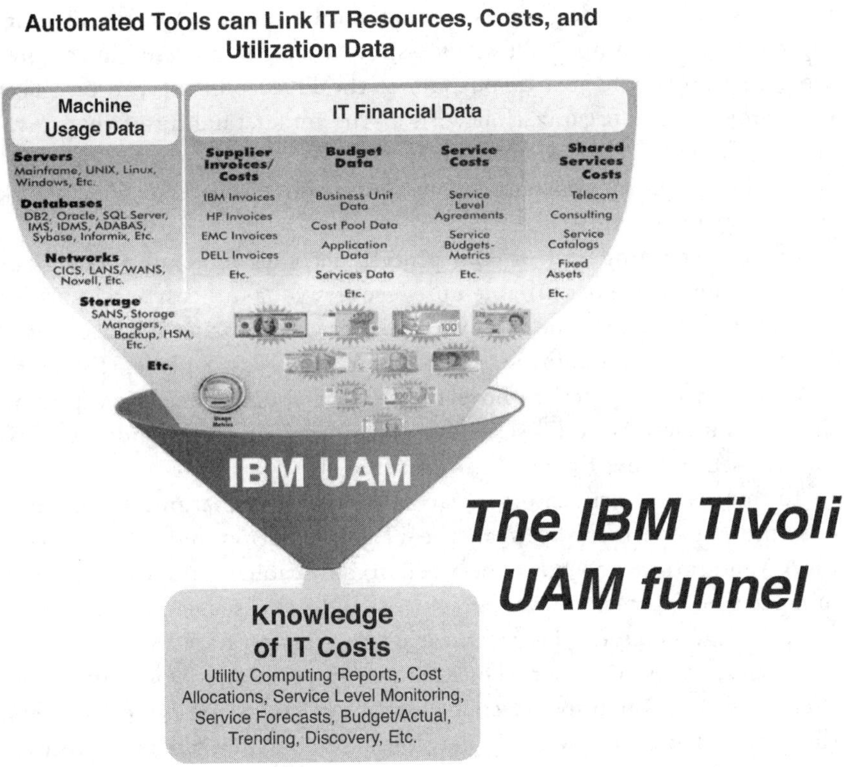

Figure 4-6 Automated tools can link IT resources, costs, and utilization data.

Automated tools that link the IT business office with the IT operational assets can be powerful enablers of mature IT financial management practices, providing the IT organization with resource-based charging capabilities. Automated tools provide the IT organization with the potential to know the exact costs of any IT asset, tie this cost with the IT organization's service catalog, and evaluate IT spending based on exact costs.

However, implementing these tools can be challenging. As with any complex software implementation, the initial and ongoing costs can be substantial. Moreover, even if the IT organization implements these solutions effectively, the difficulty of applying them effectively can be substantial. The culture of the IT organization has to see the ongoing value of mature IT financial management practices and incorporate financial discipline into daily IT operations.

Improve IT Budgeting Based on the Service Lifecycle

Effective IT budgeting will identify all IT expenses related to a particular service or customer for a given period of time. Budgeting for IT expenses combines previous commitments, such as reoccurring hardware or software maintenance, and new expenses, such as additional staff to determine the resources for a given service or activity.

The following sections focus on maturing an IT organization's budget process beyond a reactive organization, which does not proactively budget for IT resources. These sections also suggest ways to link your budgeting process with business cases and the value-added financial management practices that follow this section.

It is critical that the budgeting process not be done in isolation. If you aim to develop a given budget for an IT service, it is often helpful to link this effort to your service level management, service portfolio management, and business cases. We summarize these related efforts in detail in Chapters 3 and 5.

Cost-Focused IT Budgeting for IT Services

An IT cost center often has an internally focused budgeting process that seeks to break even over a specific period of time. If an organization seeks to become a cost center, it should develop a budget through evaluating historical expense information with forecasted needs to meet the agreed-upon service levels.

The organization should first gather expense information regarding prior years' expenditures. These expenses are largely those expenses discussed in detail in the accounting and charging section. A key mistake that cost centers must avoid is strictly basing the IT budget on prior years' expenditures or a flat allocation from the business units. This practice is shortsighted because it disregards the fact that the business and IT operational needs are rarely on an annual basis. For example, if an organization purchases a storage expansion every other year, it should not budget for this expense each year.

Instead of just relying on historical expense information, you should also determine future operational expenses based on agreed-upon service levels. These operational expenses should reflect the capabilities needed to support the service levels reflected in your service catalog or SLAs. If they do not exist, you can internally determine the service levels you plan on achieving in a given year.

Together, this historical and forward-looking information should then be the basis of the annual budget.

The structure of the budget itself should closely follow the cost types identified in the IT accounting section. As you will see in Table 4-9, this budget form simply mirrors the form developed in the IT accounting section.

Table 4-9   IT Budget Form for Web-Hosting Service

Budgeting Form for Web-Hosing Service		
Cost Type	Budgeted Amount (FY10)	Prior Year Expense (FY09)
Hardware Costs		
UNIX servers		
UNIX servers' maintenance		
Load balancer		
Load balance maintenance		
Storage		
Software Costs		
Operating system		
Web software		
Staff		
Salaries and benefits		
Facility		
Space		
Power		

Improving Your Budgeting to Become a Profit Center or Business Partner

As an organization improves its budgeting process to reflect its view of IT as a positive ROI, it discounts all IT projects and their cost by some discounted cash flow (DCF), develops its budgets strictly based on the organization's service catalog, and implements a continuous improvement effort through business intelligence and business cases.

Review Budgets Using Portfolio Management and Service Investment Analysis

As an organization's budgeting process becomes more mature, it evaluates its IT budget through the business impact and business objectives. It uses increasingly sophisticated financial tools, such as subjecting all significant projects within its budget to an NPV calculation, to determine which projects bring the most financial value to the organization. ITIL also identifies a range of other measures to evaluate budget items, including operational, strategic, and industry-specific items that are summarized in both Chapter 2 on service portfolio management and Chapter 5 on developing different types of business cases. To evaluate a given service or project's business impact, refer to the service portfolio management sections in Chapters 2 and 5.

Service-Based Budgeting

As an IT organization's budgeting process matures, it aligns its budgeting process to its service portfolio. By developing budgets associated with a particular service, an organization ensures that any expenditure results in some benefit to its customer. By establishing the annual cost of an IT product or service, the organization can evaluate the budgeting needs based on the number of customers, opportunity for expansion of customers, and operational needs of that particular IT product or service.

IT Budgeting Continuous Improvement through Business Cases

As an IT organization's budgeting process matures, it develops continuous improvement initiatives, which encourage disciplined budgeting throughout the year. Continuous improvement of IT financial management practices is a critical success factor in the ongoing, continued maturation of IT business practices, and specifically IT financial management practices.

Business cases, discussed in detail in Chapter 5, are excellent tools for continuous improvement efforts. In developing a business case, an IT organization or business unit will evaluate the business impacts and risks and develop recommendations. The amount of financial and operational rigor used to develop the business case increases with the organization's IT financial management maturity. As an organization becomes more mature, it often develops more linkages between the business case and its budgeting and charging process. It develops more collaboration between the business unit and the IT department, as reflected by the operational and financial data collected in the business case. It increases the number of alternatives it must evaluate before making the purchase. For a detailed guide to developing a business case, see Chapter 5, which discusses this process in detail.

Improve Value-Added Financial Management Activities

Accurate financial information can be used to improve service and lower cost through more a range of advanced IT financial management activities, including service valuation, service provisioning, cost optimization, investment analysis and demand modeling.

We summarize three of these activities and selected practices below and continue this discussion in Chapter 5 on how to use business cases to implement service investment analysis and service portfolio management approaches to maximize IT investments.

Service Valuation

As an IT organization develops and matures, IT financial management values services contained in the IT service portfolio. This linkage clarifies the service offerings and the rates for internal and external customers. It also provides discipline for the IT pricing. For example, if a customer would like a service beyond those services offered on a service catalog, the organization would establish a process to determine if this exception is truly feasible and cost-effective.

The cost, or provisioning value, of the service is based on actual IT accounting information. Establishing the value over and above the cost, referred to as the service value potential, is more difficult. We recommend that as your service valuation matures, you leverage the below approach to define the tangible and intangible benefits from IT investments.[8] As the customers begin to perceive that the IT organization consistently provides a positive return on IT investments, the IT organization will begin to act as a business partner to its customers. More mature pricing allows for more accurate collection of fees for IT products and services through SLAs, and more accurate pricing of IT products and services in the IT service catalog.

Service value from tangible benefits of IT services are directly observable and measurable. They include IT investments that reduce cost, improve quality of service, and expand available system and storage capacity. Tangible benefits specifically tied to financial measures include direct cost savings as a result of a completed and implemented IT project. These costs are often quantified in a business case (summarized in Chapter 5) that might also include future cost avoidance from a variety of sources, such as lower maintenance costs from a newer IT system.

To determine the value of a service, an IT organization might also quantify cost savings as a result of continuous improvement activities, such as improved quality of service through continuous improvement activities related to server outage history, server utilization statistics, business criticality, outage impact, service levels, and processing speed. For example, a tangible benefit of an enterprise resource planning (ERP) solution that replaces a number of existing applications might be consolidation of software and hardware, which might lead to cost savings.

Intangible benefits are much more difficult to measure. Professor Baruch Lev of New York University and others define intangible benefit as a perceived value to an organization of an activity, but this benefit may not be directly observable or measurable. This difficulty of identifying intangible costs is in part related to the current accounting regulations, which do not allow companies to record all intangible assets as an asset for financial reporting purposes. Professor Lev has pointed out a number of examples in his writings. For example, he cites Cisco's Internet-based product installation and maintenance system generated $1.5 billion in savings from 1996 to 1998.[9] This system—aside from the actual hardware and software costs—was not allowed to be recognized as an asset for accounting purposes. However, the IT organization should no doubt have included these cost savings in its quantification of benefits in a business case. As an organization that views IT as a positive ROI or a business partner, it begins to develop processes to identify and account for these intangible benefits to determine the service's value. Table 4-10 highlights different examples to measure intangible benefits through a process developed by Baruch Lev and others.

Table 4-10 Sample Ways to Measure Intangible Benefits

Quantitative Example	Standardized Categories	Empirical Evidence
Reduced risk of cyberattack	Reduced risk	Fewer IT costs related to spam and malware
Improved server uptime	Greater reliability	Increased uptime and, as a result, lower opportunity costs
Improved metrics for quality of service	Improved quality	Fewer service desk calls and lower cost of service
Reduced costs for service transactions	Improved speed	Increased cycle time and lower cost of utilizing IT resources

Demand Modeling

As the IT financial management process matures, an IT organization works with its customers to understand and forecast demand. By understanding this demand, an organization can understand future financial needs and evaluate investment options to maximize ROI. For example, an organization can model the demand for a given service at different prices to determine what additional capacity may be needed.

Without this demand modeling an organization may incur unnecessary cost or not be able to meet a customer's requirements. For example, in the case of a reactive IT organization, instead of knowing that a server might soon reach capacity and planning for a new expense, the reactive organization often purchases this server on an ad hoc basis. As a result, the organization might not have the time to collect quotes from alternate vendors to purchase this server at the lowest cost. Because these IT resources are budgeted on a reactive basis, the organization also might not be able to decide whether this server purchase is actually necessary.

If financial management practices had been in place, the organization could have used information from the IT charging and accounting process to model future demand and understand the cost of unpredictable increased capacity. Instead of purchasing this resource on an ad hoc basis, effective demand modeling with accurate financial management information could have enabled the IT department and business work together to develop a detailed business case to maximize their investments by perhaps determining that virtualization of existing servers could in fact provide additional capacity and be a cheaper solution to the problem.

Optimizing Costs through Service Provisioning Optimization

IT organizations must take a systematic approach to optimizing the cost of providing a given service. In Chapter 8, "Success Stories: Improving Service and Lower Costs," we discuss in detail the successful efforts of the Department of the Navy CIO to execute systemic application and infrastructure consolidation to evaluate the cost-effectiveness of the services that they provide.

Improving the cost of providing the service and determining whether this service should be provided by the IT organization is the function of service provisioning optimization. This activity takes a systemic, rigorous look at specific services and determines their financial viability and areas for improvement. There are a number of ways to measure the financial effectiveness of your services:

- **Conduct a financial analysis:** Conduct a financial review of the service using standard cash flow techniques to determine the service's viability.

- **Benchmark your service against competitors to find areas for improvement:** By benchmarking your service against other financial measures, you can determine which area may need improvement. For example, specific cost types, such as hardware or software, may need to be consolidated to be cost-effective.

- **Develop a business case for your service and alternatives:** Subjecting your service to a business case can help determine whether it is viable and meets specific business objectives.

It is unfortunately all too common to find a range of IT services being supported that have only one customer or that generate revenue that is easily exceeded by the commitment of resources to maintain these applications. By rigorously scrutinizing these activities with accurate financial information, services can be provided at a high level of value based on the service and cost.

Next Steps

This chapter has provided you with a roadmap to improving your IT financial management processes of accounting, charging, and budgeting. As you consider how to improve your financial management processes, keep in mind the importance of integrating these efforts with service level management, service portfolio management, and business cases. To that end, we recommend you build on the information from Chapters 2 and 3 as you move into the next chapter.

Endnotes

1. "Gartner Says Worldwide IT Spending on Pace to Surpass $3.4 Trillion in 2008," Gartner Press Release, Gartner Research (2008), www.gartner.com/it/page.jsp?id=742913. Accessed April 11, 2009.

2. Broussard, Frederich W. *IT Service Management Needs and Adoption Trends: An Analysis of a Global Survey of IT Executives* (IDC, 2008).

3. IT accounting framework adopted from ITIL best practices, including Sharon Taylor, et al., *ITIL Version 3: Service Strategy*, (The Stationary Office: 2007), 102–15.

4. Jessica Twentyman, "Valuing IT Assets: Managing IT Assets Can Bring Big Rewards," *Financial Times* (October 7, 2008), www.ft.com/cms/s/0/91fe4a80-91bb-11dd-b5cd-0000779fd18c.html?nclick_check=1

5. Ibid.

6. Term *profit center* adopted from material developed for "IBM Accounting and Charging Course" by Linda Boyd, et al.

7. Rick Schoenmann and John Ryan, *Scorpion Update: An Evolving Method of Analyzing and Optimizing the Corporate IT Server Infrastructure* (IBM white paper, 2003).

8. Baruch Lev, *Intangibles: Management, Measurement, and Reporting*: Brookings Institution Press.

9. *Business Week* (September 13, 1999). This source was found in Lev's *Intangibles*.

5

IT Business Cases: Realizing IT Value

IT organizations and their customers need to determine the costs and benefits of financial investments made in IT services. These benefits must clearly support the overall strategy and mission of your organization. A standardized business case should be used to determine the overall benefit of IT investments. A business case is a rigorous, standardized method to capture the benefits, costs, and risks associated with investments in IT projects and services.

Depending on your organization's IT business practices, we recommend that the business case process can be part of your service portfolio management and service investment analysis practices, which together seek to improve service and lower cost by maximizing IT investments in your IT services. Developing your business cases in the context of your services will ensure that IT resources are focused on those services and those investments with the highest value to your customers by providing outcomes desired by customers at a reasonable cost and service level.

This chapter provides a roadmap for developing and using a standardized business case to quantify the financial rate of return for an investment in new or existing services and techniques to determine which investments to fund and not to fund. This business case should also be used throughout an IT investment's lifecycle (see Chapter 2, "IT Service Lifecycle: Improving Business Performance," for a discussion of the IT service lifecycle) to measure the benefits generated by the investment. Several financial techniques can be applied to determine the value of an IT service, project or investment. The most common are

- Return on investment (ROI)
- Payback or break even
- Net present value (NPV)
- Internal rate of return (IRR)

Realizing adequate value from IT investments has been at best an inexact science and created tremendous frustration between IT organizations and their customers. Each investment in an IT service must provide benefits to your organization and provide as an outcome a level of value adequate to justify the use of organizational resources, time, and budget for the investment. Many organizations establish, and periodically adjust, a minimum return on investment for all funded IT investments.

Use Business Cases to Improve the Value of Your Services

A business case should be used to evaluate all IT investments, whether to determine the value of a specific project to improve an existing service, implement a new service, or retire an existing service. To evaluate investments, business cases should begin with a discussion of the service the investment will support and the related business objectives. In a best practice IT service organization, all funded IT projects should enable the services the organization provides. A business case can be a powerful tool to enforce this discipline and make sure that these investments are focused on the most high-value services for the organization.

Because business cases may be used for either projects that enhance a given service or to evaluate a new service, we discuss business cases for both scenarios. These principles are the same in either scenario. For example, business cases for a project to improve the functionality of an existing service should be used throughout the lifecycle of a project, and the business cases for a service should be applied throughout the service lifecycle. Business cases for both projects and services should support business objectives and tie to a new or existing service.

Business cases should be linked to two important ITIL activities, service portfolio management and service investment analysis. Service investment analysis, introduced in Chapter 4, "IT Financial Management: The Business of IT," evaluates new solutions, improvements to existing solutions, and other IT investments. By using business cases to evaluate the value and cost of an investment in the context of a given service, you will be able to not only improve service, but also screen those investments that may not support your customers' needs or provide a minimal rate of return.

Because business cases should be used to evaluate IT investments in projects that create new services, enhance existing services, or retire existing services, we generally refer to these decisions as deciding on IT investments. In the case where we refer to an investment in an IT project, we define these projects as being related to a service. Without this link to a service, this investment should generally not be made.

The Intent and Purpose of a Business Case Process

We recommend a simple process for developing and using business cases to determine and realize the projected value of your IT investments. This overall business case process and specific business case methodology is based on IT Infrastructure Library (ITIL) and other best practices that will help you to align your IT investments with your organization's strategy.

ITIL refers to a business case as a "decision support and planning tool that projects the likely consequences of a business action."[1] According to the U.S. Government Accountability Office (GAO), which is an organization that evaluates the efficiency of the use of US taxpayer funds, a business case "includes an analysis of business process performance and associated needs or problems, proposed alternative solutions, assumptions, constraints, and risk adjusted cost benefit analysis."[2] Indeed, a business case should bring together all in one place the necessary information to explain, justify, and support a decision to move forward with a given IT project or service.[3] This business case can then be used throughout the lifecycle of the investment to measure its ROI. This process can apply to services large and small—from the purchase of a single server to the implementation of a new enterprise resource planning (ERP) service.

An effective business case includes both qualitative and quantitative measures of the business impact of a potential IT investment on achieving a given business objective. A business case should be a simple document that provides a common basis for the IT department, chief information officer (CIO), and chief executive officer (CEO), and others to develop, evaluate, select, and manage an IT project, investment, or initiative.

A business case that is part of the entire IT service lifecycle will help you generate measurable value from your IT investments by driving the selection of high-value IT services for investment. This simple result of achieving value from your IT investment will differentiate you from your peers and competitors.

Many IT organizations fail to achieve their desired outcomes from IT investments. According to IBM's "Making Change Work" survey of more than 1,500 project leaders, project sponsors, and change managers worldwide, only 41 percent of projects are considered successful in meeting project objectives within planned time, budget, and quality constraints. As shown in Figure 5-1, the remaining 59 percent of projects missed at least one objective or failed entirely.[4]

Organizations Achieving Benefits in IT Projects

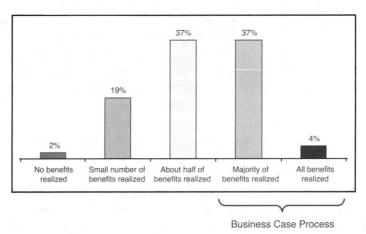

Business Case Process

Figure 5-1   IBM's 2008 global study revealed that only 41 percent of organizations achieve targeted benefits.

If you do not develop a process for selecting the highest-value investment option for funding and measure these IT projects against the business case goals, your IT organization will not realize key benefits it could otherwise achieve. A business case must be used throughout a project or service's lifecycle to measure the realization from the value from an IT investment. Figure 5-2 summarizes the usage of a business case at each step in a typical IT lifecycle.

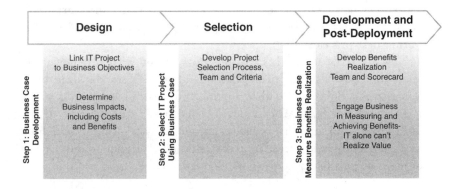

Figure 5-2   Business case used across IT investment's lifecycle

For each potential IT investment, an effective business case clearly identifies the role a funded IT project will play in furthering the business objectives of your organization. The business case will also identify the business impacts through a measurable cost and benefit analysis and link these impacts to a desired business objective.

During the selection phase, the business case document should be used to communicate, review, revise, and decide the merits or outcomes of a potential IT investment. At the conclusion of the selection phase, the business case should be used to select the highest value alternative, among viable alternatives, to executing this initiative. An example is determining which server virtualization solution provides the best ROI for an organization.

Finally, during the implementation and following deployment, the business case can be used to measure the investment against the business case goals and make any changes during or after the initiative to achieve these goals.

This chapter first summarizes how to develop an effective business case process that reflects the entire IT project or service lifecycle. This process is critical to realizing the value from your IT investments because it helps you develop the business case, select the right project or service, and measure its success against the goals stated in the business case. Aligning the business case with the IT project or service's lifecycle facilitates the adoption of this process within both the IT and business organizations.

After summarizing how to develop an effective business case process, this chapter then summarizes the key activities, staff, and outputs in three phases of a business case development, which are aligned to ITIL and other best practices.

The overall structure of this chapter provides you with a framework to develop your business case process and a supporting standardized business case methodology. We also provide information indicating where you can access free business case development tools. For example, if you would like to apply more rigorous techniques of risk scenario modeling, you can use the value measuring methodology, offered free online at www.cio.gov, published by the CIO Council.

Benefits of an Effective Business Case Process

A business case captures and documents a range of financial and organizational benefits from any potential IT investment. Some organizations incorrectly believe the sole rationale for development and documentation of a business case is to provide a document to support having a project approved for funding. This shortsighted approach ignores the many benefits of a rigorous analysis of any potential IT investment, most notably a way to measure and improve the ROI of total benefit to your overall portfolio of IT investments throughout the service's lifecycle and the impact of this investment on improving IT services. These benefits illustrate the business cases role in a range of ITIL best practices, including service portfolio management and service investment analysis that help an organization allocate resources to improve service in a cost effective manner.

The terms *ROI, NPV,* and *IRR* have a range of meanings and often differ within and between organizations. In most organizations, they are just financial methods to demonstrate an IT investment's value, as measured by netting of potential benefits against the potential costs incurred to achieve these benefits. The finance organization of many enterprises will establish a target (or hurdle rate) for ROI, NPV, and IRR. Then for each option under consideration, its calculated ROI, NPV, or IRR value must be greater than the established hurdle rate for that calculation. A hurdle rate is usually applied when the cost of capital, cost of funds, or discount rate is included in the financial calculations. Consistent with this approach, ITIL defines ROI in the service management context as "a measure of the ability to use assets to generate additional value... it is the net profit of an investment divided by the net worth of the assets invested."[5] For the balance of the chapter, we will use ROI for illustrative purposes.

Regardless of this definition, a growing number of companies have recognized the benefits of a standardized business case methodology and are developing documented, standardized approaches to financial techniques, such as ROI calculations. These companies that apply some form of ROI method have a higher overall success rate with their IT investments. Figure 5-3 demonstrates the advantage of adoption and use of a business case process. According to IBM's "Grocery Manufacturers Association IT Survey," projects that have an ROI program in place report a higher overall success rate.

In addition to generating higher ROI from your IT initiatives, developing and applying an overall business case process generates significant

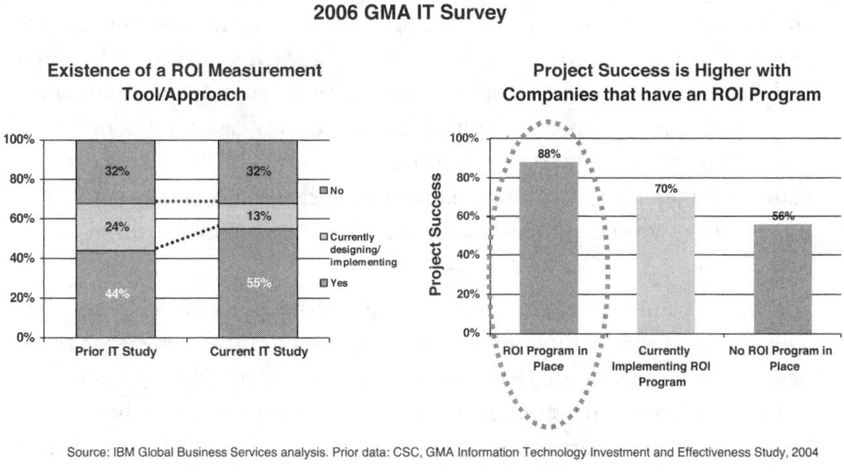

2006 GMA IT Survey

Source: IBM Global Business Services analysis. Prior data: CSC, GMA Information Technology Investment and Effectiveness Study, 2004

Figure 5-3 The advantage of business case processes: IBM's "GMA IT Survey" indicates that projects that have an ROI program in place report a higher overall success rate.

benefits to your CIO, CFO, IT staff, finance department, and your organization as a whole. These benefits reflect the business cases' role in service investment analysis:

- **Planning that demonstrates an ability to think through problems ahead of time:** Instead of running into problems during an IT investment related to a service improvement or implementation of a new service, a business case process forces you to think about and quantify significant potential risks and implementation problems before the initiative begins. Although you will not be able to avoid all risks and problems, you need to develop mitigation strategies to minimize these potential risks and problems before they occur.

- **Longer-term benefits:** By aligning IT investments with business objectives and measuring the investment based on the business case goals, you measure the achieved benefits that can enable the overall strategy or mission of your organization. By working with finance, marketing, HR, and business units to scrutinize IT investments, you can select those investments that better enable your organization's long-term strategy and mission, instead of funding those IT investments that may fit only an immediate, reactionary need.

- **Demonstration of the value of IT as a strategic business partner:** For IT organizations, particularly the CIO, one of the most significant challenges is demonstrating the business value of IT investments to the organization and specifically customers. By working with business units and finance departments to develop and agree to your overall business case process, and supporting standardized business case methodology, you will be better able to demonstrate the value of IT investments to your customers. The result for many of your customers is that your IT organization will be viewed as a business partner, instead of simply a cost center.

- **A focus on the organization's business culture and the value of IT:** The most significant intangible benefit of a business case process is the development of a culture that focuses on the value of IT investments that can be clearly demonstrated to customers. As discussed throughout this book, corporate culture can be resistant to change, but change can often enable better business practices for organizations. This process can help link the activities of IT, business, and finance with the organization's overall business objectives.

- **Improved communications and collaboration between business and IT organizations:** A related intangible benefit of the business case process is improved communication and collaboration between your internal IT organization and your internal customers and users.

> ### TIP: USE FREE (OR INEXPENSIVE) BEST PRACTICES BEFORE SPENDING FINITE IT RESOURCES!
>
> Your organization can use free methodologies to develop business cases for simple and complex IT investments. Throughout this chapter, we identify these free resources to help you improve your business case method and supporting processes where appropriate. We caution you, however, that these resources can be more than you need for many investment decisions, and you should consider using them when they are appropriate, such as for your most expensive tier of investments, outlined as follows:
>
> - Microsoft's® Rapid Economic Justification (REJ) can be used to develop a business case for deciding enterprise-level decisions. This document provides a wealth of free checklists and excellent guidance that can be applied to any IT investment. You can find this document at www.microsoft.com.
> - The Government Accountability Office also provides several free public reports, such as "Information Technology Investment Management: A Framework for Assessing and Improving Process Maturity." You can find this and other documents at www.gao.gov.
> - If you are looking for a standard business case format, you may want to use the Office of Management and Budget's (OMB) Circular 300 as a starting point. You can find it at www.omb.gov.
> - Although written a few years ago, the CIO Council's "ROI and the Value Puzzle" and "Value Measuring Methodology" also remain industry-accepted sources of information on a range of topics, including business cases and other topics addressed in this chapter. You can find these documents at www.cio.gov.

Establish Process: Developing an Effective Business Case

This section summarizes how you can develop an effective business case process that includes a standardized methodology to measure the

ROI of your IT investments, provides decision makers with the information to select the highest-value IT alternative for investment, and measures progress toward these benefits during the life of the implementation, post-deployment, and during the operation and maintenance phases.

Although many organizations have some business case process in place, most organizations only *develop* business cases. The business case is not revisited periodically throughout the lifecycle of a project or service to determine actual activity, versus the initial projections in the business case. At the end of the year, the business unit and IT department are unable to understand whether the IT investment has actually created value. Table 5-1 compares business case–only processes to a more robust, overarching business case process that spans the lifecycle of the entire IT investment.

Table 5-1 Comparison of Business Case–Only and Business Case Process

Topic	Business Case–Only	Business Case Process
Purpose and timing of business case and related activities	Secure funding for IT project during the assessment and/or selection phase of an IT investment	Used to assess, select, and measure investment based on business objectives
Cost and benefit analysis	Unclear methodology that often does not state (or mistakenly states) costs and benefits	Clearly states ROI by identifying qualitative and quantitative costs and benefits in business terms
Duration	Used only during assessment and selections phases of the IT project	Used throughout the project's or services' lifecycle
Measurement of benefits	Benefits not measured	All benefits measured during and after the investment
Business impact	IT and business organization unclear if benefits have been realized	IT can clearly identify measurable business impacts related to key business objectives
Business objectives	Unclear whether IT project supports overall business objectives	IT project linked to business objectives
Measure risk	Little or no mention of risk	Evaluates risk during assessment and selection; mitigates risk during project

One of the critical factors of a successful IT investment is the selection and deployment of a cross-section of managers and staff from various departments, such as the finance department or business units, to compose the business case team. The following sections help you

- Identify a team to focus on the business case process
- Define key terms to facilitate communication
- Develop a simple three-step business case process (design, selection, and deployment and post-deployment)
- Select investments based on service portfolio management and service investment analysis

Identify a Team to Focus on the Business Case Process

A collaborative, inclusive approach that includes the IT organization, finance department, and business units can ensure that the business case is realistic and the organization realizes these benefits. Stakeholders should be actively involved in developing inputs into the business case, especially in identifying the business objectives, business impacts, risks, and contingencies. End users and IT customers are a critical stakeholder group in any IT investment because their satisfaction with the IT service is the ultimate measure of success.

A business case process team should consist of staff from the IT department, finance department, business units, and if feasible, key customers. IT staff should generally lead the development of the business case, but obtain significant input from the business unit and financial staff. Input from the business unit helps the IT staff understand business impacts and business objectives, which are critical to maximizing the IT investment. Table 5-2 summarizes the core team members to develop a business case process.

Table 5-2 Core Business Case Process Team Members

Staff	Role	Benefit
IT staff	Responsible for managing the development of the business case.	Creates culture of focusing on value for IT investment. Holds IT staff accountable for IT investment.

Table 5-2 Core Business Case Process Team Members

Staff	Role	Benefit
Financial staff	Conducts financial analysis or provides financial information to IT staff.	Provides accurate financial projections. Opens a line of communication between the IT staff and financial staff.
Business unit	Helps provide subject matter expertise to the project, including identification of business impacts and business objectives.	Input ensures that the IT investment is linked to business and service or end user impacts and business objectives.
Executives	Executives communicate to IT, financial, and business unit staff accountable. They may be involved or provide sponsorship in larger investments.	Executive sponsorship. Facilitates communication among organizations.
External stakeholders	For larger projects, you may want to involve a larger group of staff (generally called external stakeholders) to socialize the project.	Helps to gain input and critical support early in the business case process to identify the key benefits that the core team may not be aware of.

The time commitments of each team will vary according to the size and complexity of the investment. For example, in developing a business case for a new low-end server for an application development service, staff may spend only a few hours gathering purchase orders and completing basic information. For a larger investments, such as an implementation of a new ERP service, each individual may have a greater involvement that could take upward of weeks or months.

The sponsor for the business case is the individual in charge of oversight during business case design and development and possibly during project execution. This individual should be an executive-level position such as a program manager, business unit leader, CIO, or CTO.

Define Key Terms to Facilitate Communication

Miscommunications and misunderstandings over expected outcomes from IT investments, especially around key terms such as ROI, are two of the leading causes of failed IT projects, which began with a poorly documented business case. We recommend that you identify, define, and prioritize each term (such as value, cost, benefit, risk) and financial techniques (such as ROI, NPV, and so on) that are used in each business case, and reach agreement between the IT team and stakeholders on each term.

> ### TIP: FREE INDUSTRY INFORMATION TO EXPAND YOUR BUSINESS CASE TEAM FOR MORE COMPLEX PROJECTS
>
> Several major consultancies have business case methodologies available free on their websites, including Microsoft's REJ model and IBM's Zodiac method for IT infrastructure investments. You also should refer to the ITIL and ITSM websites and other sources we listed in Chapters 2 and Chapter 3, "Adopting IT Service Management Using ITIL." These methodologies provide a good guide to expanding your team for complex IT projects. The sections on the roles, responsibilities, and average time commitments can provide you with a simple tool to communicate to a larger group of individuals brought into the project.
>
> When using an expanded team, make sure that staff can dedicate the time to the business case. If they can't dedicate the time to contributing to the business case, do not include them. Having too many ancillary staff results in a bureaucratic business case process that will hurt the credibility and success of the effort.

Developing a common set of terms does not have to be difficult, but it should be done. Indeed, you can simply use a public source of information to get started, such as the following definitions of ROI from a number of publically available sources:

- The U.S. GAO defines ROI as follows: "A financial management approach that is used to explain how well a project delivers benefits in relation to cost."[6] Most organizations use NPV, which compares a project's cash inflows to a project's cash outflows.
- The Federal CIO Council's "ROI and the Value Puzzle" presents a number of definitions of ROI by stating "descriptions of ROI generally fall into one of three categories: a mathematical equation, some combination of quantitative and qualitative techniques, and a broader definition referring to an investment's total value."[7] By *total value,* this source refers to items such as intangible benefits that you may not be able to truly measure.

We recommend that you primarily use quantitative measure, such as NPV, to measure ROI. As we discuss in Chapter 4, there are a number of challenges to measuring intangible costs and benefits. However, you can overcome these challenges by using a standardized approach that we define in Chapter 4 or by linking business impacts to business objectives (summarized in the following business case section). Using these methods, you can make a compelling and clear case for any intangible business impact that you or your team may identify for each IT project under consideration for funding.

Develop a Simple Three-Step Business Case Process

After you have selected and staffed an internal business case team and defined key terminology and goals, you should develop a standard process for developing a business case, selecting alternatives for funding, and measuring the realized value from each funded IT project. The three steps of a business case are:

- Design
- Selection
- Deployment and post-deployment

During the project design phase, your business case process team's primary focus should be developing an effective business case. Building a business case includes the following key activities:

- Identify the business objectives and the IT service that the investment supports.
- Develop a solution overview and business requirements for the IT investment.
- Document the methods and assumptions used in your business case.
- Define business impacts and link them to your business objectives and IT service.
- Identify risks and contingencies.
- Develop recommendations.

During the selection phase for selecting the best alternative for funding, you should develop a standard method to decide or screen investments. Without a standard process with a consistent approach to screening IT investments, potential IT investments with an ROI exceeding your IT organization's hurdle rate may not be funded. Moreover, the

CASE STUDY: PROBLEMS RESULTING FROM THE LACK OF ROI DEFINITIONS

The management staff of a new data center, which provided premium managed hosting services, decided to deploy a new virtualized server offering. This data center was under pressure to lower costs; otherwise, customers would potentially outsource their data center support to lower-cost external service providers. To respond to these pressures, the organization set a goal to increase revenue and lower costs because it would be able to offer a cheaper hosted server option. Thus, the organization's measure of ROI was positive net income.

The IT staff viewed the virtualization solution as just a way to provide another premium solution to customers. Their measure of ROI was simply to develop another premium solution. They were not aware of management's desire to offer this solution at a low cost. As a result, in developing the solution, they built such a premium virtualization offering that the cost was not significantly lower than the organization's standard dedicated server offering.

This lack of communication resulted in a solution that failed to achieve management's ROI. The premium virtualization solution did not achieve the goal of competing with low-cost providers because it was too expensive.

lack of a consistent, transparent funding process opens the door to a "political" choice, whereby the best option is ignored to respond to a perceived crisis or short-term pressure. This often results in funding initiatives that do not support your organization's strategy or mission, funding projects below the hurdle rate, or target ROI, or projects that do not relate to an IT service for IT investments.

During the deployment and post-deployment, you should develop and implement a process for measuring progress against the goals summarized in each business case. This measurement is a critical success factor for ensuring your IT investments provide the benefits to the organization projected in your initial business case or point to potential risks to successful completion that require corrective action during project implementation and ongoing support.

During the implementation and at the end of its implementation, you should determine whether you achieved the goals defined in your initial business case. Changes are likely to occur after development of each business case that require adjustments, or corrective action, by those implementing the initiative, but an ongoing comparison of projected activities to actual activities is critical to successful completion. Another benefit of this process being clear is that it makes the business case process team aware in the design phase that these benefits will be measured, so they will craft more realistic benefits.

Select Investments Based on Service Portfolio Management and Service Investment Analysis

After you have developed a team to focus on the business case process and have a supporting business case, you should use key elements of your service portfolio management and service investment analysis approach to evaluate alternatives based on commonality of size, complexity, potential risks, and required funding levels over that time period. The level of detail of your supporting business case for each potential IT investment should be tailored to the logical groupings, or tiers, of IT investments under consideration for funding. There are a number of ways to group IT investments, including the following methods:

- **Service portfolio management process:** These investments should be made in the context of your efforts to offer those services that best meet your customers' needs. These investments then support your current services in your service catalog and can be used to evaluate current and future services in your service pipeline.

- **Monetary amount:** Many organizations establish a monetary threshold to include in the business case. For example, some organizations will state that projects likely to be $10,000 require a basic business case, projects likely to be $50,000 require a comprehensive business case, and projects likely to be $500,000 require a team that includes executive-level participation. Although this is a simple view, it ignores that some smaller investments may actually have a larger impact on the business.

- **Business impact or objective:** Other organizations require business cases for projects that cause a significant business impact or relate to a particular business objective.

- **Governance or enterprise strategy:** Another way to evaluate business cases is their relation to your governance or enterprise strategy. For example, you may require a business case for the key areas of your governance practices, while other lower priorities may be required to complete a simpler business case.

An additional approach you should consider to create tiers of potential IT investments is the framework that was developed by Weill, Broadbent, and Keen, which creates tiers of IT investments into the following four IT asset classes by strategic purpose:[8]

- **IT infrastructure:** Provides the foundation of shared IT services (both technical and human, including servers, networks, laptops, shared customer databases, help desk, and application development) used by multiple IT applications. The disruptive nature of enterprise wide infrastructure implementations creates high upfront costs and long benefit time horizons.

- **Transactional investments:** Are made to automate processes, cut costs, or increase the volume of business a firm can conduct per unit cost. This type of investment is often made in the form of outsourcing to commercial service providers.

- **Informational investments:** Provide information for managing, accounting, reporting, and communicating internally and with customers, suppliers and regulators. These investments can support the responsiveness, control, reliability, and adaptability of firms and enable more effective decision making.

- **Strategic investments:** Reposition firms in the marketplace by supporting entry into a new market or the development of new products, services, or business processes. Successful strategic investments typically change the nature of service delivery or organizational processes in an industry, but become nonstrategic when competitors commoditize the capability.

The optimal approach you should use for your IT organization to logically group potential IT investments must be tailored to the unique environment in which your IT organization operates. However, any method should tie investments to your service strategy and your service portfolio management to ensure they are improving service and achieving your business objectives.

Each method of developing project tiers for business cases has advantages and disadvantages. The method you use should be based on your organization's needs, tolerance for ambiguity, and the degree of precision. Moreover, although all potential IT investments do not need a comprehensive business case, we strongly suggest that you require all projects to submit a scaled-down version of the business case, such as identifying which business objective and business impact the project is likely to support.

Key Mistakes to Avoid When Developing a Business Case Process

Flawed initial development of an accurate, comprehensive business case process is unfortunately common in today's IT industry. Business cases are often considered too complex and confusing. They are also not used to track the progress of a project. Using the three-step process and developing and implementing a standardized business case methodology will help you to avoid these mistakes, but we have also highlighted business case traps in Table 5-3.

Table 5-3 Avoiding Common Business Case Traps

Trap	Evidence	Recommended Solution
Do not tie into services	Investments fail to improve existing or future services.	Require all investments to be linked to a service.
Overly complex business cases	Business case costs more money than the investment.	Simplify business case format.
Overly simplified business case	Business case does not provide useful information.	Align your business case with business objectives and services.
Unrealistic benefits	Benefits fail to be realized.	Identify benefits and assumptions.
Unclear benefits and financial methodology	Benefits fail to be realized.	Clearly state assumptions and risks.
Benefits too often focus on only IT	Project not approved or fails to achieve business goals.	Clearly state business objectives.
Fail to measure risks	Project fails due to unidentified risks.	Use a simple process to identify and rank risks.
Develop business case but fail to use it ever again	Organizations fail to realize benefits.	Monitor benefits post implementation.

Project Design: Develop the Business Case

You have established a team and a process for developing business cases and selecting investments. So how do you develop the business case to measure a project's benefits, costs, and risks?

Business Case Structure

During the design phase for each potential IT investment under consideration for funding, you should develop a business case that evaluates alternative IT technical approaches, provides sufficient background on each alternative, and recommends a course of action. We suggest using an adapted version of the ITIL business case format, outlined here.[9] This format can be used as a common framework for investments large and small because each section can include more or less detail. Although the structure and content of business cases varies based on the organization and IT investment, the following framework provides an effective starting point:

Business Case Structure
Section 1: Introduction and Business Objectives

- This section presents the business objective addressed by the IT product, service, or IT project. This section should also identify the service it seeks to create or enhance.

Section 2: Solution Overview and Requirements

- This section summarizes the requirements, both technical and nontechnical, to make the solution successful.

Section 3: Methods and Assumptions

- This section summarizes the process, such as costs and benefits, used to develop the business impacts, risks, and recommendations.
- Defines the boundaries of the business case, including time limitations, cost allocations, and benefits

Section 4: Business Impacts

- This section identifies the expected financial and nonfinancial results and a tangible measure.

Section 5: Risks and Contingencies

- This section, often referred to as business impact analysis, identifies key project risks and mitigation plans

Section 6: Recommendations

- This section provides recommended actions and next steps.

Section 1: Introduction and Business Objectives

To develop this introduction and identify business objectives that your IT investment supports, you should work with business units, executives, end users, and others to identify a comprehensive set of business objectives. This list should include performance indicators to determine progress in achieving these business objectives and the target outcome for each business objective expected from funding and execution.

Developing an Effective Introduction

A business case introduction provides appropriate background, historical information, and context for the proposed investment. This background, ideally in nontechnical terminology, helps a wide range of stakeholders understand the current challenge to the organization that will be solved by funding and execution of the proposed investment. This background is particularly helpful to nontechnical staff who may not be aware of the IT challenge. This introduction is critical to helping non-IT personnel understand the need for the proposed solution and the rationale for the specific choice. Although seemingly straightforward, an effective introduction can make or break your business case. A key part of the introduction is to translate IT terminology into business terms. The introduction helps you to establish a clear set of terms that you can use throughout the business case process.

Determining Business Objectives

Section 1 of the business case helps you determine how the proposed IT project is aligned with the business objectives defined for this project. A business objective is a strategic objective that is critical to the overall success of your organization. Your IT project should support key business objectives. You may define a business objective, such as increasing shareholder value, increasing sales, or reducing costs. In this case, your challenge is to identify the IT project that best achieves this objective. In other cases, you may have identified an operational IT need, which should be communicated in business terms.

If the business objective is not apparent, consider the organization's strategic goals from the point of view of key stakeholders. One way to identify the business objectives is to first identify the stakeholder and then its desired objectives for this investment. The most effective way for IT projects to align with these objectives is for IT departments and business units to discuss the objectives with key stakeholders. After you identify the key stakeholders, such as the CEO, CFO, business unit executive, or senior manager, ask questions such as the following:

- What are the major pain points and/or issues?
- What are the new capabilities that the business or end user needs from the investment?
- How do you compare industry benchmarks in a particular area?
- How would the business benefit from the new functionality/capability?
- Given a set of benefit ranges, where does the business think it should be?
- What key changes and/or enablers are required to realize the benefits?

After discussing business objectives with key stakeholders or reviewing key documents, such as a company's strategy document, you may determine basic goals such as the CEO would like to increase shareholder value or net income; the CFO would like to reduce costs and increase sales; and the COO would like to reduce operating costs, inventory, and improve the supply chain. This information can then be developed into a simple introductory paragraph, such as the following notional example for the new Maximo® Asset Management system:

The new Maximo Asset Management system will deliver a range of organizational, operational and financial benefits across all maintenance and operations functions. This initiative will restructure the entire maintenance function by simplifying and standardizing workflows, optimizing the efficiency and effectiveness of the maintenance operations, and shifting work to lower-cost labor. This program will drive significant benefits to the business that goes beyond cost reductions, including faster maintenance activities, reduced risks and improved information for business managers to support business decisions.

You must also develop a performance indicator and target to meet these objectives, including the time interval for achieving the target performance level. As a result, these goals can then be broken down into specific areas, such as the ones shown in Table 5-4 for asset management software, which may seek to achieve the following broad goals based on the following performance indicators and targets.

Table 5-4 Business Objectives, Performance Indicators, and Targets[9]

Goal Area	Objective	Performance Indicator	Target	Time Interval
Operational	Decrease maintenance cycle time	Duration of a single maintenance call	−10%	
Financial	Reduce cost of maintenance activities	Maintenance costs	−10%	
Strategic	Provide superior customer service	Fewer follow-up activities	−5%	
Industry	Increase market share of maintenance market	Market share	+5%	

Section 2: Solution Overview and Requirements

Section 2 of the business case typically summarizes the proposed technical solution and the requirements to complete the solution. The requirements may include, but not be limited to, business commitment, organizational resources, time, operational budget, and capital expenditure. To effectively communicate the solution and the required resources, you should translate the key features and technical requirements of the solution into plain English or business terms. Typically, this section includes a "base case" alternative, which is the "no change or do nothing" approach, along with each alternative. You will need to limit the number of alternatives presented in each business case. One of the objectives in the initial scoping of a an investment into a defined business case is to succinctly define the viable alternatives for execution and to make the case why the recommended alternative provides the overall best value for your organization.

Many IT staff lack the training or experience to translate an IT solution into business terms for purposes of a business case. Similarly, many business or financial staff cannot translate their needs into IT requirements. Here are a few helpful strategies to bridge these gaps and develop an effective solution overview:

- **Link to a service:** Linking the investment to a service helps you define the specific benefit to the customer. You should ask questions such as, will the investment create benefits for an existing service or reduce its cost?
- **Link to the business objectives:** One helpful way to present this overview is to link investment to the business objectives in the first section. Figure 5-4 shows linking IT infrastructure to IT service and then to a business unit.

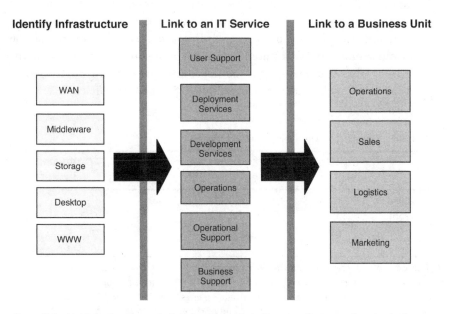

Figure 5-4 Link infrastructure projects to improvements in IT services that generate value for the business.

- **Link to the stakeholders:** You should also link the business objectives and other content back to the relevant stakeholders. This approach is effective in describing the solution. For example, if you are summarizing the solution to a COO, you can summarize a new asset management system in the context of improving an area such as inventory management.

- **Demonstrate system:** A number of IT directors and CIOs have taken a tool for a test drive to demonstrate the system.[10] Showing tools, such as a data warehouse, helps bring the project to life for business staff. Then you can ask them to describe the project in their own business terms.

- **Draw a non-IT picture:** For some projects, especially complex solutions, Section 2 should include a summary of the proposed IT project's architecture. It is helpful to use this picture to show non-IT staff the IT project components and what they may be used for.

The solution and its requirements can also be stated as a *value proposition* or *value statement.* Sometimes this is described in terms of the pain or problem and how the solution resolves that. Sample solutions might be "value-added" service or brand recognition or innovation. One method of developing and describing a value statement is to identify the level of the organization involved, the capability provided, the impact of the solution, along with associated metrics and specific economic benefit. Multiple value statements may be developed for each alternative solution included in the business case. Table 5-5 is an example of this.

Table 5-5 Example of how to Develop Value Statements

	Capability	Impact	Metric	Economic Benefit
Extended Enterprise	Electronic publishing	Introduce flexibility of choice	N/A	N/A
Corporation	Electronic publishing system's website and email delivery	Reduced costs to publish and distribute catalogs, texts, and teaching materials	Savings in staff costs, printing, postage	$175K
Functional area	Reduced typing (Online entry)	Access to measurement and benchmark data	Improved HR management Reduced typing/ administration Admin staff costs	$50K

Table 5-5   Example of how to Develop Value Statements

	Capability	Impact	Metric	Economic Benefit
Individual	Online entry	Convenient and expanded access to administrative, class, and research materials	Admin staff costs	$70K

Although the solution overview and requirements section is not included in the basic ITIL business case framework, it provides a common basis for understanding a proposed solution and its requirements. This section is sometimes included in the methods and assumptions section, but including it as a separate section is helpful for a number of reasons. When you summarize the solution and alternatives, a range of stakeholders can provide input into the solution itself. A nontechnical explanation of the solution also enables nontechnical staff to identify any needs it might have.

Section 3: Methods and Assumptions

Section 3 summarizes how you should document the methods and assumptions to develop your business case. The methods and assumptions section includes the data used to summarize the process, such as cost and benefits used to develop the business impacts, risks, and recommendations. This section should define the boundaries of the business case, including time limitations and scope of the project. For example, if your organization's tolerance for assumptions is relatively high, you should state that fact in this section of the business case. Finally, you should also list stakeholders who were part of the business case process team and considered as part of the process.

We often recommend standardizing the structure and format of the methods and assumptions section. This helps to ensure a standard set of assumptions across business cases and to enable the reader to quickly identify any new assumptions.

Section 4: Business Impacts

Section 4 summarizes how to assess and document the business impact of a given IT investment and how to link this business impact to overall

SAMPLE METHODS AND ASSUMPTIONS

Clearly stating methods and assumptions is critical to the value and credibility of the business case. Following are some clear assumptions based on IBM's Scorpion method, which produces business cases for IT optimization:

- UNIX Server to FTE ratio: 6:1.

  Salary FBR: $73,000 per annum based on 38 percent burden UNIX.

- Intel® Server to FTE ratio: 20:1.

  Salary FBR: $73,000 per annum based on 38 percent burden.

- We assumed all current Intel and UNIX servers and software are expensed in the year of purchase; therefore, there is no annual write-down cost (depreciation or amortization).

- Discount rate for NPV.

  Assumed at 3.0 percent.

- Server administration salary.

  Inflation estimated at 5 percent.

business objectives. Simply stated, a business impact is any tangible or intangible benefit or cost that relates to a business objective. Business impacts are a more tactical measure of a potential IT project than a business objective. For example, a business impact may be improved inventory management, which will help achieve business objectives such as lower cost, improved customer satisfaction, and improved revenue. These are cascading measures of performance, which are discussed in detail in Chapter 6, "IT Performance Management: Defining Success."

ITIL provides an excellent framework for helping develop a business case that includes business impacts. ITIL states that you must consider financial and nonfinancial impacts because "a business impact has no value unless it is linked to a financial objective."[11]

Developing clear and accurate business impacts from IT investments is critical to determining an accurate measure of overall project ROI and enables data-driven analysis in support of IT investment decisions. To develop a business impact, you must determine the costs and benefits of a given investment. To identify these two critical elements of an IT investment, you must consider the result or outcome rather than the technology.[12] Figure 5-5 summarizes how you can link operational metrics to direct benefits and costs.

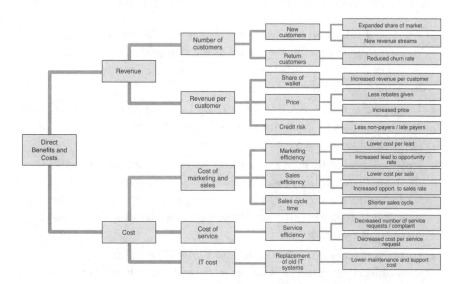

Figure 5-5   Direct benefits: How do operational metrics link to revenues and costs?

Next, we summarize typical direct and indirect IT benefits and costs.

Identifying Benefits to Measure Business Impacts

IT benefits from a funded investment should be summarized from both a business impact perspective and the value that the organization can derive from a funded IT investment. One academic paper described an IT investment such that "IT has no inherent value."[13] Although this statement is provocative, the authors make an excellent point that any benefits from IT result from an organization's use of these IT investments, not the IT assets themselves. For example, a customer relationship management (CRM) software package provides benefits only if the organization is able to collect and use customer information to achieve the organization's goals, such as marketing more effectively or delivering superior customer service.

Microsoft's REJ rightly states that "benefits must be expressed... in the language consistent with... business decision makers—the language of business, money, and finance—not features and benefits of a specific

IT application."[14] Translating these benefits into the language of business and money can be a challenge.

IT benefits are generally divided into two categories: direct benefits and indirect benefits. Examples of direct benefits include the following:

- **Increased sales and revenue:** This is perhaps the best way to demonstrate the direct benefits for private sector IT organizations. The key performance indicator is either increased total revenue or related to a particular channel, such as the Web.

- **Improved service:** A CRM software package may improve service. This can be measured by decreasing the cycle time to respond to a customer request and future increases in repeat business.

- **Improved reliability:** A new backup system for your services will improve the reliability of your website, thereby increasing total revenue by decreasing the downtime of the website. One way to measure this benefit is to link reliability to increased sales, such as reduced opportunity cost of a down server.

- **Improved access to information and impact (relating to your business objective):** Especially for governmental and nonprofit organizations, improved access to information and impact can be measured by identifying the number of constituents served or people contacted.

Organizations have different approaches to considering indirect benefits, such as cost avoidance and future savings. Some organizations disregard these benefits, stating that they may not be realized. Other organizations consider these costs but require strict tracking to make sure they are realized. The three most common types of indirect benefits are as follows:

- **Cost avoidance:** Given the increase in operating and maintenance costs within IT organizations, identifying cost avoidance is often one of the easiest areas to address. For example, by adopting server consolidation or cloud computing, you can avoid the need to purchase new data center space. From a business perspective, an IT project may help an organization avoid cost related to a regulation or charge as a result of a late shipment.

- **Cost savings:** Most organizations are focused on the cost savings portion of a given IT project. They often identify areas such as improving business processes and/or eliminating duplication of IT systems.

One common mistake is to assume too many (or the same) cost savings for a given set of IT projects. Failure to deliver these cost savings can cause resentment between IT and business staff and skepticism of the business case process.

■ **Risk mitigation:** Many organizations need to implement new technology to keep pace with competitive actions by alternative service providers in their industry. Many IT investments in infrastructure, while difficult to measure in terms of revenue and market share, enable higher customer satisfaction on transactional processing that indirectly benefits your organization.

Identifying Costs to Measure Business Impacts

In evaluating ways to improve the ROI of IT projects, most organizations focus on ways to decrease costs. Doing so often makes sense because IT is one of the largest portions of capital expenditure (CAPEX) spending and has increased dramatically over the past 20 years. Later we summarize a number of typical direct and indirect costs of a typical IT project.

Direct costs are the direct financial costs of organizational resources committed to each of your funded IT projects. An effective financial management process, as outlined in Chapter 4, enables you to quickly and easily identify these costs, which include hardware, software, staff and consulting time, training, and other items. Many organizations segment these costs into total cost of acquisition (TCA), or the deployment costs.[15] These costs, however, should also include predictable ongoing hardware, software, and IT operations costs. For example, you should include any annual license costs in addition to the initial operating system costs. Chapter 4 provides you with templates and suggestions on how to collect costs and break them down according to a service.

While many organizations are focused on the direct costs, most fail to capture indirect and non-IT costs, including those of the business unit. These costs often exceed the total direct costs of an IT project and often account for a project's failure. For example, consider a simple purchase of a new replacement server. Whereas the direct cost will be the server and perhaps some new peripheral hardware, the indirect costs likely include staff time to provision the server and possible lost revenue from business unit downtime while the IT group replaces the server.

Using Methods to Identify Benefits and Costs

There are a number of ways to identify benefits and costs with a given IT investment. These methods include:

- **Create a link with your existing financial management process (Don't re-create the wheel!) :** You can simply leverage existing benefit and cost information from the financial management process. For example, you can gather information about hardware, software, staff, and other direct costs, as well as information about direct and indirect benefits. Leverage this existing information before you begin to collect new spreadsheets and data on costs and benefits.

- **Decide scope (again with your financial management process in mind):** Your financial management process should largely determine the scope of your business case. For example, do you have the data and process to support a TCA or a TCO business case? Most organizations do not know the complete range of their IT assets or IT costs. Although a TCO or some consideration of ongoing costs is preferable, you may not have the process in place to collect these items. Keep in mind that you should fix these issues within your IT financial management process. For your business case, recognize these limitations and document them in your methods and assumptions section.

- **Develop a standard cost and benefit table:** Using the tables included in Chapter 4, you can develop a standard set of cost types and benefits that can be applied to each investment. For example, you can quickly determine (on a yes/no basis) whether these cost types apply to your investment. You can also develop a standard set of business objectives and business impacts to measure against.

- **Link infrastructure to service to business units:** You can also link infrastructure to a service to a business unit to identify costs and benefits. This visual grouping will enable you to brainstorm with stakeholders the different costs and benefits that are likely to occur.

- **Identify costs and benefits through working with stakeholders:** Another way to identify costs and benefits is to link investments with services and stakeholders. To use this method, work with stakeholders, often in a brainstorming session, to identify those benefits and costs that are likely to occur. You should specifically include a segment of end users in this type of effort.

- **Separate costs and benefits into discrete measurable units:** All costs and benefits should have measurable units associated with them.

For example, if you are going to reduce staff costs, state by how much and who will likely be reduced. These measures help the organization to compare alternatives and realize benefits when the project is in progress or complete.

- **Develop a CIO and CFO view of the project:** For top-tier investments, such as high impact or high cost, you should develop a high-level project summary, which likely simply identifies the business objectives that you will achieve.

Presenting Costs and Benefits

You should present costs and benefits in a manner that provides both executives and staff a clear understanding of a given project. Figure 5-6 is from IBM's Zodiac method for evaluating server consolidation. This example highlights a high-level business case. It includes sufficient detail for a significant investment. This particular business case focuses on the benefit of cost avoidance and cost savings, while identifying a range of new IT costs associated with the virtualization proposal.

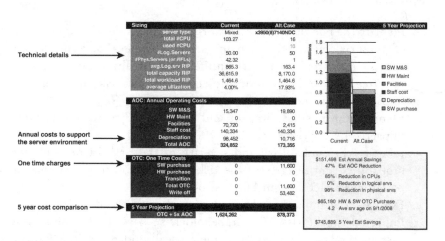

Figure 5-6   Sample method for demonstrating cost savings from the IT initiative

Section 5: Risks and Contingencies

Section 5 summarizes how you can identify key potential risks and contingencies associated with an IT investment. A risk is a potential foreseeable occurrence that can result in a delay to your IT project. The business case should include measurements of areas of risk, reflecting uncertainty associated with cost and benefit estimates, and should identify areas of possible risk mitigation. Many organizations look at risk only qualitatively. You should quantitatively determine the range of severity these risks place on the predicted future likelihood of timely project completion for each IT project.

The failure to identify, consider, and measure risks and contingencies is one of the most common mistakes of a business case. Even if business objectives are clear, most companies experience a serious gap in the ability of IT to execute against these goals. With many IT investments failing to meet deadlines, suffering budget overruns and failing to deliver on expected business value or ROI, software and systems projects are not providing the level of ROI required by today's businesses.

Risks can take many forms, though as with costs and benefits should be described in business terminology. The most common way to describe a risk is from the financial perspective. Even with a technology risk, such as the likelihood that a technology may not realize key benefits, you can determine the likelihood that the project will not reach these benefits. Establishing a process for identifying and mitigating key risks includes the following:

1. Identify the population of critical risks. You should identify the risk of potential failures to each investment option. For example, are your savings from staff costs unlikely to be realized due to human resource issues? Does your project present a risk to a business impact, such as increasing revenue?
2. Identify the business impact and business objective most likely impacted by the risk.
3. Identify the probability and severity of the risk. Identifying the probability and severity of the risk can help you to determine the potential impact on your business objectives.
4. Evaluate the impact of the risk with the stakeholder most likely impacted by the risk. The stakeholder, such as the business unit, customer, or manager, will provide critical guidance to the team to determine the need.
5. Identify a contingency plan to address the risk. This plan should be reviewed with the business unit owner

There are a number of approaches to group, rank, and measure risks and contingencies. The first method is to create a ranking system by impact and probability, such as the grid shown in Figure 5-7. One simple method is to identify all risks and then rank them by their impact and probability. Then just multiply these rankings together, and you will identify the greatest risks to mitigate.

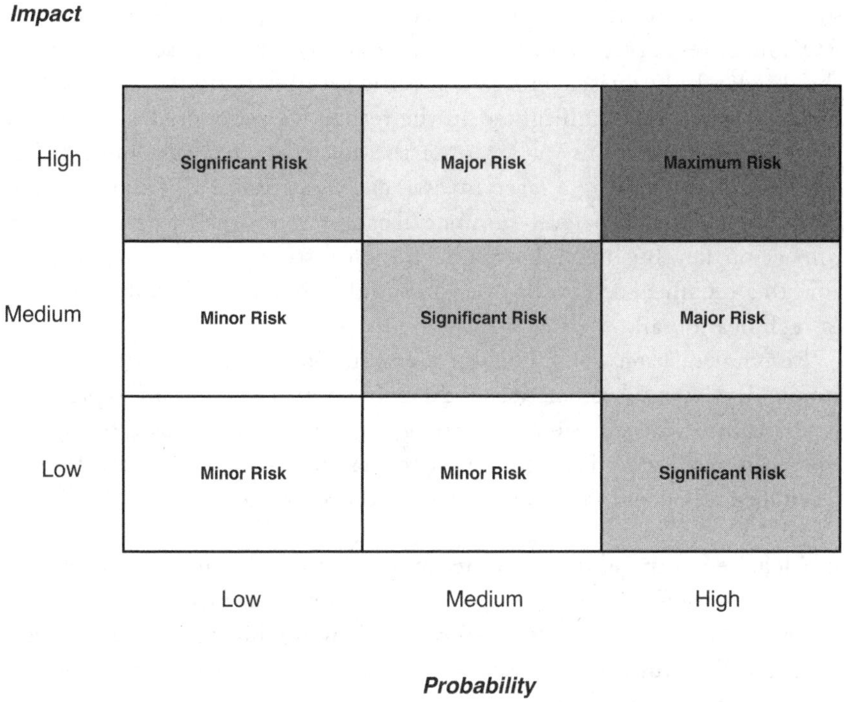

Impact

	Low	Medium	High
High	Significant Risk	Major Risk	Maximum Risk
Medium	Minor Risk	Significant Risk	Major Risk
Low	Minor Risk	Minor Risk	Significant Risk

Probability

Figure 5-7   A simple method for ranking risks related to an IT investment: probability and impact

Another method of identifying risks is to simply group them into low, medium, and high rankings. This method is an effective way to force you to identify certain groups of risks to mitigate. For example, you can decide to develop a mitigation plan for all medium and high risks. Finally, you can use simulations, sensitivity, and other analyses. Both the CIO Council's Value Measurement Methodology and Microsoft's REJ present a number of effective ways to conduct analysis of risks. We caution you that spending the time and money on this type of analysis is well beyond the scope (and needs) for most organizations. If you have the time to develop these types of simulations, we suggest that you dedicate it to improving your financial management process or other processes to improve the inputs to your business case.

Section 6: Recommendations

At the end of your business case, you should include a recommended solution. This recommendation should reflect the facts, especially the ROI measures, presented in the document. Based on these measures, it should also link investments to a specific service, business impacts, and business objectives highlighted in the respective sections. In presenting these recommendations, be aware of the audience and stakeholders. For example, in presenting a large investment to a CIO or CFO, you should likely develop a high-level summary that presents the overall ROI and impact on key business objectives. In contrast, in presenting the solution to a technical review board, you should review the recommendation in technical detail.

Recommendations should be direct and succinct. Too many organizations simply develop a robust analysis of different alternatives but fail to present a clear recommendation. Moreover, strong language should be used to support the recommendation. Following are two examples—the first of an effective recommendation and the second of an unclear recommendation:

- **Clear recommendation:** We recommend the following maintenance and operations initiative because it will improve our market share by 5 percent and decrease costs by 10 percent through improving our service levels. The project has a positive ROI based on the measures provided by our finance department.

- **Unclear recommendation with no business objective:** We recommend that we purchase server XYZ because it will increase our hosting capacity.

An additional item to consider adding to the recommendation is an initial high-level project plan with the "strawman" (or initial) timeline. For example, using project management best practices, what are the key milestones, timeline, and dependencies for the project? This plan enables the stakeholders to envision how the project might progress and where their involvement in it would most likely occur.

Finally, end the presentation of the recommendation with a set of *next steps*. They are actionable tasks for moving forward with evaluation of the business case and preparing for the project selection phase.

IT Investment Selection: Choose the Most Valuable Investment Option

After you have developed a business case, your next step should be straightforward: Decide whether to move forward with the recommendation or an alternative, including the always-available "do nothing" option. To make this decision as simple and effective as possible, we recommend the following key steps:

- Develop an evaluation team.
- Develop common evaluation criteria.
- Establish a quick and transparent process.

Develop an Evaluation Team

Your team for evaluating business cases should include a standard group of management, staff, and subject matter experts. If this is a large investment, you should include both those individuals who contribute to the business impacts and business objectives affected by the IT project and those who do not. One common mistake is to include only senior management in this selection process. Too often this results in a political or convenient choice. By including staff and stakeholders, you will also give more credibility to the process and help garner buy-in among staff.

For lower tiers of business cases, we recommend that you establish two screeners: someone from a business and financial perspective and someone from a technical perspective. This ensures an effective review after you establish the common evaluation criteria described next.

Develop Common Evaluation Criteria

Next, you should develop a common set of criteria to evaluate business cases. These criteria should consist of an agreed-upon scorecard of priorities. We recommend that you develop a common scorecard and common set of priorities before reviewing the business case for the investment. For example, you should establish the goal of the project to meet the business objectives and business impacts. Some organizations also set out a baseline number of alternatives, commonly three, which must be evaluated in the business case.

You should also decide whether you will consider intangibles or qualitative measures. For example, some businesses will disregard any business impact that is not measured or doesn't relate to a business objective.

As part of your evaluation criteria, determine what assumptions you will tolerate. For example, we recommend that you do not tolerate undocumented estimates. We also recommend that you recheck any estimates, such as ROI, NPV, and key cost and benefit calculations.

Establish a Quick and Transparent Process

You should establish a quick means of screening investments. The worst thing the screening phase can become is a bureaucracy that needlessly delays improvements to your new or existing services. If your staff cannot commit to reviewing the business case, change the process. Similarly, if business cases simply stack up on desks, choose another reviewer. We have found that one of the worst—but common— outcomes of a bureaucratic business case is that staff begins to find ways around them. For example, a large IT service provider asked us to investigate why they weren't seeing business cases, despite the substantial effort they dedicated to developing a format and a process. After a brief investigation, we determined that because the budget officer routinely delayed in completing the form, the staff would purchase items below the threshold required to complete a business case.

Equally important is developing an evaluation process that is transparent. For example, you should be clear about the time, selection criteria, and team involved in the selection. If the selection process isn't transparent, staff will avoid the process or find other means of avoiding it.

Deployment and Post-Deployment: Measure and Realize the Benefit of Your IT Investment

The next section summarizes how to use business cases to measure the progress of an investment. These measurements will help you realize key benefits from an investment. During implementation of the IT investment, you can use the business case to measure progress to achieving the business objectives and desired business impacts. At the end of a project, you can determine whether you have realized the benefits.

Despite the growing attention to developing business cases, most organizations do not track their benefits. According to one survey, fewer than 10 percent of the largest U.K. companies have a formal benefits tracking process.[16] This lack of attention to benefits presents challenges for both the business and IT organization. From a bottom-line standpoint, it leaves business leaders with little knowledge about their IT investments. From the standpoint of IT executives, it gives them little information to demonstrate the value they bring to the organization and business units. As a result, the IT organization is viewed as a cost center, which is why securing funding for it has become more difficult.

Translate the Business Case into an IT Scorecard to Track Benefits

Based on the business case, you should develop an overall IT scorecard of IT investments. There is a range of formats for scorecards (often called balanced scorecards), from automated tools to a simple one-page document. The key elements of these scorecards are similar. First, a scorecard should list the benefits, including the business impact and business objective, from the business case. This document should also list the metrics, including any qualitative measures outlined in the business case. Finally, it should list those responsible for achieving the business objective or impact.

For information about performance management and balanced scorecard approaches, see Chapter 6.

Get Business and Users Involved

As stated in our discussion about cost and benefits, business units, finance staff, and others must be involved in realizing any benefit from an IT project. These individuals are involved in using the IT project to develop the value; they must also be involved in tracking and realizing the benefits. For example, a client recently asked why it was not realizing key benefits from a new ERP system to track and manage assets and inventory. In discussing the business case process with the business units, the client identified a number of challenges with the implementation that resulted in fewer benefits being realized. As a result, the IT staff adjusted the ERP software, which resulted in fuller realization of benefits.

Make Your Value Tracking Actionable

You must make your tracking process actionable. One common mistake is that organizations track outcomes, such as increased revenue, without being able to attribute the revenue to a given IT investment. To make your value

tracking actionable, follow up on your business case efforts to link IT infrastructure to service, to business impact and objective. This linkage will help
you measure the benefits to know why something may or may not be occurring.

Correct the Business Case

If you see an error in the business case, correct the business case. Too
often, organizations manage the project toward the business case, even
when the business case is flawed. For example, during implementation
of a new asset management system, we discussed the business case with
key executives and staff involved with the implementation and the people who would use the system in the future. After our discussion, we
determined that the business case was wholly inaccurate. Although
doing so was difficult, we developed new measures and a value scorecard,
which resulted in benefits being achieved.

Preserve the original or initial version of the business case as a baseline. It facilitates lessons learned and continuous improvement. As these
are identified, review the process and determine what could have been
done differently during execution of the process to avoid errors or inac-
curacies in estimating costs and benefits.

Figure 5-8 demonstrates the value of the business throughout the
project lifecycle. This value changes throughout the project lifecycle.

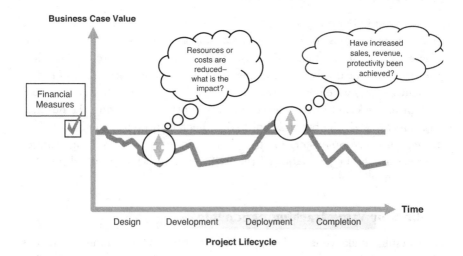

Figure 5-8   The value of the business case fluctuates throughout the project lifecycle.

Next Steps

This chapter presented a roadmap for developing and using business cases to quantify the financial justification for an investment, how to determine which investment to fund and which potential IT investments should not be funded. Building on this approach, you should use the other chapters in this book to clearly define the level of detail and scope of your approach. For example, you should consider how to integrate your business efforts with the IT financial management activities within Chapter 4. You should also consider how this business case will support the IT service portfolio management approach highlighted in Chapter 3. This tactical business case approach will help you to ensure that you improve service and lower costs across your IT organization.

Endnotes

1. Sharon Taylor, et al., *ITIL Version 3: Service Strategy*, The Stationary Office, 2007, 112.

2. David Powner, et al., "Information Technology Investment Management," Washington, D.C.: Government Accountability Office, 2004, 114.

3. Loosely adapted from USDA's CIO IT Capital Planning and Investment Control.

4. IBM's "Making Change Work" Survey, www.ibm.com.

5. Taylor et al., *ITIL Version 3*, 112.

6. Powner, et al., *Information Technology Investment Management*, 114.

7. Federal CIO Council, "ROI and the Value Puzzle," Federal CIO Council, 1999.

8. Sinan Aral and Peter Weill, "IT Assets, Organizational Capabilities and Firm Performance: Do Resource Allocations and Organizational Differences Explain Performance Variation?" Center for Information Systems Research, Massachusetts Institute of Technology, August 2006.

9. Adopted from Taylor, et al., *ITIL Version 3*.

10. Lee Pender, "How to Communicate IT Value in Business Terms," 2001, www.cio.com/article/29460/How_to_Communicate_IT_Value_in_Business_Terms.

11. Taylor, et al., *ITIL Version 3*, 114.

12. Adapted from Federal CIO Council, "ROI and the Value Puzzle."

13. Joe Peppard, et al., "Managing the Realization of Business Benefits from IT Investments." Submitted for *MIT Sloan Management Review*, April 2006.

14. Microsoft's Rapid Economic Justification, Microsoft 2006, www.microsoft.com/business/enterprise/value.mspx.

15. See, for example, Microsoft's Rapid Economic Justification.

16.. Peppard, et al., *Managing the Realization*, 2006.

6

IT Performance Management: Defining Success

This chapter provides you with an understanding of performance management and why it should be a critical, ongoing activity for your IT organization. We discuss several common industry approaches to the measurement of organizational performance, with a focus on the balanced scorecard (BSC) approach pioneered by Dr. Robert Kaplan and Dr. David Norton in 1992. We also define what factors have resulted in a somewhat mixed track record of success with BSC implementations across commercial, government, and nonprofit organizations, and how the BSC approach is being adapted by leading IT organizations using ITIL, performance benchmarking, and other techniques.

The capability of IT organizations to develop, and successfully adopt, a meaningful performance management framework is increasing, but the alignment of IT performance measures to organizational strategies and related measures, often proves elusive. Determining what to measure is the first critical step for your IT organization but requires a systemic approach to ensure that your IT organization measures the following:

- Meaningful performance management that can be used to continually improve your IT services
- Activities that align to the overall strategy of your organization and achieve key business objectives
- Activities that assist senior IT leaders, managers, and staff in continuously improving your IT activities to achieve key business impacts
- Activities that determine the level of customer satisfaction related to your IT products and services to enable for ongoing course corrections to your customer activities
- Activities that determine the level of satisfaction of your IT managers and staff in your IT organization

From their initial work in the development of the BSC framework, Kaplan and Norton evolved the BSC to include cascading scorecards to measure performance at different levels of the organization. Kaplan and Norton use the term *cascading* to link scorecards at different levels of the organization. The term *cascading* indicates that organizational direction is determined by senior leadership, and their direction provides the basis for cascading down the organization for development of scorecards that link up to the organization's overall strategy. These cascading scorecards need to be linked to consistently measure the overall health of an organization. We discuss how IT organizations currently adapt the basic BSC framework and ways you can leverage these approaches for your IT organization. In addition, we discuss how to make your IT performance measurement framework conformant with leading IT practices such as the ITIL framework.

The software industry has developed a number of highly useful software tools to support the systemic application of performance measurement to your IT organization. We discuss the changes in the performance measurement of the software industry and how this impacts any performance management framework you may consider or are currently trying to implement for your IT organization.

Finally, we discuss the role of benchmarking in the development and ongoing use of an IT performance management framework. When properly applied, benchmarking is a significant tool for improving your IT operations but must be applied carefully to gain meaningful results.

What Is Performance Measurement for IT Organizations?

There are several definitions of performance measures, including:

Performance measures are quantitative and qualitative ways to characterize and define performance. They provide a tool for organizations to manage progress towards achieving predetermined goals, defining key indicators of organizational performance and customer satisfaction.[1]

The key elements of this definition include two broad categories of performance measures: quantitative and qualitative measures. Most organizations, including IT organizations, can quantitatively measure some aspects of the performance of their organization. This type of measurement focuses on data relatively easy to capture, measure, and report. Typical measures in this category include measures of volume, workload, and performance time. For example, typical quantitative measures can include the number of servers provisioned, lines of code written, mean time to repair, and system uptime.

Qualitative measures focus on activities that are intangible and often more difficult to measure. Customer satisfaction is a common intangible measure. Many organizations use customer surveys and a variety of measures of a help desk and service desk to provide the foundation for measuring customer satisfaction. However, customers are often reluctant to provide feedback on their level of satisfaction, either through indifference, time constraints, or a perception that their feedback will not be used to improve IT operations. As a result, many organizations either ignore intangible performance measures or use misleading indicators.

Although performance measures provide individual measures of specific elements of organizational performance, *performance management* is a broader term to define the processes organizations use to apply performance measures to the continual improvement of organizational performance. Other definitions of performance management include:

Performance management is the process whereby an organization establishes the parameters within which programs, investments, and acquisitions are reaching desired results.[2]

Performance management is the process of assessing the progress made (actual) towards achieving the predetermined performance goals (baseline).[3]

Kaplan and Norton evolved the process of performance management into a specific method of managing performance defined by the BSC:

The Balanced Scorecard is a management system (not only a measurement system) that enables organizations to clarify their vision and strategy and translate them into action. It provides feedback around both the internal business processes and external outcomes in order to continuously improve strategic performance and results. When fully deployed, the Balanced Scorecard transforms strategic planning from an academic exercise into the nerve center of an enterprise.[4]

Lingle and Schiemann further evolved the definition of performance measurement to include "measurement-managed organizations."[5] The focus of Lingle and Schiemann's work is on organizations that have adopted a balanced set of key performance indicators (KPIs) to tightly manage their businesses to both execute organizational strategy and to manage to profitability. These types of organizations do not use performance management as a bureaucratic exercise, a task that must be accomplished, or another management report to be completed. Rather, these organizations culturally embrace the value of performance management discipline to provide meaningful information that they use to make sound business and operational decisions to enable their mission.

The key element common to both the BSC and management-measured organizations is the link to organizational strategy and key business objectives. Performance measurement should ultimately be applied to help your organization, and specifically your IT organization, to perform as efficiently and effectively as possible to achieve key business objectives, such as increased net income for private organizations or constituents served for certain public organizations.

One of the biggest challenges in the development of an effective IT scorecard is the development of measures appropriate to each level of your organization. The measures developed to determine organizational performance at a strategic level are different from the detailed measures used at a lower level in your organization. Consistent with ITIL's perspective on measuring the return on investment (ROI) of an IT project or service, we see performance measures developed that are:

- Strategic
- Tactical
- Operational

All performance measures must ultimately support the strategy or mission of the organization. Kaplan and Norton have used the term *cascading* scorecards to capture the criticality to organizations of measuring performance at multiple levels within the organization, but ensuring that measures are linked, or cascade, between organizational levels. For example, in developing an effective business case, ITIL suggests that you develop business impacts that support business objectives. All measurements start with a clear organizational understanding of the overall strategy and goals of each organization. These goals are often referred to as the business objectives.

Organizations also use a variety of terminologies to define what they measure. Although we use the terms *performance measures* and *key performance indicators* interchangeably throughout this book to define measures of organizational performance, various terms are in use, including *desired business results* and *measured outcomes.*

An unlimited number of performance measures are available for any organization to adopt at all levels of the organization. One of the critical success factors for any organization desiring to utilize performance measures for effective decision making is the ability to select a limited set of meaningful performance measures in use at all levels of your organization. Balance—achieving a set of performance measures at each level of your organization that assists your organization's senior leadership, managers, and staff to measure and adapt performance to achieve the strategy or mission of your organization—has proven to be an elusive goal for achieving organizational success. This situation occurs primarily because organizations do not spend enough time when first developing performance measures to determine what performance measures will provide meaningful information, on a timely basis, to decision makers in their organization. Organizations make the mistake of either attempting to define and capture more performance measures than can be reviewed and used by decision makers or using too few performance measures so that the organization gets an incomplete picture of current operations to make meaningful decisions.

A common way to achieve this balance through the BSC and measurement-managed organizations is to focus on developing a balanced set of measures, which includes the measurement of internal processes using ITIL. This element of performance measurement is growing in importance as ITIL adoption increases in IT organizations worldwide. As IT functions and organizations reorganize around ITIL, their performance measures must adapt to these best practices. As ITIL and other best practice frameworks have defined, standardized business practices can be used to effectively drive continually improving performance for your IT organization. Performance measures applied to the ITIL practices adopted by your IT organization can further enhance your IT organization's adoption of an industry frameworks like ITIL. Many available performance measurement systems are "ITIL conformant," or accepted as common measures in use in IT organizations. We strongly recommend considering ITIL-conformant systems and methods as you develop your approach going forward.

Why Use Performance Measurement for Your IT Organization?

Academics, businesses, and government organizations have conducted a number of studies to determine the benefits of adopting some type of systemic performance measurement, or a scorecard, to measure and improve their performance. Lingle and Schiemann conducted a seminal study that defined the characteristics of such organizations, as shown in Table 6-1.[6]

Table 6-1   Characteristics of Organizations Using Performance Measurement

Reported	Measurement-Managed Organizations	Non-Measurement-Managed Organizations
Clear agreement on strategy among senior management	93%	37%
Good cooperation and teamwork among management	85%	38%
Unit performance measures are linked to strategic company measures	74%	16%
Information within the organization is shared openly and candidly	71%	30%
Effective communication of strategy throughout the organization	60%	8%
Willingness of employees to take risk	52%	22%
Individual performance measures are linked to unit measures	52%	11%
High levels of self-monitoring by employees	42%	16%

Three key findings from this study of the elements of a management-measured organization versus a non management-measured organization require further examination:

- An agreement on strategy and effective communication of strategy throughout the organization is necessary.
- Unit performance measures are linked to strategy, and individual performance measures are linked to unit measures.
- Information in the organization is shared openly and candidly.

Agreement on Strategy

We are continually surprised by the number of clients whose managers and staff cannot clearly articulate the strategy and business objectives of their organizations. Caught up in the operational details of daily work life, managers and staff often gradually lose focus on what strategy and goals their organization must achieve and how their organization is planning to achieve them. The daily tumult of operational activities, and the constant reaction to challenges that are perceived as crisis slowly draw managers and staff away from the overarching mission or strategy of their organization. This challenge is especially difficult for geographically dispersed, decentralized organizations. Also, as organizations operate in a rapidly changing global environment, senior leadership must constantly adapt their strategies not just for today, but also for the future. They must adapt their organizations to deal with emerging threats and opportunities.

When you drive your car, you utilize a number of "indicators" on the dashboard to regulate your performance. You carefully monitor the speedometer against the legally posted speed limits. You periodically review the fuel gauge to ensure you have an adequate supply to reach your destination, or you plan ahead for a refueling stop to keep your supply adequate. With advances in technology, it is increasingly common to use a navigational system to monitor the location of your car and determine the optimal route to get to your next destination. But the most critical decision you make every time you step into your car is fundamentally this: Where are you going?

An organization's strategy sets the overall decision about where an organization is going. A performance measurement scorecard or a balanced set of performance measures your organization uses to measure and correct performance can be automated into a dashboard your organization can use at multiple levels in your organization to measure and correct performance. A common reference in industry at this time is to refer to an automated performance scorecard as a "digital dashboard." Your digital dashboard performs the same function for your organization that your car's dashboard performs for you when you are driving. The digital dashboard provides a visual, easy-to-understand, limited set of performance indicators that you can use to take corrective action to get to your desired destination.

But the foundation of any BSC is strategy. If your senior management, managers, and staff do not agree on the strategy for your organization, it is difficult to get to an organizational destination when that destination is not known or is not commonly understood. Your IT organization will not be able to create a meaningful IT scorecard that links to higher-level organization strategy, when that strategy either does not exist or at a minimum is not understood or agreed to.

When a valid organizational strategy does exist, it is a critical success factor for any organization to communicate this strategy consistently to all levels and physical locations of the organization.

Linked Performance Measures

The most basic, fundamental failures of implementation and ongoing adoption of performance measurement scorecards are a result of failing to

- Create appropriate, meaningful measures at differing levels of an organization to continually improve organizational performance.
- Link measures from the employee, up to the unit, up to the division, and ultimately up to the highest, strategic level of an organization.

To avoid these two mistakes, all levels and departments of your organization and your IT department must be willing to be measured. Your organization must embrace the discipline that comes with a properly developed, implemented, and periodically adjusted system of measures that you will use to adapt the performance of your organization in executing your organization strategy or mission. Performance measurement must be integrated into the culture of your organization. Your senior leadership, managers, and staff must see the value of performance measurement to both their individual success, and the success of the organization, for performance measurement to yield the incredible benefits to the organization that can be obtained by a disciplined, consistent measurement approach.

The senior leadership of your organization must be clear, consistent advocates of systemic performance measurement, which is the underpinning of performance management. While setting a clear strategic direction for your organization, your senior leadership must also put in place a performance management system to guide organizational performance and derive business value. With this clear direction in place and communicated throughout the organization on a consistent basis, your IT organization can develop an IT scorecard for use in measuring ongoing operations.

Your IT scorecard must include a clear link with your overall strategy and direction. Your IT scorecard must also cascade down to the scorecards of each organizational component of your IT organization and link even further directly into the individual development plans (IDPs) for each manager and staff in your IT organization. Performance management is at its most powerful as an enabler of organizational success when each individual in your organization, and specifically your IT organization, can see how individual performance goals cascade directly down from the overall organizational strategy.

In Chapter 8, "Success Stories: Improving Service and Lowering Costs," we discuss in detail the successful implementation of a BSC set of performance measures at the city of Corpus Christi, as well as the use of performance measures in the IT organization of Neighborhood America, an entrepreneurial social networking company in Naples, Florida.

How do you make this happen for both your overall organization and specifically for your IT organization?

Information Sharing

Performance management is not effective if used as a punitive tool to point out performance below targets. Performance management is best used as an early warning system of performance-missing target measures and a means of identifying the need for a corrective action plan to correct this lag in performance. If your organization is unaware of a developing area of lagging performance, the organization cannot develop and implement a corrective action plan. Most of us would not want our cars to run out of fuel before realizing the level was getting low. We use the fuel gauge to warn us of any pending need to refuel our car. However, we recognize the reality that employee compensation is often linked to the achievement of specific performance levels, so the culture of your organization must consider environmental factors that impact the achievement of specific performance levels. If an economic downturn occurs, performance goals must be adapted to the changing realities of macro environmental factors.

The culture of your organization must support performance management as a wise use of organizational resources to enable success for both the organization and the individuals that compose each organization.

Studies of management-measured organizations such as the study by Lingle and Schiemann make a compelling case for the value of using performance measurement when linked to overall organizational performance, as shown in Table 6-2.[7]

Table 6-2 Linking the Use of Performance Measurement to Organizational Performance

Measures of Success	Measurement-Managed Organizations	Non-Measurement-Managed Organizations
Perceived as an industry leader over the past three years (1999–2002)	74%	44%
Reported to be financially ranked in the top third of their industry	83%	52%
Three-year ROI	80%	43%
Last major cultural or operational change judged to be very or moderately successful	97%	55%

Although a compelling case can be made for the benefits of systemic performance measurement to the overall organization, the individuals that make up your organization at all levels must also see the value of this approach to their individual careers.

In many organizations, the senior leaders, managers, and staff understand through trial and error what behaviors are rewarded by their organization. In many cases, the rewarded behavior is not consistent with the stated goals of each organization. A successful performance measurement approach ensures consistency of cascading performance scorecards, down to the individual level, to drive a high level of performance by a consistent, measured vision of organizational success that all members of an organization can recognize and embrace in all their activities on behalf of the organization. To achieve this requires commitment and acceptance from across the senior leadership, managers, and staff of your organization. Although performance measurement is challenging to implement, the rewards in terms of organizational performance are significant and justify the commitment of organizational resources to achieve.

The Balanced Scorecard Adapted for IT Organizations

In 1992, Kaplan and Norton first published their work on the BSC. While including financial measures as a portion of the BSC, Kaplan and Norton expanded their basic measurement scorecard to include measures across four focus areas, or perspectives, including:

- The financial perspective
- The customer perspective
- The internal business process perspective
- The innovation, learning, and growth perspective

Although measuring performance in a number of focus areas is commonplace now across organizations, the original BSC was groundbreaking in broadening the measurement of organizational performance beyond traditional financial measures. The original BSC is represented in Figure 6-1.

The BSC acts as a link from the strategy of your organization to the daily operational performance of all components of your organization. The specific measures of the BSC can be further categorized as follows:

- **Leading indicators:** These are forward-looking measures, such as customer demand and customer satisfaction.
- **Lagging indicators:** These are measures that indicate where the organization has progressed, such as ROI and financial results.

Many organizations have adopted this construct of four focus areas for measurement of organizational performance, but they must specifically tailor it to the unique operating environment and customers of IT organizations. Driving IT organizations to change their culture to a more performance-driven, strategic focus requires adapting the basic BSC construct to fit the IT environment.

A number of leading IT organizations have already begun significant work in this area. Forrester and Gartner have both published IT

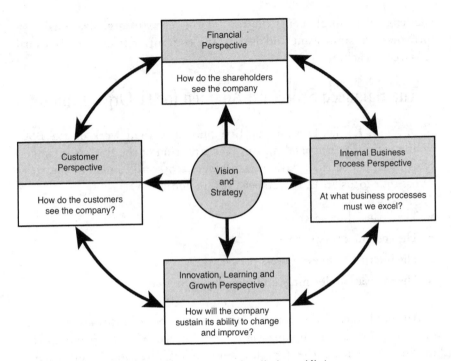

Figure 6-1 The original balanced scorecard concept from Kaplan and Norton

scorecard perspectives that translate the four perspectives in the initial BSC into potential IT scorecard perspectives, as shown in Table 6-3.

Table 6-3 The Original Balanced Scorecard Concept Adapted to an IT Scorecard

Balanced Scorecard	Becomes	Forrester[8]	Gartner[9]
Internal processes	⇒	Operational excellence	Operational excellence
Customer	⇒	User orientation	Customer
Financial	⇒	Business value	Business contribution
Learning and growth	⇒	Future orientation	Future

Next, we examine each of these four BSC perspectives and how they are tailored to the IT environment.

Internal Processes and Operational Excellence

The current IT industry focus on the adoption and use of IT best practice frameworks, such as ITIL, supports the validity of using the internal process perspective from the BSC as one of the initial building blocks for an IT scorecard. But what is the significance of modulating this initial BSC terminology to become "operational excellence" under any potential IT scorecard?

One common definition of *operational excellence* follows:

Operational excellence is a philosophy of leadership and teamwork resulting in continuous improvement throughout the organization by focusing on the needs of the customer, empowering employees, and optimizing existing activities in the process.[10]

Four elements of this definition will be critical to the success of your IT organization in the next three to five years, including:

- **Philosophy resulting in continuous improvement:** An organizational philosophy is a common set of values or behaviors accepted as appropriate for an organization. An organization that has a philosophy of continuous improvement demonstrates a focus and commitment in daily operations to identify, scope, and execute improvements to all aspects of organizational performance.

- **Focus on customer needs:** In an approach made popular by Edward Deming, an organization exists to serve its customers, and all aspects of organizational performance should exist only if serving a tangible customer need.

- **Empowering employees:** Empowerment is an approach that relies on employees at all levels of an organization executing their work activities and the activities of the organization in the most efficient and effective manner possible. This approach does not rely on top management being directive down the organization on how to optimize operations, but rather empowers employees to lead change in the organization on operational efficiency.

- **Optimizing activities within processes:** Processes are composed of discrete activities. Much focus in industry today is on optimizing processes, but a significant amount of process optimization work is substantially complete in many organizations. Organizations now need to focus on improvement at a detailed level below the process level (the activity level).

Best practice IT organizations embrace these four elements of operational excellence. These best practice organizations recognize that it is not enough to focus on the development and optimization of technology. In addition to rewarding strong technical skills, these best practice organizations also focus on operational excellence through innovative methods such as cross-training IT staff in financial or customer relationship skills, as discussed in Chapter 7, "IT Business Skills: Enabling Customer Outcomes."

Performance measures also encourage IT organizations to focus on the customer. With the intense competition between internal and external IT service providers, your IT organization must be increasingly focused on honing in on who the customer base is and what the current and future needs for IT products and services are. Edward Deming had it right: You start with your customer and work backward to create an IT organization that can deliver outstanding customer outcomes at a market price in a timely manner to the customer needs. Customer focus is gradually becoming equal to technological prowess in terms of the characteristics your IT organization will need to adapt to be successful.

Performance measurement also helps IT organizations in their constant, competitive battle to attract and retain IT professionals who can deliver the constantly evolving range of IT products and services needed by your internal customers. No longer can your IT executives and managers succeed with only a focus on a few siloed technical skills. Your IT leaders must gain and exhibit a broader range of skills to be successful, including a focus on customers and financial/project management. In return for your IT leaders developing this broader range of skills to enable the success of your IT organization, you must be better able to create a working environment and long-term career path needed to retain these skilled IT professionals. In a highly competitive labor market, your IT organization must work with your Human Resources organization to develop comprehensive compensation methods that reward IT professionals and increase your rate of retention of IT managers and staff.

Performance measurement also helps you focus on optimizing the discrete components that make up a process: the activities. Although business process reengineering and business process improvement efforts do an outstanding job of creating new or optimizing existing optimal processes, the level of best practice detail provided in leading IT process frameworks, such as ITIL, allows for improvement at a more microlevel in your IT organization. Specifically, when your organization is identifying continual improvement opportunities, you should focus your improvement efforts at improving specific organizational activities. Many IT organizations are increasingly using Lean and Six Sigma to analyze and improve specific IT activities that compose your critical operational processes.

But, by far the most critical element of this definition your IT organization will need to examine and adopt is the "philosophy of teamwork and leadership resulting in continuous improvement." We equate philosophy to organizational culture, using the Edgar Schein definition of *organizational culture:*

> *A pattern of shared basic assumptions that the group learned as it solved its problems of external adaption and internal integration, that has worked well enough to be considered valid and, therefore, to be taught to new members as the correct way you perceive, think, and feel in relation to those problems.[11]*

According to Schein, culture is the most difficult organizational attribute to change, outlasting organizational products, services, founders, and leadership and all other physical attributes of the organization.

To adopt operational excellence as a cornerstone of your IT organization, and therefore as a cornerstone of your IT scorecard, requires your IT organization to either utilize an existing culture of commitment to operational excellence, or design and adopt a culture of operational excellence as part of all aspects of your IT operations.

Achieving all aspects of this definition of operational excellence is a challenge for your IT organization, and using operational excellence as the first component of your BSC-based IT scorecard will provide your IT organization a critical enabler to measure, adapt to, and achieve operational excellence in its complete form.

The Customer and User Orientation

The second component to allow for when considering a BSC-based IT scorecard is a component focused on either *customers* or *user orientation.* Are these two terms synonymous?

Some common definitions of *customer* include the following:

Customer is one that buys goods or services.[12]

Customer is an entity that receives or consumes products (goods or services) and has the ability to choose between different products and suppliers.[13]

The common elements to these definitions are those individuals or organizations that buy, receive, or consume goods or services and who have the ability to choose between multiple service providers. These definitions underscore a critical distinction between the customer that buys, in this case, IT products and services, and the customer who receives and consumes IT products and services.

In many operational or business units within an organization, the organizational component responsible for purchasing IT products and services is distinct from the organizational component that receives and consumes IT products and services. For example, if a warehousing organizational unit purchases a new software tool from its internal IT organization to track goods and services in each organizational warehouse, the finance or accounting component of this business unit may "buy" the new software tool, and the line managers and staff in each warehouse may receive and use the software tool.

A user, by definition, uses IT products and services according to a common definition of *user:*

User is a person who uses a computer or internet service, and may have a user account that identifies the user by a username, screen name, or handle.[14]

A further distinction of users of IT products and services are *end users,* who can be defined as follows:

End user is a concept in software engineering, referring to an abstraction of the group of persons who will ultimately operate a piece of software.[15]

So, should an IT scorecard create and track a series of measures around customers or adopt a user orientation?

Through cooperatively developing service level agreements (SLAs) with internal and external customers, you can effectively address both the end user and customer. The end user is actually a subset of customers, and therefore an effective IT scorecard should adopt as its second critical component a customer orientation, but with a focus on measuring the end user requirements and experience. Based on the requirements in an SLA, you can effectively measure both the end user's experience with a service and the customer's requirements. For example, the SLA can define that the end user may need a particular functionality for an application, but that the paying customer, often the parent organization, is willing to pay only a defined amount of money for a given change request. Developing this level of detail in your SLA or similar document helps to balance and measure these sometimes competing needs.

Financial and Business Value

For most organizations, and especially commercial organizations that have shareholders and other investor-owned organizations, financial measures are the most important performance measures. The primary evolution on this component of the BSC framework has been a growing focus on not only measuring financial activity, but also focusing on the use of organizational resources producing value or contribution to the organization.

This evolution of the financial component of the BSC framework is especially relevant for your IT organization. Senior executives in organizations increasingly expect that your IT organization is investing in IT projects and IT infrastructure that directly contribute to the execution and achievement of the overall strategies or mission of your organization. IT executives, and specifically the CIO, must increasingly show the direct correlation between IT investments and spending and overall organizational success.

Many IT staff lack the training or experience to translate an IT solution into business terms for purposes of a business case. Similarly, many business or financial staff cannot translate their needs into IT requirements. In Chapter 5, "IT Business Cases: Realizing IT Value," we summarize a number of strategies to bridge these gaps and develop an effective set of financial performance measures.

ITIL provides an excellent framework for that, by including links between IT projects, business objectives, and business impacts (see Figure 6-2).

The methods for defining the business value of IT investments summarized in Chapter 5 can also be applied to developing effective performance measurement methods. This is a critical aspect of your performance measurement system.

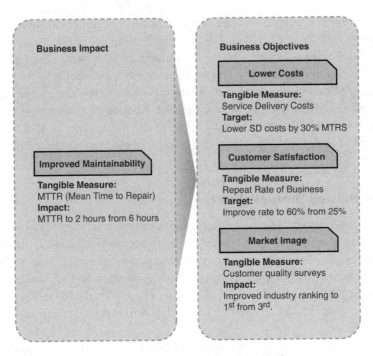

Figure 6-2   A single business impact can affect multiple business objectives.

Learning and Growth/Future Orientation/Future

What is the future? One common definition of the *future* regarding business follows:

> *Future is a prospective expected condition, especially one considered with regard to growth, advancement, or development.*[16]

Being successful today is no guarantee your IT organization will continue to be successful in the future. Numerous external and internal factors drastically impact the ability of your IT organization to continue to be successful. In professional sports, the same team does not win the championship every year. However, certain franchises are able to be highly competitive on a regular basis, when a majority of franchises enjoy only infrequent success. What characteristics are common to franchises that win on a more consistent basis?

Among the key factors for success are the following:

■ The ability to recruit and retain talented players who commit to continual success

- The ability to develop new strategies for success to meet competitive challenges

- The ability to retain existing successful strategies so the franchise is not in continual flux

- Owners and senior leadership who continually communicate the commitment to and expectation of winning

- Continual study of competitors for new strategies that can be adopted or competitor weaknesses that can be exploited

Including these factors in your performance measurement system will help ensure the future success of your IT organization by having a workforce with the skills and abilities to execute your performance management system.

This focus on learning and growth in your performance management system will also address a critical success factor for any IT organization: new or emerging technology that your customers will eventually demand to execute their business. With so much focus on maintaining the existing IT applications and infrastructure, and the continual need to consolidate and retire aging technology, few IT organizations have the time and organizational resources to devote to tracking and developing emerging technologies. There is simply too broad a range of new hardware, software, and targeted applications for any IT organization to track the full range of new technologies.

In addition to new or emerging technologies, much of your current technology is going to continue to evolve through almost continuous new releases, upgrades, and patches that require attention. Your IT organization will continue to reach inflection points where your IT leadership will need to make course corrections to keep pace with technological change. The popular media do a great disservice to internal IT organizations by presenting new and emerging technologies often as appearing available on a commercially viable scale when new technology is only in the development stage. Business and operational unit managers read about new technology and expect their internal IT organization to have answers to a range of questions about these technologies, when much of the resources of an IT organization are focused on the daily challenge of keeping the existing applications and infrastructure running.

Although new or emerging technologies can be interesting from a technical view, your IT organization should track and scope the viability of only new or emerging technologies that are relevant to the industry, market, or mission space of your overall organization. For example, many companies assumed there was tremendous value for their organization using the Internet when it first came into common commercial use in the 1990s, but after much trial and error, a portion of businesses realized that the Internet was not a key enabler of their business model.

One place to look when scanning the market for relevant new or emerging technologies is the new technologies being adopted or targeted for adoption by competitors in your marketplace. The area of business intelligence has evolved rapidly in the past few years. Many companies have purchased and utilized a variety of business intelligence tools (we include under business intelligence customer relationship management, corporate performance management, and knowledge management) to segment and dissect the buying patterns of key customer segments. Even if a competitor either comes to market or utilizes a new business intelligence tool that your IT organization had not identified and targeted for implementation, the speed with which your IT organization can adopt and implement either the same tool or a similar tool is a critical success factor for your IT organization.

Looking to the future does not mean your IT organization has perfect vision for new or emerging technologies that enable your overall organizational strategy or mission. What looking to the future does mean is that your IT organization exhibits due professional care to do the best job possible with your available organizational resources to scan the IT industry and competitors for enabling tools that your organization can adopt. It also means that if your IT organization does miss a potential IT enabler for your organization success, the organization can react, adapt, and implement this technology in a reasonable time frame to counter the moves of competitors.

How Many Components Do You Need for Your IT Scorecard?

Although the original BSC construct has four focus areas (or perspectives), each organization is unique and should adapt this framework to its own specific structure. This focus is a critically important concept to understand and apply. Specifically, your IT organization can adopt the four perspectives in the original Kaplan and Norton model, but this is not necessarily the optimal approach for a specific IT organization.

There have been numerous stumbles and outright failures in BSC implementations, and one of the consistent, root causes of these failures is the attempt to take the basic BSC construct and apply it directly to your IT organization. This approach can work in limited situations, but understanding the original BSC construct is only a starting point for developing and using an effective IT scorecard for your IT organization.

A critical concept to understand and apply to your IT scorecard is that you can have as many or as few focus areas for your IT scorecard that produce meaningful data for your IT organization to make decisions to continually improve your IT operations.

We discussed four potential focus areas for your IT scorecard: operational excellence, customer, business value, and future orientation. However, our discussion points to additional potential focus areas that would warrant a distinct additional component to your IT scorecard. These areas include employee commitment, user orientation, environmental scanning, and innovation.

We recommend a phased approach to the development of your IT scorecard based on your unique IT organization. Specifically, for the development of your initial IT scorecard, we suggest adding three components:

- Customer
- Operational excellence
- Business value

This recommendation is based on the fact that your IT organization must attract and retain customers. The customers must perceive that your IT organization is providing IT products and services that enable the customers to add value to the overall achievement of their organizational strategy and mission. You drive achievement of satisfied customers by driving waste out of your IT operations, and you do this by adopting or enhancing a philosophy of excellence in all aspects of your IT operations.

Achieving an effective IT scorecard that captures meaningful KPIs in these three components will take significant time and commitment of organizational resources. The next two components for an IT scorecard you should consider are:

- Future orientation
- Employee commitment

These components should be developed as your IT scorecard matures as a decision-making enabler for the IT organization.

After you have created your initial groupings, the IT scorecards must contain the appropriate level of detail to produce meaningful data for your IT organization to make decisions to continually improve your IT operations. Defining your IT scorecard components clearly and concisely provides the boundaries for development for the specific KPIs you will track and utilize as an organization.

A successful IT scorecard will develop and adopt to many components or focus areas by defining a grouping of individual KPIs to utilize within each component. Resistance to the use of an IT scorecard and individual KPIs is not uncommon in IT organizations. Part of this resistance is a legitimate concern that many IT scorecards in use do not produce meaningful information for IT decision makers to make course corrections to IT operations. However, resistance to IT scorecards also occurs because some IT managers and staff do not want to be measured.

Common Performance Measurement Software Tools

The business intelligence software market, which includes performance management tools, has consolidated significantly in the past several years. These software tools provide managers with robust methods to develop performance management systems. The three largest software vendors in this market space are:

- IBM, primarily through the acquisition of Cognos® in November 2007
- SAP, primarily through the acquisition of Business Objects in October 2007
- Oracle, primarily through the acquisition of Hyperion in March 2007

Although these are not the only software offerings in the business intelligence market space, these acquisitions point to a consolidation of the software available as a foundation for an organizational performance management system. Specifically, they point to the development of a specific IT scorecard for your IT organization.

Your initial consideration of an approach to development of a new IT scorecard, or enhancement of any existing IT scorecard, should consider whether you are utilizing any of the three software offerings listed previously somewhere in your broader organization. This exercise may seem simple, but in highly decentralized, geographically dispersed organizations, it may be difficult to determine whether any of these software offerings are already in use in your organization.

Managing Development and Use of Your IT Scorecard

Many of the steps to successful development, deployment, and ongoing use of your IT scorecard are similar to the process for adoption of the ITIL framework for your IT organization. You must do the following:

- Obtain executive sponsorship for your IT scorecard project.
- Select and empower a cross-functional internal team to develop the initial IT scorecard.
- Consider use of an external consultancy or individual expert to guide your project.
- Charter the project with a clearly defined timeline to completion and measures of success, define key milestones, and define the total organizational resources required to execute the project.
- Develop a list of key stakeholders to the project and reach out to these various stakeholder groups on a regular basis to communicate ongoing project activities.
- Rigorously track the progress of the project and take corrective action if at any time the project is failing to achieve key milestones and successfully achieve project measures.

So what is different about an IT scorecard development and adoption project versus an ITIL adoption project?

There are five factors you must consider in your IT scorecard project that are unique to this project:

- You should determine whether you are going to have committed, full-time staff dedicated to an organizational unit in your IT organization to track and report on your IT scorecard or embed these activities within existing organizational components in your IT organization.
- You should consider segmenting out your application development and application maintenance performance measures from your performance measures for your infrastructure/ongoing operations performance measures.

- You should consider the use of benchmarking to compare both your current performance measures and desired future state performance measures against some measure of desired performance commonly accepted in the IT industry.

- You must include your enterprise architect or specifically your data architect in the development of the IT scorecard because most IT organizations have a tremendous amount of existing data that can be mined using business intelligence tools to populate the performance measures you decide to track using actual data.

- You should be sure whatever IT scorecard you develop is ITIL conformant.

Organizational Positioning of Your IT Scorecard Activities

When an organization is taking on a new skill or activity, it is common to create an organizational component to specifically tackle this new activity. A focused, rigorous approach to performance management is often a new activity for many IT organizations. Therefore, many IT organizations will create a dedicated performance management organizational component to be the focal point of performance management activities. Although this organizational component can be relatively small compared to the overall IT organization, many IT organizations use this approach of a dedicated performance management team to signal to the IT organization that this is a significant focus for the organization requiring dedicated resources and to emphasize that this organizational component will apply and also continue to develop organizational expertise around IT performance management. Frequently, this performance management organizational component is embedded into a continual service improvement (CSI) unit.

This approach presents several risks. The most significant risk of this type of organizational model is that the performance management team becomes disconnected from the daily operations of your IT organization and quickly becomes ineffective at tracking meaningful performance measures for IT decision makers. Without being directly embedded in each of your IT organization's business units, the performance management organizational component will become quickly marginalized because it does not work within the IT units to track performance measures. One approach to minimize this potential risk is to rotate IT line managers and staff through the performance analysis unit on fixed rotations.

The importance of performance measurement must be communicated continuously within your IT organization, reinforced as being part of a culture of CSI, and positioned organizationally and physically, to indicate its significance to the ongoing IT operations.

There are two effective alternatives to creating a stand-alone performance management organizational component:

- Embed your performance management analysts within each of your existing IT organizational components and have these analysts report in a matrix organizational design to a senior IT leader, such as the deputy CIO, who has a view across the IT organization.

- Have a small, dedicated performance management group but have this group report directly to the CIO or deputy CIO. The CSI unit should contribute to any service improvement plans (SIPs) resulting from reviews of performance measures.

The benefit of both of these organizational designs for your performance management units is that it shows the importance of these activities to your IT organization. It does so by the positioning of being a direct reporting function to the CIO and deputy CIO and providing meaningful information to key IT decision makers without any potential filtering or intervention by lower-level IT managers or staff.

Segment Your Application Development and Application Maintenance Performance Measures

Application development (AD) and application maintenance (AM) consume a large portion of the overall resources in some IT organizations. In these cases we recommend that you develop an IT scorecard specific to AD. This AD scorecard should be a more tactical, detailed scorecard than the overall IT scorecard you develop to measure and improve the performance of your overall IT organization. Using the Kaplan and Norton framework, this cascaded scorecard should be consolidated into your overall IT scorecard.

AD and AM continue to receive significant focus in IT organizations. Application projects typically are not started without a rigorous

PERFORMANCE MEASUREMENT CASE STUDY

We were at a client site and attended a meeting of the performance measurement team (PMT) that was responsible as part of a large-scale system implementation for developing and tracking performance measures. What was immediately evident was that the PMT had limited knowledge of what activities were occurring within the software and hardware development teams and had limited, if any, contact with these development teams. The PMT was physically operating in a building in a different part of the city from the development teams and was relying on posted information of development activities on an intranet site to attempt to develop initial performance measures, targeted future state desired performance levels by performance measures, and time intervals for achievement of the targeted future state performance levels. Although senior leadership at the client clearly had communicated the importance of cycle time for selected organizational activities as critical success factors, the PMT was primarily focused on common project management performance measures, including lines of code (LOCs) and error rates. Following were some of the drivers of this apparent disconnect:

- The PMT leader indicated that the PMT perceived that they were an unimportant activity to the overall organization, and that their efforts were marginalized by leadership of the project.
- The physical separation of the PMT created a perception of being disconnected from the project.
- The PMT leader and staff indicated that the culture of their organization was not committed to CSI.
- The PMT leader indicated the PMT staff in general were poor performers, or "short timers," who had been staffed to the PMT as a place to "keep them busy."

When we discussed the situation with the overall project leadership team, they indicated that they considered performance measurement to be a critical part of the project. This indicates that some level of disconnect was occurring within the project, and it was related to the effective tracking and use of performance measures.

business case analysis, and with each business case producing a target rate of return that exceeds the target hurdle rate for IT investments in your organization. A majority of common application performance measures in use by IT organizations would fall in the two components we defined for your overall IT scorecard of operational excellence and business value.

Under the AD and AM scorecard component of operational excellence, we put performance measures related to productivity and quality. Productivity measures in the AD environment should focus on the productivity of your developers in general. This component would focus on throughput—specifically, how many LOCs your developers generate on a consistent basis. Quality measures would focus on the error rate in the generated LOCs. Generating a high volume of LOC is virtually meaningless if both the error rate in the generated code is excessive and the functionality being created by the generated code does not meet the required functionality of the customer. The functionality issue is a performance measure linked to the "customer" segment of your AD scorecard but is mentioned here to stress the connectivity of the various components of the AD scorecard. We recommend also including in this component a measurement of time required to repair errors in generated code.

Under the AD scorecard component of business value, we recommend grouping your financial measures of the financial return generated by the commitment of organizational resources to specific AD projects. Your organization should commit organizational resources only to AD projects that produce software that enables the execution of your organizational strategy. The link of your AD investments directly to your organizational strategy must be measured and acted upon. AD projects that do achieve the projected financial returns defined in the initial business case for each project must be reviewed for either termination, if the AD project does not appear to be able to generate sufficient financial returns to justify the ongoing commitment of organizational resources, or targeted for corrective action so that the original projected financial returns can still be obtained with a focused intervention. Your AD scorecard can prove invaluable as an early warning system for AD projects that are not on schedule to obtain required results for your organization.

Use Benchmarking for Your IT Scorecard

Benchmarking is a continual improvement tool that can be highly effective in improving organizational performance when properly applied. Benchmarking is not a solution to all the failures of any organization. It is a tool. It is one among many business discipline tools that can be used to solve specific, well-defined problems, but it is not a cure-all for poor organizational performance.

In general, benchmarking is a process organizations use to compare their performance against the performance of external organizations that are considered to have "best practices" in a specific area relevant to your organization. For example, Company ABC might have a highly efficient accounts payable process, supported by technology enablers. If your organization is struggling to make payments on a timely, accurate basis, you may compare your processes and supporting technology enablers against the payment approach at Company ABC to determine whether it is economically justifiable for your organization to adopt the payment practices at Company ABC. This is a common benchmarking effort. You select specific areas of lagging performance in your organization for improvement. You identify external organizations that are considered to have leading performance in the specific area you selected for improvement within your organization. You study the specific activities in use at this external organization and determine whether you can adopt these activities into your organization to improve performance.

Benchmarking is often a misunderstood and misapplied business discipline. Xerox is generally credited with developing and using the concept of benchmarking in the early 1980s. One common misconception about benchmarking is that you select only external organizations in your industry as target benchmark organizations. There are several ways to select target organizations, including:

- **Functional benchmark organizations:** You may have selected your payment processes for improvement. Although your organization may be a commercial bank, you can select target benchmark organizations from across any industry segment that exhibit best practices in payment processing. Payment processing is a functional skill, not specific to a specific industry. Best practice payment processing may occur in a retail company, not a commercial bank, but is applicable to your banking organization.

- **Internal benchmarking:** You may have multiple organizational components in your organization that execute a common activity, such as payment processing. Before looking outside your organization for target benchmark organizations, consider looking internally across the organization to see whether a best practice approach to payment processing exists within one of your organizational components, and share this approach across the organization. This is a common approach to benchmarking in large, geographically dispersed organizations. For example, your operating unit in Ireland may have best practices for payment processing, but these best practices are not in common use across your global organization. An internal benchmarking approach is often a cheaper, faster alternative to external benchmarking.

- **Competitor benchmarking:** This is a common approach to benchmarking. When attempting to improve your operations in a skill set specific to your industry, you may target benchmark organizations only within your competitor community. For example, if your ATM operations for your commercial bank are lagging behind your competitors in the banking industry, you may look only within your competitor community to find best practices for ATM operations.

A number of commercial organizations provide benchmarking services and publish benchmarking reports on specific areas under common study across industries, such as payment processing. A number of the large consultancies provide benchmarking services, either on common areas of benchmarking, or will conduct customized benchmarking studies for specific clients.

The biggest risk of benchmarking, however, is it limits the creative process within the organization to look for new solutions to lagging internal performance. Benchmarking is inherently copying the approach to a performance area that another organization is already executing. Benchmarking is not a tool to develop new solutions to existing problems, so by using this tool, you are limiting the number of solution alternatives you can generate. What, then, is the relevance of benchmarking an IT organization?

Benchmarking should be applied against three areas of your IT organization: processes, performance measures, and organizational design.

SHARED SERVICES CASE STUDY

Our client organization wanted to create and run a shared services center to handle basic transaction processing activities in accounting, human resources, and Information Technology. The client organization had ten sites geographically dispersed across the United States. Each site had staff to perform this basic transaction processing activity just for its specific site. The driver to create a shared services center was to eliminate this duplication of effort and consolidate this activity in one location.

In developing a shared services model for this client organization, we took the client project team to five shared services centers across a number of industries. After visiting the five benchmarking sites, the client project team was able to discern common best practice elements to a shared services center. The shared services center was not a core activity for the client organization or for any of the five benchmark partners visited by the client project team. This is an example of highly effective functional benchmarking to strive toward industry best practices.

PROVISIONING CASE STUDY

A client organization wanted to reduce its backlog of servers to be provisioned and improve average cycle time for server provisioning. Given that this was a specific, limited problem, the client decided to benchmark internally to see whether a best practice existed within the current IT operations. This IT organization consisted of five operating units, and unfortunately from an efficiency perspective, all five operating units were provisioning servers in the primary data center. After forming a cross-functional internal benchmarking team to study the provisioning backlog, a new approach was created for server provisioning based on existing practices within one of the five IT operating units. This approach solved the provisioning problem without chartering a long-term benchmarking project.

Process Benchmarking

In our view, common best practice IT frameworks, such as ITIL, attempt to capture the full range of best practices needed by IT organizations across the globe. While capturing best practices for IT organizations in both performance measurement and organizational design, the ITIL framework is primarily focused on the processes within IT organizations. Therefore, a common and effective approach to IT benchmarking is the use and adoption of either ITIL or other leading IT industry best practice frameworks. Adoption of portions or all the ITIL framework is discussed in detail in Chapter 3, "Adopting IT Service Management Using ITIL."

Performance Measures Benchmarking

After you have selected the overall components of your IT scorecard and the specific performance measures you will target for adoption in each component, you need to consider the following:

- What is the current performance level of your IT organization against each individual performance measure you select to track and use for CSI?

- What is the target, or future, performance level your IT organization wants to achieve? (This is where the use of industry benchmarking is most effective.)

- What is the time interval for achieving your target performance level for each individual performance measure?

For example, if your IT organization has a mean time to repair (MTTR) for a system outage currently of 6 to 8 hours, your IT organization should consider benchmarking, or comparing, this MTTR against average performance levels for target benchmark organizations. If leading IT organizations have an MTTR of 5 hours, your IT organization could adopt a target, or future, performance level of MTTR of 5 hours. The next decision your IT organization would need to make is how quickly a target performance level of MTTR of 5 hours can be consistently achieved. We refer to a desired future performance level as a *target* and the length of time needed to achieve the target as *time intervals.*

Two key considerations your IT organization will need to make in the development of targets and time intervals for your IT scorecard performance measures are:

- Does your organization need to achieve best practice performance levels?
- Do the benefits to the organization of achieving best practice perform-ance levels justify the commitment of organizational resources needed to obtain these performance levels?

Many of the activities performed by IT organizations for their cus-tomers are not mission-critical activities for the customers. Therefore, IT organizations do not always benefit their customers by achieving best practice performance levels on activities that are not mission-critical to their customers. Achieving high performance levels often comes at a cost to any organization. As you develop your IT scorecard, you must give significant cost considerations to which performance measures track per-formance that are critical to your customers. Many of your customers will have a select portion of the applications that your IT organization runs as being considered mission critical. Your customers will expect, and sometimes demand, high performance levels related to support for this segment of mission-critical applications. Other applications, not considered mission critical by your customers, will not be expected to perform at a best practice level of performance.

When you work with your customers to develop the performance measures that are embedded in negotiated SLAs, your customers will indicate the priority of the various applications you will support for them based on their manifested need for high performance out of selected, mission-critical systems. Benchmarking activities targeted at performance measures in your IT scorecard should focus on specific per-formance measures that tie to customer satisfaction.

Some specific IT benchmarking organizations benchmark specific areas of IT performance. Among these IT benchmarking organizations are:

- **Standard Performance Evaluation Corporation (SPEC):** This non-profit was formed to establish, maintain, and endorse a standardized set of relevant benchmarks that can be applied to the newest generation of high-performance computers (www.spec.org).
- **Transaction Processing Performance Council (TPC):** This nonprofit was founded to define transaction processing and database benchmarks and to disseminate objective, verifiable TPC performance data to the industry (http://tpc.org).

Gartner and Forrester Research also provide high-quality benchmarking studies conducted at specific performance areas for IT organizations. While most major consultancies also provide strong benchmarking capabilities, SPEC, TPPC, Gartner, and Forrester are among the industry leaders in IT benchmarking and provide excellent starting points for your IT scorecard development and evolution.

Organizational Design Benchmarking

Although benchmarking of IT processes and related performance measures have a large body of existing service providers and supporting quantitative data, the area of benchmarking of organizational design for IT organizations is more embryonic.

Much discussion continues to occur in the IT industry around the federated, centralized, and decentralized IT organizational design models. However, no clear best practice model has emerged. This is largely due to the wide diversity of size and scope of commercial, nonprofit, and government organizations. This diversity of organizations makes development of a one-size-fits-all solution to IT organizational design difficult to achieve. The evolving role of the CIO and the emergence in many organizations of a chief technology officer (CTO) also results in a diversity of IT organizational designs.

Benchmarking of IT organizational designs often must be accomplished by selection of external benchmark partner organizations for study. A common approach to selecting IT organizations for potential benchmarking is to look at organizations of the same size and scale as your organizations. For example, we had a client IT organization attempting to make a decision about how to combine its legacy applications development unit with its emerging, large-scale application development unit. As part of this organizational design project, we selected several target benchmark organizations in the same industry as our client, with the same national footprint, to see how these target benchmark organizations structured their legacy and new application development groups.

Involve Your Enterprise and Data Architects Early in the IT Scorecard Development

Your IT scorecard, either at the IT organizational level or any of the cascading IT scorecards (such as an AD scorecard), must accurately capture the current performance level of each performance measure you decide to track and use to make decisions to improve the performance of your IT operations. IT organizations typically have a significant amount of existing data about the performance of ongoing IT operations. Unfortunately, this data is often captured in a variety of disparate, unconnected systems and applications that make capture and centralized reporting of performance difficult, if not impossible.

You must include either your enterprise architect (EA), or data architects, in the initial planning and development efforts around development of all levels of your IT scorecard. Nothing will doom a performance management project to quicker failure than developing a meaningful set of individual performance measures, grouped into logical components, but populated with inaccurate, if not outright wrong, performance data. Making business decisions with inaccurate data results in significant risks to all aspects of your organization and immediately undermines the credibility of your efforts toward holistic performance management.

A good data architect or data analyst can be one of the critical drivers of successful IT scorecard development and adoption. The data captured in your IT scorecard must be accurate. A lack of quality data will immediately call into question the validity of performance management in your IT organization. Recovering from a failed, initial performance management project in an IT organization is a long, difficult process. Involve your data architect early in any performance management project, especially for IT organizations that are in the early stages of performance failures. Decision makers in your IT organization need accurate performance data if they are to make decisions to improve their IT organization to better 1) align your IT organization to your organizational strategy or mission, and 2) achieve operational excellence in your IT operations, which requires accurate, quality performance data. Essentially, you need to convert data to meaningful information for the decision makers in your IT organization to utilize to continually improve performance, including the development and implementation of SIPs. ITIL takes this concept a step further and considers that your IT organization actually needs to convert data to information but further evolve information into knowledge and eventually wisdom (data $\Rightarrow$ information $\Rightarrow$ knowledge $\Rightarrow$ wisdom).

Although a number of excellent software tools exist to pull data from disparate parts of your enterprise architecture, you cannot underestimate the organizational resources that must be committed to the capture and reporting of quality data during the initial stages of a performance measurement implementation.

Ensure Your IT Scorecard Is ITIL Conformant

ITIL has become the de facto best practices standard in the IT industry. Woven throughout the various elements of the ITIL lifecycle are performance measures. As you develop an IT scorecard, consider whether the performance measures you are adopting conform with the recommendations around performance measurement of the ITIL framework. A number of consultants and software vendors providing ITIL services list their performance measurement approaches and supporting technology as being ITIL conformant.

There is no magic to your IT scorecard being ITIL conformant. Review the performance measurement components of ITIL. Compare the overall components of your proposed IT scorecard (that is, operational excellence, customer, future orientation, business value) against the ITIL framework and determine whether your IT scorecard is consistent in intent and execution with the ITIL framework. This is a good method to check that your approach to performance management, using tools including your IT scorecard, is consistent with current IT industry best practices. This will enhance the credibility of your performance management approach for your IT organization, both within your IT organization and with your critical customers and broader stakeholders. An ITIL-conformant IT scorecard indicates the IT scorecard is consistent with industry best practices, which is one indicator that an IT scorecard is capturing performance measures consistent with industry practices to use for improved decision making.

How Do You Populate Your IT Scorecard with Individual Measures?

The number of individual performance measures utilized by various IT organizations is almost unlimited. A number of excellent publications provide comprehensive lists of literally hundreds of individual IT performance measures in common use in industry, including:

- Gartner's *IT Performance Measures Quick Reference Guide,* which captures more than 300 IT performance measures, segmented by operational excellence (196 measures), customer (29 measures), business contribution (31 measures), and future (52 measures)
- Janco Associates's *Metrics for the Internet, Information Technology, and Service Management: A Handiguide*[17]

When you begin development of your initial IT scorecard, the development and selection of the initial overall components of your IT scorecard will heavily drive the selection of individual performance measures for your IT organization to utilize. In the initial stages of your IT scorecard project, your cross-functional team will have to give tremendous upfront thought to what exactly the critical drivers of performance for your organization are and how your IT organization supports execution of these drivers.

Many best practices IT organizations focus on performance measures related to operational excellence. How long was the network down? What is the average time to provision a server? What is the capacity of the infrastructure? These types of operational measures are important, typically measured by existing network tools, and are relatively easy to capture and measure on an ongoing basis.

We also recommend that you focus on developing performance measures against the high-level financial measures of an overall IT organization that are typically in place and measurable. What amount of the organization's overall budget is consumed by IT? How is the IT budget allocated among application development, operation/maintenance, and a variety of infrastructure activities? What are the trends in IT spending?

The performance measurement areas that are more difficult to define and measure effectively are measures related to customer satisfaction, including user orientation, and financial measures related to business value of IT operations to the organization, not just high-level financial measures such as IT spending as a percentage of the organization's overall budget.

Commitment of significant organizational resources to define upfront the necessary performance measures to be captured and reported on for your IT scorecard is a critical success factor for your IT organization. Much care and thought will need to be applied to this effort, and healthy, spirited debate will need to occur to truly achieve clarity on what performance measures will be most useful for your IT organization to use to continually improve service to your customers. Careful trade-offs will need to be made between the cost and difficulty of tracking and reporting on performance measures versus the benefits to your IT organization from this ongoing effort.

Links to Other ITIL Framework Components

The ITIL framework is a comprehensive body of knowledge of IT leading practices codified into a service lifecycle framework. Every component of the ITIL should be measured. Your IT scorecard and supporting cascading scorecards will need to measure the specific components of the ITIL framework you have decided to adopt for your IT organization:

- The operational excellence component of your IT scorecard should include measurements of critical business processes, including demand, capacity, and availability management.
- The business value component of your IT scorecard should include measurements of service portfolio management, chargebacks, critical financial processes (such as accounting, charging, and budgeting).
- The customer component of your IT scorecard should include service level management, specifically the management of SLAs, and customer satisfaction.
- The future orientation component of your IT scorecard should include many of the components of your service strategy and service design.

Sample IT Scorecard

Figure 6-3 illustrates a notional IT scorecard for an IT organization. This notional scorecard is composed of the three overall components recommended earlier in this chapter: operational excellence, customer, and business value. This notional scorecard is further segmented under each component into four subsets focused on operating elements of your IT organization.

The purpose of this notional IT scorecard is to show how a complete IT scorecard may be presented. Although limited in the number of

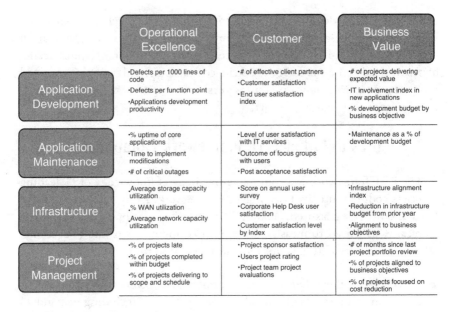

	Operational Excellence	Customer	Business Value
Application Development	•Defects per 1000 lines of code •Defects per function point •Applications development productivity	•# of effective client partners •Customer satisfaction •End user satisfaction index	•# of projects delivering expected value •IT involvement index in new applications •% development budget by business objective
Application Maintenance	•% uptime of core applications •Time to implement modifications •# of critical outages	•Level of user satisfaction with IT services •Outcome of focus groups with users •Post acceptance satisfaction	•Maintenance as a % of development budget
Infrastructure	•Average storage capacity utilization •% WAN utilization •Average network capacity utilization	•Score on annual user survey •Corporate Help Desk user satisfaction •Customer satisfaction level by index	•Infrastructure alignment index •Reduction in infrastructure budget from prior year •Alignment to business objectives
Project Management	•% of projects late •% of projects completed within budget •% of projects delivering to scope and schedule	•Project sponsor satisfaction •Users project rating •Project team project evaluations	•# of months since last project portfolio review •% of projects aligned to business objectives •% of projects focused on cost reduction

Figure 6-3   Notional IT scorecard

performance measures in use, it provides a view of how IT performance measures can be grouped both by the BSC components tailored to IT organizations, and by organizational components or focus areas for IT organizations.

Next Steps

The development and implementation of a meaningful performance management framework for your IT organization is challenging but can be accomplished through thoughtful work and commitment. The BSC concepts provide a strong foundation for a performance management framework and can be adapted for use in your IT organization. Performance management is a part of all aspects of your IT organization. You must measure yourself to commit to a culture of CSI, which is a critical success factor for IT organizations going forward. You need to strike a careful balance between the commitment of your organizational resources to performance management and measurable benefits to your organization from its use. In addition, your IT managers and staff must have the required skills to develop, execute and evolve performance management. In the next chapter, we discuss the critical need for IT organizations to identify both critical skill sets needed to execute current operations, but also to identify future skill sets needed for your IT organization, and develop and execute a plan to obtain these skills.

Endnotes

1. "NYS Project Management Guidebook: Release 2," New York State Office of Technology, Section II: 4 "Performance Measurement," 2003.

2. Office of the Chief Information Officer (OICO), Enterprise Architecture Program (2007), Treasury IT Performance Measures Guide.

3. Ibid.

4. Balanced Scorecard Institute, "What Is the Balanced Scorecard?" http://www.balancedscorecard.org/basics/bsc1.html. Accessed April 16, 2009.

5. John H. Lingle and William A. Schiemann, *Bullseye, Hitting Your Strategic Targets Through High-Impact Measurement* (New York, New York: Simon & Schuster, 1999).

6. Ibid.

7. Ibid.

8. Liz Barnett, "Metrics for Application Development," *Forrester* (May 2, 2005), pp. 1–3.

9. Gartner, "IS Performance Measures Quick Reference Guide." Roswell, Andy. April 6, 2007. www.gartner.com

10. http://en.wikipedia.org/wiki/Operational_excellence

11. E. H. Schein, *Organizational Culture and Leadership*, 3rd ed. (San Francisco: Jossey-Bass, 1985–2005).

12. *American Heritage Dictionary.*

13. BusinessDictionary.com

14. http://en.wikipedia.org/wiki/User_(computing)

15. http://en.wikipedia.org/wiki/End-user_(computer_science)

16. *Houghton Mifflin Dictionary.*

17. Victor Janulaitis, *Metrics for the Internet, Information Technology, and Service Management: A Handiguide* (Janco Associates, 2007). Derived from various templates of Janco Associates, Inc. 2001.

Suggestions for Further Reading

Balanced Scorecard Institute, "What Is the Balanced Scorecard?" www.balancedscorecard.org/basics/bsc1.html.

Barnett, Liz, "Metrics for Application Development," *Forrester*, May 2, 2005.

Gartner, "IS Performance Measures Quick Reference Guide."

IBM Global Services, "Balanced Scorecard: Technique Paper," Version 1.0, July 2001.

Improvement Skills Consulting, *Measuring Process Performance*, 2008.

Lingle, John H., and William A. Schiemann, *Bullseye, Hitting Your Strategic Targets Through High-Impact Measurement*, Simon & Schuster, 1999.

Office of the Chief Information Officer (OCIO), Enterprise Architecture Program, 2007, Treasury IT Performance Measures Guide.

Rooney, Tim, "Applying ITIL Best Practice Principles to IPAM," *BT Diamond IP*, August 2008.

Schein, E. H. *Organizational Culture and Leadership*, 3rd ed., Jossey-Bass, 1985–2005.

Symons, Craig, "The Five Essential Metrics for Managing IT," *Forrester*, April 14, 2008.

7

IT Business Skills: Enabling Customer Outcomes

Effective IT business skills are critical to helping an organization achieve its goals and maximize the return from IT investments. These business skills and activities should be aligned with the two primary goals of this book: to improve service and lower costs. We first discuss examples of how IT business skills contribute to these goals. This chapter then provides a method for identifying whether your IT organization has the required business skills to execute business activities within your IT organization. Then, we discuss options for addressing any skill gaps that may exist in your existing business skill sets.

Changing customer demands and previous IT managers who lacked business skills affect an IT organization's capability to align with the business. IT organizations have transformed from centralized services that focused on supporting core technologies to working with customers to identify projects that achieve key business objectives, such as driving revenue growth. At the same time, the required skills for IT organizations have forced IT managers and staff to expand their skill sets from solely technology-focused skills to financial and business-practice skills.

Historically, IT organizations began supporting a mainframe, group of services, or set of applications that achieved a given level of availability. This required skilled technical resources to resolve technical problems and provide technical solutions that enabled customer outcomes. However, as IT organizations transformed to business partners and consumed an increasingly larger amount of an organization's capital expenditures, those IT organizations have increasingly been required to take on responsibility of key areas such as:

- Reporting performance measures defined and tracked across the IT organization
- Reporting program and project management activities performed at both a portfolio and individual project level
- Tracking IT budgets for hardware, software, property, equipment, and human resources
- Executing and tracking continual service improvement activities
- Managing procurement and purchasing activities to acquire goods, general services, and technical services needed to execute ongoing activities
- Tracking and financial reporting of ongoing IT operations

This chapter will help you to identify the IT business skills to effectively execute these activities to improve service and lower costs.

The IT Business Skill's Goals

Effective IT business skills improve service levels by enabling IT organizations to work with customers to identify and track key IT projects, facilitating continual service improvement activities, and improving key business practices using industry best practice frameworks, including Information Technology Infrastructure Library (ITIL). IT organizations focus on these and other business activities with the goal of identifying methods to reduce costs across the IT organization. These activities include improving key IT business practices using ITIL, leading financial management activities, managing vendors, tracking performance measures, and supporting continual service improvement activities.

IT Business Skills Improve Service

Your IT organization can improve overall service levels by managing all aspects of the relationship between your IT organization and each customer, tracking performance measures, supporting continual service improvement activities, and improving key processes using industry best practice frameworks, such as ITIL.

These IT business skills help you to coordinate and support key service level processes using industry frameworks, such as ITIL's configuration management process. These skills help you to standardize application of IT processes across the IT organization. For example, if your IT organization maintains a configuration management database (CMDB) to track IT assets, it can link this information to the financial management process to account, charge, and budget for these assets.

IT business skills help you to maintain customer focus, consistent with the ITIL service level management (SLM) process. From developing standard service level agreements (SLAs) formats to ensuring that the financial management supports these SLAs, these skills will establish clear benchmarks for customer satisfaction and ensure that the IT operations and finances are aligned to these customer needs.

IT business skills play a critical role in understanding the needs of an operational and business unit, translate information between your IT organization and key customers, and monitor the performance of key activities using agreed-upon performance indicators. Specifically defined roles in your IT organization include relationship managers (RMs). RMs work to translate customer needs and requirements into actionable requirements documents for the IT organization. In some IT organizations, RMs are considered so critical to their success that they may be a distinct organizational unit or reside within the IT organization itself.[1]

These IT business skills can help drive disparate parts of your IT organization to support specific IT service offerings. From development of a service catalog to helping align application development projects with infrastructure, IT business skills enable your staff to ensure that IT spending and supporting activities are aligned with services that help achieve overall business objectives and the desired business impacts. For example, these skills may help your staff to implement your service catalog management process by aligning the different IT activities within your organization with a defined service, such as managed hosting or a web-hosting application.

Finally, these skills are critical to reporting performance measures defined and tracked across the IT organization. For example, it should develop and deliver reports on program and project management activities performed at both a portfolio and individual project level. It should also execute and track continuous improvement activities.

IT Business Skills Lower Cost

IT business skills also focus on lowering cost by tracking financial management of ongoing IT operations, streamlining IT business practices, and managing vendors through overseeing procurement and purchasing activities to acquire goods, general services, and technical services needed to execute ongoing IT operations.

Your IT business skills play a critical role in connecting key elements of your service portfolio to efforts to cut costs. IT business skills take elements of the service portfolio, including the service catalog and SLAs, and links these activities to key financial management functions (such as accounting, charging, and budgeting). As part of this effort, the IT organization focuses on how to support these service levels yet minimize costs.

IT organizations increasingly rely on external service providers and vendors. Forrester Research stated that "in the near future, we expect the vendor management function to increase in importance." Forrester and other industry research groups argue that centralizing this function is one of the most effective ways to reduce costs, consistent with an organization's overall business objectives.

Tracking vendor costs and negotiating with vendors using ITIL's supplier management process is one of the most basic ways an IT organization monitors costs and identifies opportunities for cost savings. Supplier management activities to secure value for your IT spending with vendors can be combined with the financial management activities discussed in Chapter 4, "IT Financial Management: The Business of IT." An effective way to both manage and reduce costs is to develop some basic form of asset tracking system.

Configuration management can also be an effective way to reduce costs through better managing your assets. Many IT organizations use Excel spreadsheets that execute many of the functions of a CMDB and link this database to key hardware and software licenses and costs. Even if you do not have a distinct IT organization, you can develop a process to execute this activity. For example, your organization's finance department, which often manages software agreements with vendors, can work with your application maintenance department to identify those applications that are rarely used. As a result, the organization may be able to consolidate rarely used applications, thereby reducing the cost of software licenses, unused infrastructure, and staff that may be supporting these IT functions.

IT business skills help you focus on cost cutting through coordinating the activities of the application development and maintenance organizations and the infrastructure groups. For example, you can develop more effective business cases that take into consideration not only the one-time cost of a given server, but also the ongoing software maintenance costs and personnel costs of an application maintenance organization.

A third area of reducing cost is to use the ITIL framework to identify opportunities to improve IT service management by potentially eliminating any problems or waste in your critical IT processes. As a result, the organizational resources required to execute a given IT process can be reduced. For example, many IT organizations have lengthy server provisioning and application development processes that result in delays for key customers. As a result, your customers may face a competitive disadvantage because they cannot respond quickly to the marketplace with a given product or service offering. Using the ITIL framework as guidance to break down these challenges into key processes, you can identify where the waste or delay is and use continuous improvement efforts to eliminate them. Figure 7-1 highlights how your IT organization can translate key elements of your service strategy into your financial management activities.

These are some of the many ways your organization's activities can help to improve service and lower costs. To effectively execute these activities, you should make sure you have the skills to address these concerns.

IT Business Skills

Developing key IT business skills is critical to effectively executing business operations. These skills can be broken down into the following five categories:[2]

- Business processes
- Financial accounting and finance
- Managerial accounting

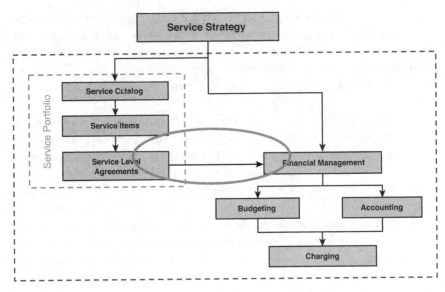

Figure 7-1 Example illustrating how an IT organization connects IT activities with financial management

- Regulatory skills
- IT skills

Most organizations have employees with varying degrees of these required business skills both inside and outside the IT organization. For example, IT business functions often are executed and placed organizationally in the finance or administration departments. Given the varying degrees of existing business skills in your IT organization, we recommend a combined approach to identifying and developing IT business skills. This combined approach includes training IT staff and integrating skills from outside the IT organization, to bridge any skills gap on IT business management with existing business skills possessed by the managers and staff in your IT organization. Two effective examples of integrating skills from outside the IT organization include cross-training IT, finance, and business unit staff and developing integrating structures within the organization. To cross-train staff, a member of the IT organization may work within the finance organization for a year rotation, thereby building this financial knowledge. In the case of an integrating organization, the IT organization and business unit may develop a monthly meeting to discuss key business topics related to IT investments.

Business Process

Your IT organization should have a strong working knowledge of business processes. This knowledge will be the underpinning of your effort to improve key IT business practices. For example, your IT organization should have working knowledge of the key business practices summarized in this book, including those related to ITIL, performance management, and financial management. From a tactical level, these skills should enable your organization to analyze and improve workflows through the development of process diagrams and evaluate which area of a given process should be improved to achieve your desired outcome. These skills should also enable your organization to document key ITIL operational processes, such as change and configuration management.

You can develop these skills through a range of formal certifications, including Lean Six Sigma (LSS), ITIL, and basic business process improvement courses. Although these formal certifications are helpful, many free resources are available from websites such as CIO.com and the Federal CIO Council. Moreover, just as important as these basic certifications is the way to use these skills. For example, in developing a basic business process, your staff should be able to document key activities and develop a workflow, such as the workflow summarized in Figure 7-2, to identify key challenges and opportunities. These IT financial management practices are discussed further in Chapter 4.

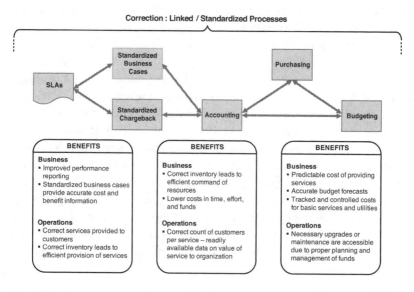

Figure 7-2 Example of how business process skills can identify opportunities for improvement

Financial Accounting and Finance

Your IT organization should also have access to staff with basic financial accounting and finance knowledge. For example, selected staff of your IT organization should be able to understand key concepts and principles of financial accounting, such as financial statement analysis. This understanding will help you understand how your IT investments achieve key business objectives, such as increasing net income or reducing costs. Your IT organization should also have access to staff with awareness of more advanced concepts of financial accounting, including leases and intangible assets.

There are many strategic benefits from these skills related to financial accounting and finance. For example, your IT organization may be able to avoid fixed costs for hardware and software purchases through leasing hardware instead of purchasing it. When discussing the value of your IT activities with business units, be aware that although an internally developed application may not be valued on the balance sheet because it is an intangible asset, it does contribute to a business activity that generates a significant amount of net income.

Your IT organization should also have access to key corporate finance skills, such as methods to evaluate the cost of capital, which helps determine the net present value (NPV) of your IT investments. A working knowledge of different valuation models can also help you determine how to value an IT investment to contribute to business objectives and achieve desired business impacts.

These financial accounting and financial skills are two key areas where you can leverage other parts of the organization. For example, your finance or administration organization likely has a robust corporate finance and accounting capability. It is important that you develop a standard practice, such as a monthly meeting or key point of contact, to access these skills. Without these skills, it is difficult to develop a credible argument for IT contributing to key business objectives, such as lowering annual expenses or increasing an organization's net income. There are many basic methods to establish links to these skills. For example, establish a monthly checkpoint with your corporate finance department and accounting department to review your IT budget, expenses, and projects. Before this checkpoint, establish a key agenda that summarizes what you need from your perspective to effectively manage your IT budget.

Managerial Accounting

Managing IT financial management practices—accounting, charging, and budgeting—requires managerial accounting skills. These skills help you translate financial cost accounting into IT operational activities. For example, you use managerial accounting to establish a process to group your IT expenses into forecasting the cost of a given IT service and develop your IT rates.

To effectively link financial accounting with a given IT service, you should have knowledge of key cost concepts, such as the difference between a variable and fixed cost. If your organization wants to create a chargeback model, as discussed in Chapter 4, you should have a basic understanding of transfer pricing, operating budgets, and different costing methods, such as activity-based costing.

In most organizations, managerial accounting is the skill of linking financial information to operational information, usually in the form of an Excel spreadsheet. At their best, managerial accounting skills quickly and effectively translate between the IT departments, business units, and the financial or administrative organization. For example, these skills help to identify relevant operational information, such as application development and maintenance activities, and their financial costs, to group them into a single process for tracking their costs and benefits.

At their worst, ineffective managerial accounting can cause frustration between the IT organization and business units, or generate misleading information across the organization. Table 7-1 summarizes common managerial accounting challenges and solutions.

Table 7-1 Common Managerial Accounting Challenges and Solutions

If You're Facing This Challenge	Try...	Why...
Hardware or software expenses: You can't find information to price your IT expenses such as software...	Make the vendor do the work by using new quotes for the software or other expense.	Approximate detail is better than rough estimates.
Staff costs: For application development projects, you can't create a tracking tool to determine the true staff costs...	Create a spreadsheet to estimate people's time against each project.	This will enable you to start tracking estimates for each project. Each week you will get better.

Table 7-1 Common Managerial Accounting Challenges and Solutions

If You're Facing This Challenge	Try...	Why...
Process: You don't have the staff or skills to translate accounting data into the cost of a service...	Use the cost sheets in Chapter 4 or in publically available templates, such as Microsoft's Rapid Economic Justification (REJ).	They provide you with the best practices that at least help you estimate your costs.

Regulatory

Depending on your industry, your IT organization should have a working understanding of relevant regulatory issues. You should understand the impact and constraints government regulations place on your business. For example, if your organization wishes to undertake a significant application development initiative in the healthcare sector, you must be aware of issues such as the Health Insurance Portability and Accountability Act (HIPAA), which govern medical privacy. Similarly, if these regulations require privacy standards for specific applications, your change management processes may be significantly limited.

You may also need to develop knowledge of contract regulations and taxation issues. For example, to maximize your IT dollars, you may want to develop an IT budgeting process whereby vendors compete for a series of IT projects. Although this may be an effective way to save resources, your IT organization must have significant knowledge of your existing contacts to avoid any regulatory infractions.

Information Technology Skills

Finally, your IT business organization (often referred to as the IT front office, or IT controller's office) must have relevant information technology skills. Although this advice may seem obvious, many IT business organizations simply consist of contracting, purchasing, or budgeting staff who have little knowledge of the organization's IT environment. This lack of knowledge can lead to a range of faulty IT business practices.

A basic understanding of IT can be largely broken down into two segments: infrastructure and application development/maintenance activities. Your IT organization should have a working knowledge of key IT infrastructure components, including servers, storage, load balancers, networks, and key infrastructure projects. Depending on the size of your organization, a working knowledge of data and network communications, such as your local area network or wireless area network, is also helpful. For application development, your staff should have a basic understanding of your key applications, their software components, and the staff dedicated to maintaining and developing them. These skills should include knowledge of your software licenses, database software, and the application development process.

These skills are the foundation for your IT organization translating between your IT operations and business units. For example, without these skills, your organization's efforts for effective relationship management and vendor management may prove ineffective. In the case of relationship management, if your IT organization does not understand the core components of your IT organization, it might not be able to develop, monitor, and address concerns about SLAs. If your IT organization does not understand key aspects of your information technology, it will also not be able to lower costs through vendor management efforts. For example, many organizations may be able to lower their overall software costs by switching from individual software licenses to enterprise licenses. Without an understanding of these types of licenses, you may not be able to effectively reduce these costs.

Improving Your IT Business Skills

To improve service and lower costs, IT leaders recognize the need to improve how their organizations are aligned with the business. These efforts to improve organizational alignment can largely be broken down into two areas: improving the structure of your IT organization and building your IT organization's business skills. This section focuses on improving your IT business skills.

Building IT Business Skills for Your Existing Staff

Regardless of the organizational structure of your IT organization, your staff should have some level of skill related to key IT business functions.

Although IT and business leaders commonly cite improving IT and business alignment as a top priority, few provide a detailed plan on how to develop their employees' skills to get there. One study by Vanson Bourne highlighted this gap with training related to ITIL V3. Although 62 percent of IT leaders surveyed stated that they planned to migrate to

V3, only 17 percent had a plan and timeline in place to do so. Training was a key issue, with 67 percent of IT managers and directors saying that they were not equipped to support ITIL V3.[3]

Most organizations do not have sufficient resources to train all employees in a formal classroom. In his article "IT Training's Impact on the Bottom Line," Eddie Kilkelly suggests a useful blended learning approach, which combines in-person learning and virtual learning with practical skills. This blended approach also helps to tailor training to individuals with different needs. For example, because the key ITIL processes include operational processes such as change management and configuration management, many IT staff involved with these activities may have different levels of experience with these functions.[4]

After you develop your approach to improving your IT business skills, you can develop a plan for implementing that approach. Common challenges, solutions, and ways to implement these improvements are displayed in Table 7-2.

Table 7-2 Developing a Plan to Improve Your IT Business Organization

IT Business Skill Challenge...	Try...	How...
You need to integrate skills from across your IT operations...	Using monthly checkpoints and documenting a process	Conduct monthly checkpoints to discuss key IT business practices.
		Document key processes and identify ways to work with IT operations.
		Develop a configuration management database, or an Excel worksheet, to work across different departments.
You have fragmented IT business analysts...	Developing common tools and processes	Develop a common set of tools, such as standard business cases, budgets, and chargeback models.
		Develop a common process to unify their efforts to prevent them from "going native."
You have no resources for IT business skills...	Formalizing IT business relationships with other departments	Identify finance, administration, vendor management, and other staff currently performing functions.
		Develop a monthly checkpoint with these staff, such as a monthly process to receive information on IT spending.

Identify Skill Development Needs and Gaps

To identify skill development needs, first identify any skill gaps in your IT business roles. To do this, we suggest that you identify the individuals responsible for each key process, the skills they need, and whether they have some or all of these skills. Here are the identifying steps to do this:

- **Identify the key business process or function:** Identify the key IT business processes, such as financial management, ITIL, and performance management that you would like to evaluate to discover whether you have the necessary skills. In many cases, this is a list of your key IT business processes and functions.

- **Identify the individuals responsible for these processes:** For each process, identify the individuals responsible for its key components. For example, your IT business analyst may be responsible for your business case process; your IT team leaders may be responsible for key ITIL tasks; and your budget director may be responsible for financial management tasks, such as budgeting, accounting, and charging.

- **Identify the needed skills:** For each individual and task, identify what skill they need. For example, to execute the financial management process, your staff should have some skill in basic accounting and management accounting skills. To improve your service levels using ITIL, your staff should have basic ITIL and business process improvement skills.

- **Identify the skills your staff possess:** For each person responsible for the process, identify which skills that person has. For example, for financial management, does the staff responsible for this process have some skill in basic accounting and management accounting?

After you have completed these tasks, use the skill gap method highlighted in Table 7-3 to identify the gaps in your IT business skills.

Methods to Improve IT Business Skills

After you have identified those who need training, we suggest a combined approach to developing your IT business skills. This approach helps to ensure that you target any training to those who need it. In many cases, an organization will provide formal training across the organization, which may not be the most effective use of resources. This

Table 7-3 Skill Gap Framework

	Process		
Process	**Financial**	**Management**	**ITIL Configuration Management**
Individual			
Skill Required			
Current Skill			
Gap Between Required and Current Skill			
Development Needs			

approach helps to ensure that your precious training dollars are used most effectively.

First, you can provide in-person or web-based training to those individuals with key IT business skill gaps. When you provide formal training, using a blended approach of in-person, web-based, and experiential skill development helps to maximize the effectiveness and return on investment (ROI), of your training resources. Table 7-4 summarizes key formal training related to IT organizations.

Table 7-4 Comparing Formal IT Business Certification

Consider This Topic	...If You Have Training Funding	...Or If You Have No Funding
ITIL	Use online e-learning to provide your staff with the basic tools they need to complete the ITIL Foundation certification.	Develop a core reading list of ITIL whitepapers to develop a basic understanding of IT service management.
Project management professional (PMP)	Sponsor key staff (and only key staff) to complete the PMP certification.	Use the Project Management Body of Knowledge (PMBOK) and other resources to develop a basic internal PMP course to highlight key project management topics.
Financial skills	Provide key financial and accounting skills to your key IT managers.	Ask your finance and/or accounting staff to provide an overview of key topics to your staff.
Regulatory	Send your IT staff to the relevant annual association conference or a local course.	Ask your industry association for free whitepapers on the regulatory topic.

Another way to build skills within your IT organization is to identify those individuals outside your organization who can lend their skills to your efforts. For example, if your organization lacks key financial skills, reach out to the corporate finance or accounting staff to help develop a method to track your IT expenses. In developing business cases, the business unit or customer often is willing to provide insight into its development, which can be helpful to ensure that the costs and benefits are accurate. Table 7-5 highlights common staff that may be useful to develop your IT organization.

Table 7-5   Common Staff Outside the IT Organization That Can Be Particularly Useful

Seek Out These Staff	To Find This Information
Finance/accounting/audit/ administration	Financial data on staff, purchase order, accounting
IT team leaders	Linking cost data with your IT services and infrastructure
Marketing	Methods your business can support your marketing and sales efforts
Customer relationship	What your customers are saying about IT
Legal/regulatory compliance	Regulatory issues you should be aware of
Project management	Key project milestones you should follow and track

Cross-training and job rotation can be an effective way to broaden the skills of your IT and business staff. Internal IT department job rotations can be extended to the IT business department. Although IT rotation programs are frequently used to develop functional IT skills, this is an effective way to also build business skills. The business-to-IT job approach (and vice versa) is used less often, but is more effective way to improve business alignment and these key skills. This effort not only builds key business, financial, and managerial skills, but also helps IT staff understand the challenges of the business.

Next Steps

This chapter recommended approaches to improve your IT organization's alignment with your customers. We suggest that you combine these approaches with the key ITIL processes outlined in this book to develop an effective IT service management approach. Through improving your IT organizational alignment, designating clear process owners for key ITIL processes, and implementing an effective continual service improvement (CSI) function, you can improve service and lower costs for your customers.

Endnotes

1. Marc Cecere, et al., "Forrester on IT Organizational Design" (September 2005), www.forrester.com/ER/Research/Report/Summary/0,1338,37113,00.html.

2. See, for example, www.theiia.org/itaudit/.

3. Eddie Kilkelly, "IT Training's Impact on the Bottom Line," *TJOnline* (July 2008), www.trainingjournal.com.

4. Ibid.

8

Success Stories:
Improving Service and
Lowering Costs

This book presented a number of methods and approaches for your IT organization to improve service and lower costs. These methods and approaches can be used as stand-alone tools or combined into an integrated approach to achieve your business goals. Striking a balance between 1) the adoption and use of multiple tools to improve service and lower costs and 2) the commitment of IT resources to implement these tools, requires careful thought and analysis. In Chapter 9, "Going Forward," we present a number of near-term and long-term opportunities to use the methods summarized in this book. To develop an overall framework for these improvements, we suggest using the Information Technology Infrastructure Library (ITIL) continual service improvement (CSI) framework to identify and improve key services.

IT organizations exist in all shapes and sizes, with a wide range of organizational structures, governance, workforces, missions, and supporting infrastructure. These IT organizations also exist within a wide range of organizations—nonprofits, commercial, government, and academic organizations. Your approach to implementing organizational change in your IT organization is dependent on the IT organization itself, the organization it exists within, and the broader environment the organization exists and operates within.

Change is constant in all aspects of an IT organization. The demand for IT services from internal customers is constantly changing as business units try to continually adapt to changing market and economic conditions. From natural disasters, to the economic downturn of late 2008 and into 2009, organizations cannot plan for every risk and contingency. However, when deciding what methods and approaches to adopt to improve service while lowering costs, successful IT organizations make measured, thoughtful decisions, supported by the best information available at the time. Throughout this book, we have provided you with alternative approaches to develop a framework for effective decision making. In Chapter 5, "IT Business Cases: Realizing IT Value," and Chapter 6, "IT Performance Management: Defining Success," we discuss alternate approaches to identifying key risks related to IT services and investments. Chapter 2, "IT Service Lifecycle: Improving Business Performance," provides a method to improve the focus of your IT investments through service portfolio management.

Recognizing that organizations come in all shapes and sizes, this chapter provides you with a number of examples of organizations that have used effective IT business processes to improve service and lower cost. We organize these examples into the following five success stories of IT organizations of varying size, shape, and industry. These organizations have selected and successfully implemented elements of the methods and approaches we have recommended in this book to improve service and lower costs.

Swiss Re[1]

Swiss Re is a leading global reinsurer based in Zurich, Switzerland, and operates in 25 countries. Swiss Re offers financial services products that enable risk taking essential to enterprise and progress. New insurance acquisitions have driven tremendous growth at Swiss Re. To help manage this growth, Swiss Re is moving from a silo, manual approach in managing key IT processes to an end-to-end service management model in which IT processes are standardized, automated, and aligned with business needs.

According to Heinrich Waldhier, head of process management in IT at Swiss Re, "Whenever it is possible, we try to automate processes to ensure that we have sustainability for growth." One area where this shift can be seen is in the organization's handling of change and release management processes.

Standardize Change and Release Management Processes

The company's IT organization is under tremendous pressure to manage growth resulting from multiple acquisitions without substantially increasing its budget. Doing so required that staff move from a silo, manual approach to an end-to-end service management model. The company had 40 change processes in use, and sought to consolidate to one, standard change process. To improve change and release management processes, Swiss Re staff sought to:

- Align best practice processes for software delivery with business requirements to accelerate development and deployment of new services
- Predict IT requirements for new business services and assess how changes will affect service availability
- Automate previous manual processes to help ensure that necessary tasks occur on time as planned, reducing manual labor and the risk that errors are introduced in the environment

Improving Scalability, Flexibility, and Quality of Service

Swiss Re began its journey toward an IT service management model that has enabled it to achieve the scalability, flexibility, and the quality of service it requires. As a first step, Swiss Re staff developed a comprehensive IT governance framework that enabled staff to advance from ITIL V2 to ITIL V3 best practices. In addition, Swiss Re management and IT staff evaluated the company's policies, enhanced its IT governance solution, and defined guiding principles. From this, the team created an IT governance handbook that aligns IT processes with business needs and clearly outlines roles, responsibilities, and governance processes.

Following the establishment of standard processes through which change managers and release managers could deploy those changes, the company began evaluating vendor tools that would help automate asset management, configuration management, and release management processes.

After the selection of an automated tool, the team created a fully automated deployment engine based on ITIL V3 best practices that consolidates the 40 change processes into 1 and enables:

- Application owners to understand the dependencies of their applications and the potential impact on other applications or infrastructure component changes.

- Developers to forecast new infrastructure requirements and communicate them to IT staff. In cases where new technologies are needed to support an application, staff can gain approval early in the process to avoid unnecessary delays.

- Automatic implementation of change requests based on business practices.

- The ability to audit all changes in the production environment.

These changes have also been essential in helping Swiss Re meet regulatory requirements and minimize risk. By creating a framework and standardizing and automating the deployment of changes, with a clear audit trail, IT staff can easily justify changes and adhere to principles set forth in regulations.

Key Points

Swiss Re is a large, geographically dispersed organization that had made a number of acquisitions in a relatively short period of time. To manage these changes, Swiss Re standardized key processes defined under ITIL V3, specifically standardizing change and release management. Many large, geographically dispersed IT organizations face similar challenges to standardize key business processes to help improve IT services across the organization. This implementation of standardized processes also leveraged the review, and selection of an automated tool. This reflects how many successful ITIL V3 implementations combine IT business practices with software tools to support the service lifecycle and continual improvement initiatives.

The City of Corpus Christi[2]

The city of Corpus Christi, Texas, is the largest city on the Texas coast with 280,000 residents, and as a municipal government, it strives to improve the quality of life for its citizens while lowering operating costs. The city mayor and senior leadership team ("the City") reviewed its management of water, wastewater, utility, and storm water services, and decided to make some changes in its management systems, with an eye toward implementing improvements citywide.

Previously, citizen calls were routed to the appropriate department and recorded on index cards before being entered into a spreadsheet. Each utility department used its own separate system and procedures, with no citywide standards or procedures. Given the manual nature of this process, staff could not accurately track how long it took to respond to and fix problems. In addition, staff had no way to view the work history for each site, making it difficult to identify recurring problems.

Although the City had already established a geographic information system (GIS), work orders were not interfaced with the geographic information system. Therefore the City lacked the ability to spatially analyze work requests. As a result, departments could not easily determine whether a customer request represented a site-specific problem or an area-wide issue that would require more extensive support.

Leveraging Technology for Organizational Change

In response to the use of manual processes that impeded successful service to the citizens of the City, the City decided to reengineer its work and asset management processes so that it could:

- Establish and manage its success against citywide standards
- Spatially analyze work to improve resource utilization and enhance response times
- Clearly define and measure actual service levels provided
- Accurately track costs
- Time performance measures to match the City's strategy

The City decided to implement the IBM Maximo Asset Management software to gain visibility, the control, and the automation needed to achieve these goals. Throughout the implementation, the City emphasized what drove the need for change, rather than the underlying technology.

Today, citizen calls are now routed to the citywide call center where service staff can immediately record and track work orders and view work histories using Maximo software. Standardized location and priority codes help staff deploy resources based on urgency and service level requirements. Leveraging the process automation capabilities, the City can efficiently manage each job to completion.

In addition, staff can accurately measure the elapsed time for each job and associated work order and track it against the City's service level requirements (SLAs). Automated notifications are sent to City managers via their BlackBerrys so that they can keep an eye on critical issues.

Identifying Serious Infrastructure Issues

Because the software is integrated with the City's geographic information system, City staff can spatially view problem areas and planned work. This has helped service staff to avoid creating duplicate requests and better inform citizens of work in their areas.

It has also enabled departmental staff to proactively identify areas with serious infrastructure problems. For example, the Wastewater Department found that many wastewater backups were not caused by rain, signaling an issue with the pipes themselves. Staff members then used the spatial analysis capabilities to pinpoint which areas experienced problems in dry weather and implement a repair strategy.

The approach is setting a standard for other government organizations. During 2008, Public Technology Inc. (PTI) recognized the City as a winner in the GIS Technology Solutions category for "Using a Computerized Work and Asset Management System Interfaced with GIS to Improve Utility Infrastructure and Customer Service."

Improved Financial Management

As part of implementation, the City also used the integrated software with its financial accounting system from PeopleSoft. This integration helps staff accurately track department costs as well as staffing needs. For example, when the City provided flood assistance to neighboring towns, the costs were rolled into the Water Department's overall operating costs. Now, staff can track these costs separately and use the information to apply for federal funding when available.

Identifying Trends for Improved Service

Greater insight into operations has also helped the City identify trends to improve service and optimize efficiency. For example, Wastewater staff found in reviewing performance reports that nearly 33 percent of the department's effort was spent resolving problems at just 14 percent of customer sites. With this information, the City developed and implemented a repair plan to help resolve these ongoing issues and ultimately reduce costs.

Balanced Scorecard Impact

The City also can assess its own success effectively because the Maximo software provides a significant portion of the data required to rate services against the City's balanced scorecard (BSC). This BSC measures City operations in four areas: customer service, financial management, process efficiency, and sustainability.

This BSC program received national recognition in 2008 when the City was inducted into Kaplan and Norton's "Balanced Scorecard Hall of Fame." The city of Corpus Christi is only the second city in the United States to be recognized for its BSC.

Key Points

The city of Corpus Christi needed to improve service to its citizens. The city of Corpus Christi achieved this goal through the review and analysis and selection and implementation of a software tool to improve performance management. This effort provides transparency into the assets of the City, and a source for City officials to make effective decisions about how to best utilize City resources to serve the needs of its citizens.

While the software tool enabled improved service and lower costs, the City aligned its resources to make optimal use of the information provided by the tool. As the ITIL V3 framework stresses, the goal of performance measurement is to turn data into information into knowledge into wisdom. The City achieved this optimization of data and was also able to use the software tool to populate a meaningful BSC to enable better decision making for City officials.

United States Navy NETWARCOM

Because the daily actions of the U.S. Navy (Navy) are executed in cyberspace, preventing adversaries from accessing, intruding in, modifying, or blocking access to this data is vitally important to Navy readiness and overall national security. Similar to civilian IT organizations, military IT organizations are under pressure to justify IT investments. In October 2006, the chief of naval operations (CNO) initiated Operation Cyber Asset Reduction and Security (CARS) to improve shore-based information security posture, reduce the Navy's shore-based computer network, server, and application infrastructure by at least 51 percent, and to obtain full IT budget and asset visibility by September 2010. CARS is being led by Naval Network Warfare Command (NETWARCOM), based in Norfolk, Virginia, under the leadership of Neal Miller, CARS director, and Charlie Kiriakou, CARS deputy director, with direct support from the Navy headquarters and all of the Navy's second-echelon commands.

The scope of the CARS operation is across the geographically dispersed Navy footprint. When CARS was stood up, the Navy had a global portfolio of nearly 1,200 individual networks owned and operated by 25 separate Navy second-echelon commands, and included more than 100,000 servers and workstations. At the initiation of CARS, more than 50 percent of the total Navy IT systems, and 90 percent of Navy networks existed outside of Navy centrally managed networks. Navy networks are primarily composed of the Navy-Marine Corps Intranet (NMCI) for Continental United States (CONUS), and its overseas counterpart ONE-NET for Outside the Continental United States (OCONUS). CARS activities are a critical part of keeping the U.S. Navy's information secure from our adversaries and available to Navy and joint-mission partners. CARS is helping to transform the Navy IT into a more mature structure in which enterprise IT investment decisions will be made.

Improving Security and Reducing Infrastructure

The CARS mission is still in progress, and tangible results are being defined. As the number of networks is reduced, security is improved by limiting the number of potential points of attack, which in turn reduces operational risk and allows the Navy to concentrate resources and defensive efforts. The Navy network portfolio has been reduced from nearly 1,200 in 2006 to 435 by mid-March 2009, with the goal to reduce to below 200 by September 2010. Highlights of results to date include:

- Navy-wide network governance and security certification processes have been put in place, including protection of networks behind standard security suites using common security perimeter controls.

- A formal network portfolio management process was instituted: All Navy networks were reviewed and only those that met narrow conditions have been allowed to reside outside one of the Navy's enterprise networks. Only 190 of the original 1,200 networks have been found to meet these criteria—the rest have been terminated or are targeted for termination, primarily by migrating capabilities into a Navy enterprise network.

- Automating the process for creating security accreditation documents is raising both quality and consistency and significantly reducing the time and manpower required to complete necessary documentation, assess risk, and make sound risk acceptance decisions by a single Navy security approving authority (SAA).

- End-to-end disaster recovery capabilities are being improved by providing full failover capability between consolidated Navy application hosting facilities, which were successfully put to the test in New Orleans and San Diego during the 2008 hurricane season.

- The Navy is working across the enterprise to be more environmentally conscious, referred to as a "green" initiative. The Navy has embarked on server consolidation and migration to a modern, virtualized environment, which is reducing total consumption of electrical power to run and provide proper heating and cooling for the Navy's IT systems. Virtualization and consolidation also reduces fuel consumption by reducing requirements for backup generators.

- All of the Navy's public-facing websites are in the process of being consolidated to a single Department of Defense (DoD)-managed facility, thereby enforcing standards on and improving security for all Navy websites.

Leveraging Industry Best Practices in a Military Cyber-Operation

The Navy has historically operated in their IT organization as providing autonomy to IT organizations in Navy business units geographically dispersed across CONUS and OCONUS facilities. To execute this project required culture change in the Navy IT organization by requiring more centralized control of Navy IT operations in a mature structure that takes an enterprise, servicewide view. Changing the Navy IT organization from a geographically dispersed, decentralized organization to more centralized control is an ongoing effort. A long-term view and a commitment to the mission and vision by the highest levels of Navy leadership have been a critical success factor.

CARS is effectively a live cyber-operation. Because the standard military doctrine for operational planning and execution was followed, clear lines of authority were established in a format readily recognized by Navy second-echelon commanders:

- A focused planning effort up front helped CARS to identify potential barriers and to address them before becoming an issue.

- Unity of effort demonstrated by clear, frequent, and open communications at the working level and throughout the Navy chain of command has helped to ensure that policies and processes were consistently applied and required actions well understood.

- Objective measures of performance with both long-term and incremental goals have helped to manage resources.

- Flexibility to make adjustments in a dynamic operational environment has also been a major contributor to success. External factors such as new security demands at the DoD level could not be completely predicted, so authority to improvise was delegated to the CARS director.

Industry best practices for change management and large IT project management are also critical success factors:

- The Navy completed a formal Lean Six Sigma (LSS) Certification & Accreditation (C&A) project focused on decreasing the cycle time for accreditation decisions, reduction of C&A package rework/rejection rates, and increased speed to capability through timely operational risk assessments for operational commanders. A second LSS effort was conducted that improved the fidelity of data for financial savings/cost avoidance that resulted from CARS network reductions.

- For this project, the Navy has used a mix of private-sector consultants and research organizations to provide the Navy the latest thinking on best practices in IT that the Navy can apply to this project. Both general and focused research with industry leaders has helped shape the CARS operation. The Navy has extensively leveraged research from research organizations such as Gartner as well as from interservice information exchange.

- CARS has applied many of the concepts of capability maturity models to help measure and communicate progress.

- Emerging standards and process frameworks such as ITIL V3 and the Project Management Body of Knowledge (PMBOK) are being employed to leverage lessons found in industry, avoid mistakes of the past, and ensure solid alignment of the results with the Navy's vision for the future.

- A performance-based contract approach was chosen (versus time and materials) that included several subordinate initiatives. In this operation, this has provided the government with flexibility, helped to maintain focus on delivering results, and is estimated to have enabled completion of the mission at a significantly reduced total cost.

Key Points

With regard to the military community, and specifically our military IT community, the U.S. is beginning to reject the concept of "operational readiness at any cost." Instead, "the right readiness at the right cost" is demanded. The Navy IT organization has reacted to this changing environment with an enterpise-wide improvement initiative: CARS. This initiative requires a gradual, sustained change in the Navy culture, which is the most powerful enabler of improved service and lower costs.

The Navy CARS initiative involves multiple methods and approaches discussed throughout this book, including the following:

- Development and adherence to enterprise IT standards for the network portfolio

- Standardization of processes, including a number of security processes, which mitigates risk to the Navy enterprise
- Development and use of detailed performance measures to make adjustments to the operational performance of the Navy IT organization
- A committed stakeholder management plan to maintain commitment to the CARS change initiative across the Navy enterprise
- The adoption of components of industry best practice frameworks, including ITIL V3, Control Objectives for Information and related Technologies (COBIT), Capability Maturity Model Integration (CMMI), and LSS as part of a continual service improvement (CSI) culture
- The use of a PMBOK-based portfolio management approach

This project balances the ongoing challenge of the defense community to maintain operational security at all levels of the defense community while adopting IT best practices. This project is an excellent example of a real-world approach to improve service and lower costs in a unique operating environment with challenges not encountered in civilian IT organizations.

Neighborhood America

Neighborhood America (NA) is an entrepreneurial, agile social networking company founded in 1999, based in Naples, Florida. Competing in the same social networking market as large companies such as MySpace and Facebook, NA has been successful in applying a number of the business disciplines recommended in this book to streamline and apply IT products and services specifically tailored to the growing needs of their customers. NA is continuing to develop and market enterprise-level solutions. Using scalable, fast business processes, NA is developing a suite of IT products and services for their customers, summarized by the tagline "Enterprise @the Speed of Fast."

Standardization Across the Enterprise

According to Jim Haughwout, NA CIO, NA has transformed in one calendar year its IT operations in three key focus areas: 1) standardized processes, 2) technology, and 3) new product development and implementation. Transformation activities implemented by NA include:

- Development and adoption of a standardized set of processes to guide their IT operations using selected portions of the ITIL V3 framework, as well as adoption of Six Sigma for continual service improvement. NA has, since June 2008, defined eight high-level standard processes with four to six subprocesses supporting each of the eight high-level processes. These are scalable, fast processes that enable the IT products and services being offered by NA, with a focus from the ITIL V3 framework on service management, and specifically problem management. The focus of these processes is aligning to customer need, and desired outcomes, rather than aligning to providing only technology solutions to customers, without extensive knowledge of customer requirements.

- Development and implementation of a proprietary, custom-developed performance management system, "Business Command Solutions," which provides an electronic ("digital") dashboard real time of ongoing performance across a number of key performance indicators developed and adopted by NA. This proprietary system also links to NA's use of SalesForce.com.

- Changing their approach to developing customer solutions by offering a standard suite of five core services, with a limited set of options within each service to allow the customer the ability for some level of customization based on a limited range of options, instead of creating a custom solution for each customer that typically had involved extensive meetings and several months of development work. Within each of the five core service offerings, NA offers a "classic" view of each service, which is the basic service offering for each core service, before allowing the customer the limited additional options for customization by each core service.

- Streamlining of their existing business case analysis (BCA) approach to use a cross-organization core team drawn from business intelligence, sales, marketing, finance, and IT to quickly create a BCA for significant new projects, both internal and with customers. The NA CIO and CFO, Brenda Agius, sit down weekly to review significant BCAs, and utilize an Excel-based financial model that is updated every six weeks for significant changes in pricing and market assumptions.

Measurable Performance Improvement

Jim Haughwout indicates that NA has achieved the following measureable outcomes from these combined efforts to improve customer service while reducing costs:

- Reduced cycle time for product development an astounding 94 percent within one year.
- Developed a standardized set of five solution offerings (bundled under their primary solution offering ELAvate) as ELAvate Approach to Solution Execution (EASE). The differentiation for this set of solution offerings is that for the first time NA is not only selling the technology enablers for social networking, but is providing a full range of solutions to scoping, developing, implementing, and sustaining social network business enablers for NA customers to achieve their business strategies.
- Utilized real-time performance measures to continually improve NA performance in both IT and product development and marketing.
- Developed and utilized standardized templates for each solution offering to enable quicker service and response to customers.
- Improved:
    - *a.* Testing time and accuracy of new IT products
    - *b.* Development and use of IT project plans
    - *c.* The existing NA IT staffing model to optimize staff time and effort

NA has enjoyed a rapid IT transformation using a combination of business disciplines defined throughout this book, and is poised for future continued growth in revenue, while reducing IT costs, going forward.

Key Point

Neighborhood America is a success story of one of the critical elements of the ITIL V3 framework—the involvement and leadership of the IT organization in service strategy and service design. The IT organization aligns to the business strategy to not only provide IT infrastructure support, but also drive top-line revenue growth. This case also reflects the emerging role of the CIO beyond providing basic IT services, and into the business side of the organization to be a key player in organizational success.

In addition to this emerging role of the CIO, the NA IT organization has applied a number of ITIL V3 processes to achieve operational excellence in IT operations. By moving quickly to standardize key ITIL processes, the IT organization achieved key improvements in their IT operations. This IT organization automated their performance management framework, making is easier for NA leadership to use performance measures as a tool for decision making. The entrepreneurial culture of NA is a key enabler of making the IT organization nimble and agile in its execution of its multiple roles.

Forbes

According to ForbesMedia.com, "Since 1917, *Forbes* has stood, unwavering, for one overriding principle: the unshakable belief in the power of free enterprise. Our mission has also been clear and unchanging: to provide insights and information that ensure the success of those who tap into *Forbes*."[2] Forbes CIO Mykolas Rambus supports this goal by using IT to increase customer focus to find new ideas that increase top-line revenue. From recombining existing assets that create more value to working proactively with business partners on new solutions, Mr. Rambus helps to create IT business value and improve *Forbes*'s bottom line.

Mr. Rambus uses a project portfolio management process to put a stranglehold on the IT project portfolio by creating an ideas funnel to identify the most valuable projects. The result: 75 percent of their projects are now high value, up from 25 percent a year earlier. After developing this process to refocus on high-value projects, he then worked to find ideas within IT and business units. These ideas identified a range of projects that increased top-line revenue.

Increase Customer Focus

To increase the IT department's customer focus, Mr. Rambus first met with each of its 16 customer groups. Mr. Rambus then began to sit in on monthly sales calls and held regular checkpoints with the heads of each of *Forbes*'s business units. This focus transformed the role of CIO to business enabler from a cost center. Finally, he polled the IT department about how to better leverage existing IT assets to drive business value.

Finding Ideas for Top-Line Revenue Growth

Based on input from these key customer contacts and ideas within the IT department, Mr. Rambus identified a number of ways to adjust current offerings and combine existing assets to increase top-line revenue. These ideas included:

- **Enhancing ForbesMedia.com:** These discussions with the 16 business units resulted in a project to increase revenue through refocusing the ForbesMedia.com website. This project improved the information flow for media buyers seeking information about ad rates and editorial content. This improved website helps to differentiate *Forbes*'s advertising services, creating business value for its customers.

- **Improving audience development:** Mr. Rambus and his staff combined outside partner customer information with circulation demographic data to more effectively target circulation and advertising. This improved customer segmentation increases overall revenue through more effective advertising campaigns and improved value proposition for advertisers.

- **Global 2000 information:** Mr. Rambus identified an opportunity to collect information on Global 2000 companies and to combine this information with circulation and demographic information to provide improved services and generate a new income stream.

- **Survey tool:** These ideas also identified underused IT assets. For example, Mr. Rambus combined an existing survey tool with open source software to provide a new service that helped determine the effectiveness of a given advertising campaign. This improved service not only differentiates *Forbes*'s offerings to potential customers but also maximizes its own advertising dollars.

Key Points

Forbes is also a success story at one of the critical elements of the ITIL V3 framework—the involvement and leadership of the IT organization in service strategy and design. This involvement reflects one of the critical aspects of ITIL's CSI, whereby the CIO and IT leadership focus on key business objectives, such as top-line revenue growth. The IT organization can align its key activities to the business strategy to drive top-line revenue growth, not just enable operations by providing an IT infrastructure and a set of services. This example reflects the emerging role of the CIO that moves beyond managing IT infrastructure and into the business side of the organization as a key player in organizational success.

The *Forbes* IT organization also has implemented a rigorous, portfolio management approach to provide greater discipline to the IT investment process. The outcome of this rigorous approach has been a greater focus for *Forbes* on high-value IT investments. High-value investments are investments that enable the strategy of *Forbes,* while maintaining an optimized, integrated IT infrastructure and application development and other ongoing IT operations.

Next Steps

This chapter has provided you a view of how different IT organizations have improved service and lowered costs by implementing a number of the methods and approaches we discuss throughout this book. Each IT organization in this chapter approached improvement and cost savings using a mix of methods and approaches. The primary driver of the uniqueness of each organization's approach to its change initiative was the unique operating environment of its organization. An entrepreneurial commercial social networking company is faced with a widely different set of challenges for its IT organizations compared to the global footprint of the Navy. Local governments are relentlessly focused on serving their citizens, yet the need for good information to make decisions is universal to all IT organizations.

Industry best practice frameworks are a useful source of information on how to improve service and lower costs. However, the use of these frameworks must be tailored to the unique needs of your IT organization. An organization focused on security, such as the Navy, cannot benefit from industry best practices in the same manner as an international insurance company. Adoption of industry best practices must be carefully balanced against the benefits to your organization from their adoption.

Organizations such as *Forbes* and Neighborhood America can use their IT organizations to proactively drive profitable revenue growth. Other organizations, such as Swiss Re and the Navy, use their IT organizations to maximize the use of their organizational resources to maintain operational excellence, while maintaining a secure environment. Local governments can use a combination of asset management and a balanced scorecard to better serve their citizens while reducing costs. All of these efforts involve software and hardware tools that enable success.

In the next chapter, we capture key lessons learned that you should take away from the cumulative information in this book, and look ahead to near-term opportunities for IT organizations to continue to improve service and lower costs.

Endnotes

1. IBM case study
2. IBM case study

9

Going Forward

With more than $30 billion targeted to be spent on IT products and services over the next decade, IT organizations have an unprecedented opportunity to improve service and lower costs. This book has presented alternative methods to improve the business practices of your IT organization, increase the focus on your customer, and contribute to your organization's business objectives. We have provided real-world success stories of IT organizations that have selected and integrated a number of the IT business practices outlined in this book to achieve measurable outcomes.

In the immediate future, IT organizations will continue to focus on developing and refining their IT service management (ITSM) capabilities, including the adoption of ITIL, the industry best practice lifecycle framework. The adoption of ITSM capabilities happens at different rates based on the size, scope, and complexity of the IT organization. IT organizations will also continue to experience increasing pressure to lower IT costs, making the emerging body of knowledge around IT financial management critical to an IT organization's success. Conducting business case analysis before making IT investments, using the discipline of portfolio analysis to take a holistic view of your IT spending, and applying performance measures to determine how successful your IT organization is at implementing IT investments will improve service and lower costs. Although implementing these business practices in your IT organization may be challenging, doing so provides you with a range of opportunities to provide increased value to your customers, whether they are internal business units or external customers.

To help you move forward to improve service and lower costs, this chapter is divided into two major sections. The first summarizes some of the opportunities to use the methods presented in this book. We first discuss how you can use the ITIL Continual Service Improvement (CSI) framework to identify key areas for improvement. We then outline specific opportunities that are immediately available to most organizations to improve service and lower costs.

The second major section highlights some of the emerging trends that will occur over the next ten years related to IT business management and a number of associated opportunities. Indeed, organizations will likely see a convergence of IT and business, leading to successful organizations taking advantage of the opportunities to align their IT spending to business goals and objectives. Effective private sector IT organizations will generate more revenue, and public sector IT organizations will better serve citizens. Those organizations that capitalize on these activities will have a substantial competitive advantage and thrive in the future.

Opportunities to Improve IT Business Practices

All government, business, and nonprofit organizations are different. These differences influence how each individual organization adopts standardized business practices. However, a number of opportunities to improve IT business practices exist across all organizations. Although you can begin improving your IT business practices in any number of ways, from focusing on a specific process, such as financial management, to a specific opportunity, such as those outlined here, we recommend this: First, set your goals, then analyze the opportunities available to achieve your goals, and then develop a plan to achieve them. We recommend that you use the ITIL CSI framework to instill a culture of improvement—focusing on improving service and lowering costs—that will help your organization achieve these goals. We also recommend that you identify both near- and long-term opportunities, some of which are summarized next.

Using ITIL's CSI Model to Improve Service and Lower Costs

We recommend that you use the CSI model to identify and implement approaches to improve service and lower costs. This model helps you to identify key business objectives, evaluate where you are today, establish measurable targets, determine a path to reach your targets, and measure your outcome.

The model shown in Figure 9-1 highlights this approach. This CSI approach can be used to identify gaps in your IT service—including your organization/staff, technology, or key processes—to help you achieve both your long-term business objectives and near-term goals.

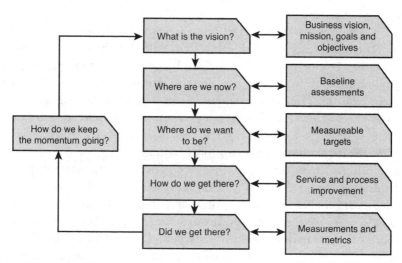

Figure 9-1   Adapted ITIL V3 CSI improvement model

As discussed in Chapter 2, "IT Service Lifecycle: Improving Business Performance," and Chapter 3, "Adopting IT Service Management Using ITIL," the CSI process to improve service should not be a one-time effort or simply a reaction to a given failure. Instead, an effective CSI process is embedded in the culture of your organization and occurs throughout the year and focuses on specific initiatives.

To identify which specific opportunities to address, you can leverage the three key elements of CSI. First, evaluate these opportunities based on the seven-step improvement process (service measurement and service reporting):

1. Define what you should measure.
2. Define what you can measure.
3. Gather the data.
4. Process the data.
5. Analyze the data.
6. Present and use the information.
7. Implement the corrective action.

Second, use the service measurement process to evaluate where your efforts are best targeted and whether they are effective. For example, if you decided to implement the key financial management processes outlined in Chapter 4, "IT Financial Management: The Business of IT," you may want to measure whether you are charging for the entire amount of the cost or value of a service, as defined by your IT accounting and service valuation activities. You can use this service measurement data to identify your need for improvement. Even if you are capturing all your costs or the entire value of the service, if your organization decides to set a business objective of lowering the cost of each service by 10 percent, you may initiate the seven-step process to lower the costs of your services. Similarly, if you are focused on leveraging the business case process outlined in Chapter 5, "IT Business Cases: Realizing IT Value," and the service portfolio management process outlined in Chapter 2, you may decide to measure the return on investment (ROI) of your IT spending. As a result, you may decide to focus your CSI efforts to improve the number of high-value IT sevices by 10 percent. Service measurement is critical to establishing and achieving these goals.

Finally, focus on service reporting, as discussed in Chapter 2 and in Chapter 6, "IT Performance Management: Defining Success." Through effective monitoring of IT performance based on business goals, you can proactively mitigate problems and challenges.

This CSI function, led by a CSI manager, will help to identify specific opportunities to improve service and lower costs. Although there are many opportunities, and they change based on your organization, we have summarized some specific typical opportunities here.

Specific Opportunities to Improve Service and Lower Cost

Many IT organizations need to improve service and lower costs, but the challenge is determining which improvement methods and approaches to apply to your IT organization. Each IT organization is unique. Key challenges for your IT organization are selecting the target areas for improvement, determining the optimal method for improving target areas, developing an organizational resourcing plan to support a change initiative, and binding and measuring each change initiative with a fixed timeline and performance goals that determine success or failure.

A common error IT organizations make is to attempt to execute a large number of improvement efforts simultaneously, with limited planning, focus, and organizational resourcing. To help you focus your efforts to improve service and lower costs, we have defined a list of potential methods and approaches discussed throughout the book and in common use in the IT industry today, as shown in Table 9-1.

Table 9-1 Focus Areas for Improving Services and Lowering Costs

Focus Area	Method/Approach	For More Information, See
Integrate and align IT and business goals.	Enhance your organization's IT business skills.	Chapter 7- IT Business Skills: Enabling Customer Outcomes
	Develop an effective service portfolio management process.	Chapter 3 - Adopting IT Service Management Using ITIL
	Implement performance management using cascading IT scorecards.	Chapter 6 - IT Performance Management: Defining Success
Optimize IT spending and achieve cost savings.	Implement a financial management framework.	Chapter 4 - IT Financial Management: The Business of IT
	Evaluate the ROI of immediate cost-cutting initiatives.	Chapter 5 - IT Business Cases: Realizing IT Value
	Financial management provides information needed to better manage the following: demand management, capacity management, and server and application consolidation.	
Improve the success rate of your IT projects.	Determine the financial performance of services.	Chapter 4 - IT Financial Management: The Business of IT
	Use standardized business cases to determine which IT projects to fund and measure ongoing performance of funded projects.	Chapter 5 - IT Business Cases: Realizing IT Value
	Utilize a performance management framework to measure portfolio performance.	Chapter 6 - IT Performance Management: Defining Success

Table 9-1 Focus Areas for Improving Services and Lowering Costs

Focus Area	Method/Approach	For More Information, See
Manage and lead IT service management initiatives.	Determine which industry best practice framework to adopt. Determine what components of the framework to implement, and plan and execute implementation. Utilize organizational change management to support service management initiatives.	Chapter 2 - IT Service Lifecycle: Improving Business Performance Chapter 3 - Adopting IT Service Management Using ITIL Chapter 7 - IT Business Skills: Enabling Customer Outcomes
Change the culture of your IT organization.	Execute an IT service management improvement initiative to improve service. Focus on the customer, beginning with a service catalog implementation or improvement. Focus on the customer with refined service/operational level agreements (SLAs/OLAs) as part of service portfolio management. Create a climate of accountability through financial tracking and measurement. Change the balance of the commitment of your IT resources to revenue growth and innovation, and reduce focus on infrastructure maintenance. Measure, measure, measure to create data to enable better decision making to achieve your strategy. Commit to developing your workforce. Align the organizational structure of your IT organization to a process-based approach aligned to the business. Reward success!	All chapters

Your IT organization is unique. Before starting any improvement initiative, you must first determine the current readiness of your IT organization for change. Only if your IT line managers and staff are ready for change will any of the change methods and approaches be effective. Timing links closely to organizational readiness for change. Many IT organizations operate on a unique annual cycle of peaks and valleys, matched to the business customers being supported. For example, within the IT organization of the Internal Revenue Service (IRS), change initiatives are not typically programmed for execution during filing season, which is a planned peak period for IT support within the IRS. You know the unique pattern to the demands on your IT organization, and you must plan your strategy for improvement within the reality of these constraints.

IT organizations are often successful at change when line managers and staff are able to recognize that their IT organization is either consistently failing to meet customer demands or is unable to keep up with normal maintenance (e.g., monthly, quarterly, or annual patch management). When your line managers and staff are ready for the message and promise of change, you can begin to analyze the various methods and approaches in use in IT organizations across a variety of industries and organizations, as presented in case studies of success in Chapter 8, "Success Stories: Improving Service and Lowering Costs," to determine what change initiative will provide the highest benefit to your IT organization while using the minimal amount of organizational resources to implement.

When your IT organization is ready for change, and you have selected the initial methods and approaches you plan to adopt in a phased implementation, you can begin to use this book as a guide to implementation to achieve higher service and lower costs.

The Future of IT Organizations

IT organizations will continue to evolve in the next decade. Competing demands on IT organizations will continue to require thoughtful analysis and decision making. You will see changes to your IT organization and should plan to proactively address these changes to continue to run your IT organization efficiently and effectively.

There are four critical focus areas for IT organizations going forward (see Figure 9-2).

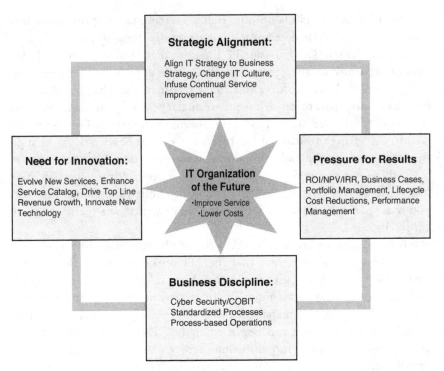

Figure 9-2   The four areas of IT organizations important to the future

These areas are:

- Strategic alignment of IT to the customer and enterprise
- Need for service innovation
- Pressure for results
- Enhanced business discipline

With the increased complexity of Information Technology and pressure for IT departments to improve their contributions to the business strategy, there will be an increasing convergence of IT and business. Whereas today most IT spending is focused on maintaining existing applications and infrastructure, in the future successful IT organizations will shift this balance and focus a majority of their resources on achieving business results. This shift will enable private-sector IT organizations to generate increased gross revenue and bottom-line profit, and will enable public-sector IT organizations to better serve their citizens.

Strategic Alignment of IT to the Customer and Enterprise

IT organizations must better align to their customers to be successful. This alignment has been elusive for many IT organizations and resulted in continued frustration between customers and IT organizations. As IT organizations adopt service management best practices such as ITIL to optimize the IT organization alignment to the strategy of the business, they will focus on the following two activities:

- **Aligning IT with buisness strategy and customer needs:** In their article "The Role of ITIL in Building the Enterprise of the Future,"[1] Art Murray and Mirghani Mohamad discuss how ITIL can provide an effective way to promote information flow and strengthen the entire IT organization. Instead of viewing the IT organization in specific functional units—such as the data center, the application management group, and the service desk—organizations can use the processes summarized in the service lifecycle to define a given service. Whether organizations adopt ITIL or other service management best practices, they will increasingly use these IT business practices to align themselves with the customer and overall buisness strategy.

- **Implementing cultural changes in the IT organization:** The cultural changes in the IT organization will continue to accelerate away from technology-focused culture to a service- and business-oriented culture. This culture will create challenges for technology-oriented staff who refuse to acknowledge the importance of the customer. Ultimately, however, those IT organizations and staff who do not focus on business outcomes will no longer be providing IT services.

- **Increasing importance of CSI function:** Best practice IT organizations will increasingly adopt a strong CSI function, seeking to improve service levels based on business objectives. Instead of reactive improvements, those organizations that use effective business intelligence and other performance measurement tools will identify those areas for improvement and exploit them.

Need for Service Innovation

While most IT organizational resources are currently applied to maintaining the existing infrastructure, the next decade will require IT organizations to achieve operational excellence in their daily operations and make available IT resources for more strategic IT operations. Strategic IT will allow the IT organization, and particularly the CIO, to drive profitable revenue growth for the organization and enable innovation in both technology and business discipline to make your IT organization a leader within your organization in growth and new product development.

- **Evolve new services and enhance the service catalog:** Organizations will shift funding away from spending most IT funding for simply maintaining existing IT infrastructure to devoloping new services as documented in a standard service catalog.
- **Drive Top Line Revenue Growth:** The most effective IT organizations will focus not only on lowering cost, but also on generating revenue. As demonstrated in Chapter 8, Forbes CIO Mykolas Rambus uses a project portfolio management process to identify the most valuable projects and services. As a result, these projects now drive top line revenue growth.

Pressure for Results

IT organizations are experiencing increased pressure to justify their funding. They need to implement more accurate financial management activities, from basic activities such as IT accounting to value added activities such as service investment analysis. At the portfolio level, IT organizations need to do more accurate, rigorous business case analysis using ROI methods before determining what IT investments to fund. After initial funding, IT organizations need to develop more accurate tracking of actual results by project against projected results. Using this comparison data, these IT organizations need to make more disciplined decisions about how to manage IT projects to completion, on time, and within budget. A performance management framework, properly implemented, can use information supplied by financial management to provide senior leadership of an organization more accurate, meaningful data to enable better decision making.

- **Integrated business and IT staff:** Business and IT staff will increasingly converge to develop a hybrid discipline. For example, the field of IT financial management will grow in increasing importance as organizations seek to know the cost of each IT service and measure how this service contributes to the organization's overall goals and more clear ROI.

- **Contribute to revenue and business objectives through business cases and portfolio management:** After developing this process to refocus on high-value projects based on the need for service innovation, the most effective IT organizations will focus on those projects that achieve business objectives, as measured by a clear ROI in standardized business cases. These business cases will help to optimize the overall service portfolio of IT organizations. Although Mr. Rambus, the CIO of Forbes.com, may currently be an exception, the most effective IT organizations will increasingly adopt these efforts.

Enhanced Business Discipline

IT organizations will increasingly use integrated best practice frameworks, such as COBIT, ITIL, and ISO, to enhance business discipline. Although clear differences exist between best practices (e.g., ISO 17799, ITIL, and COBIT), they will increasingly converge to provide a more integrated roadmap for improving IT business practices. In his article "Building Blocks of Process and Innovation,"[2] Jean-Pierre Garbani explains that ISO 17799 is the international standard for security management, ITIL helps guide service management, and COBIT addresses governance and control functions. Currently, a series of gaps and overlapping ideas exist between these frameworks. For example, many organizations struggle to connect their governance practices using COBIT with their IT service management efforts using ITIL. In the next ten years, these best practices will provide an increasingly better roadmap that will make clear how to move between one best practice and another.

As a result, organizations will use best practice frameworks to enforce business discipline. The best IT organizations will use these integrated best practices to enforce business discipline at the governance and operational level. For example, organizations will use a more integrated COBIT and ITIL to make decisions at the enterprise level and implement them throughout the organization. Or succesful IT organizations may decide to identify a larger business objective of increasing revenue and use ITIL financial management and service portfolio management to measure and screen projects to achieve this goal.

Conclusion

This book introduced a framework for determining what level of business discipline your IT organization will need in the future and how to potentially adopt an IT industry best practice framework—in this case ITIL V3—to help you achieve the desired future state of your IT organization. These practices will help your organization to continually adapt to both customer demands and emerging technologies. Given the increasing reliance on IT, developing effective means to improve service and lower costs will help you differentiate your organization. Simply put, it will help you make the IT organization and the business more competitive.

Endnotes

1. Art Murray and Mirghani Mohamad, "The Role of IT in Building the Enterprise of the Future," www.kmworld.com, (January 2007), 22–23.
2. Jean-Pierre Garbani, "Building Blocks of Process and Innovation," www.optimizemag. com, (November 2005), 93–95.

Appendix

Acronym List

A

AD	application development
AM	application maintenance

B

BSC	balanced scorecard
BCA	business case analysis
BPI	business process improvement

C

CMMI	Capability Maturity Model Integration
CAPEX	capital expenditure
C&A	Certification & Accreditation
CM	change management
CFO	chief financial officer
CIO	chief information officer
CNO	chief of naval operations
COO	chief operating officer
CTO	chief technology officer
CMDB	configuration management database
CONUS	continental United States
CSI	continual service improvement
COBIT	Control Objectives for Information and related Technologies

| CRM | customer relationship management |
| CARS | Cyber Asset Reduction and Security |

D

DIKW	data, information, knowledge, wisdom
DBR	desired business result
DR	disaster recovery
DCF	discounted cash flow

E

EVM	earned value management
EASE	ELAvate Approach to Solution Execution
EA	enterprise architect
ERP	enterprise resource planning

F

| FM | financial management |
| FTE | full-time equivalent |

G

| GIS | geographic information system |
| GDP | gross domestic product |

H

| HCM | human capital management |

I

IDP	individual development plan
IT	Information Technology
ITFM	Information Technology financial management
ITSCM	Information Technology Service Continuity Management
ITIL	Information Technology Infrastructure Library
ITSM	Information Technology service management
ITUAM	Information Technology Usage and Accounting Manager
IRR	internal rate of return
IBM	International Business Machines
ITT	Invitation to Tender

J

Not applicable

K

KPI	Key performance indicator

L

LSS	Lean Six Sigma
LOC	lines of code

M

MTTR	mean time to repair
MREJ	Microsoft's Rapid Economic Justification

N

NMCI	Navy-Marine Corps Intranet
NETWARCOM	Navy Network Warfare Command
NA	Neighborhood America
NPV	net present value

O

OGC	Office of Government Commerce
OLA	operating level agreement
O&M	operation and maintenance
OCONUS	Outside Continental United States

P–Q

PM	performance management
PMT	performance measurement team
PM	project management
PMBOK	Project Management Body of Knowledge
PMO	project management office
PMP	Project Management Professional
PRINCE2	Projects in Controlled Environments, Version 2
PTI	Public Technology, Inc.

R

RFC	requests for change
ROA	return on assets
ROI	return on investment

S

SC	service catalog
SCM	service catalog management
SC	service continuity
SDP	service design package
SIP	service improvement plan
SIA	service investment analysis
SLA	service level agreement
SLM	service level management
SPEC	Standard Performance Evaluation Corporation
SoR	Statement of Requirements
SOW	statement of work
SDLC	system development lifecycle

T

TUAM	Tivoli Usage and Accounting Manager
TSO	The Stationary Office
TCA	total cost of acquisition

TCO   total cost of ownership

TQM   Total Quality Management

TPC   Transaction Processing Performance Council

U–Z

U.K.   United Kingdom

Index

A

acceptance of ITIL in-progress surveys, 81-83

accounting, 92-93
managerial accounting, IT business skills, 227-228

actual costs, applying consistent methods to, 116

actual costs and comparing against your budget to prevent cost overruns, 119

AD (application development), IT scorecard, 203-205

adopting ITIL
identifying staff to help with, 59-61
selecting specific elements, 71-73

against budgets to prevent overruns, 119

aligning IT to the customer and enterprise, 261

AM (application maintenance), IT scorecard, 203-205

application development (AD) of IT scorecard activities, 203-205

application development organizations, 115

application maintenance (AM), IT scorecard activities, 203-205

assigning costs to services, 113

assumptions, business case structures, 163

automated tools, implementing to monitor resources, costs, and utilization, 129

averages, applying consistent methods to, 114-116

avoiding mistakes
with CSI, IT financial management, 108-109
when developing business case processes, 156

IBM Press
The Greening of IT:
How Companies Can Make a Difference for the Environment

John Lamb

0137150830 / 9780137150830
Available now

Read the following excerpt from
The Greening of IT...

Drawing on leading-edge experience, John Lamb helps you realistically assess the business case for green IT, set priorities, and overcome internal and external challenges to make it work. He offers proven solutions for issues ranging from organization obstacles to executive motivation and discusses crucial issues ranging from utility rate incentives to metrics. Along the way, you'll discover energy-saving opportunities—from virtualization and consolidation to cloud and grid computing—and solutions that will improve business flexibility as they reduce environmental impact.

Lamb presents case studies, checklists, and more—all the practical guidance you need to drive maximum bottom-line value from your green IT initiative.

All Companies Can Take Basic Steps Toward Green IT

According to Gartner research firm, the green wave has only begun to rise. The research company predicts that in 2009, more than one-third of all IT organizations will place environmental concerns among their top six buying criteria. By 2010, Gartner says, three-quarters of companies will use carbon-footprint considerations in calculating their hardware-buying strategy, and by 2011, large enterprises will develop policies requiring their suppliers to prove their green credentials through an auditing process.

Most companies are talking a good game but not actually going green where it counts. According to a survey of 124 IT operations by Forrester Research in May 2007, some 85 percent of respondents said environmental factors are important in planning IT operations. But only one-fourth of survey respondents have actually written green criteria into their company's purchasing processes. Enterprises that have started the green journey, however, have found that reducing total energy requirements can be accomplished through some fairly straightforward improvements that don't take years to implement or to bring return. The following six tasks are applicable to all green IT projects. Chapter 2, "The Basics of Green IT," gives details on the five steps used by IBM to implement green data centers. Those five green data center steps include the virtualize, cooling, and measure tasks in the following list. Also, Chapter 9, "Green IT Case Studies for Energy Utilities," and Chapter 10, "Green IT Case Studies for Universities and a Large Company," give details on the five steps used for case studies.

1. Communicate Green IT Plans and Appoint an Energy Czar

Measuring the current state of affairs, energy wise, is one of the first steps to take. A baseline on which to start measuring the impact of an organization's energy-saving initiatives in the green IT area is needed. Of course, you must also communicate your proposed energy-efficiency initiatives right away. Inform all employees about the plans and goals to save energy via green IT. Besides communicating with your employees, set up an organization to drive the effort. You may start by making one person responsible; give that person a title (like "Energy Czar"). Details on the importance of communication and collaboration for green IT is the subject of Chapter 3, "Collaboration Is Key for Green IT."

2. Consolidate and Virtualize

Consolidating IT operations, and using virtualization to reduce server footprint and energy use, are the most well-recognized and most-often-implemented efficiency strategies of the past few years. Some of the largest technology organizations in the world—including Advanced Micro Devices®, Hewlett-Packard®, Intel®, IBM, and Sun Microsystems®—have recently (2008) completed major data center consolidation projects. The projects also included server consolidation and virtualization. Details on the significance of virtualization for your IT systems in going to green data centers is the subject of Chapter 6, "A Most-Significant Step—'Virtualizing' Your IT Systems."

3. Install Energy-Efficient Cooling Units

In most cases, traditional data center design called for bulky **computer room air conditioners (CRAC)** units that are placed on the perimeter of the floor to move large amounts of air around the data center. However, in-row or supplemental cooling units have been shown to save energy. The in-row units typically enclose a row or two of servers, and the backs of all the servers are pointed into a single "hot" aisle. Heat in the aisle is contained by a roof and end-row doors, allowing cooling to be applied directly to the heat source, rather than trying to cool after the heat is dispersed into the general data center floor. Details on data center cooling strategies for green data centers are given in Chapter 8, "What About Chillers, Cooling Tower Fans, and All That Cooling Equipment Usually Ignored by IT?"

4. Measure and Optimize

In 2009, several groups (including the The Green Grid) are expected to release important deliverables in the form of metrics that businesses can use to measure the power-usage effectiveness of facilities infrastructure equipment. Most businesses can already readily identify areas where infrastructure optimization can achieve increased efficiency by simply monitoring and measuring their existing infrastructure equipment. The EPA is also working to create metrics. About 100 companies have indicated that they will provide raw power data and other information to the EPA for use in developing its new benchmark. The EPA indicated that the results of the benchmark should be available by 2010.

Until widely accepted metrics become available, businesses should make sure that the utility costs associated with their data center operations are broken out separately from those for other corporate facilities. In addition, metering specific equipment racks or types of equipment such as servers can provide valuable insight into which specific consolidation, virtualization, and optimization projects will yield the best ROI going forward. The status of energy-use metrics is the subject of Chapter 7, "The Need for Standard IT Energy-Use Metrics."

5. Implement Efficient Applications and Deduplicate Data

Software and application efficiency can be significant for green IT. The author has had a recent experience where the procedure for creating a data warehouse report was reduced from eight hours to eight minutes merely by changing the Oracle data warehouse search procedure. (For example, don't search the entire database each time when only a much smaller search is required.) During the eight hours required to create the report, the large server was running at near peak capacity. Sure, that type of significant application inefficiency has been created and fixed many times over the history of programming. But what about the cases where a few application efficiencies can make an application run 20 percent faster? That 20 percent more-efficient application can also result in 20 percent lower energy use. The steps required to improve application efficiency by a few percent are often not easy to determine; however, the added incentive of saving energy—while making the application run faster—is a significant plus.

Data-storage efficiency, such as the use of tiered storage, is also significant. **Data deduplication** (often called **intelligent compression** or **single-instance storage**) is a method of reducing storage needs by eliminating redundant data. Only one unique instance of the datum is actually retained on storage media, such as disk or tape. Redundant data are replaced with a pointer to the unique data copy. For example, a typical email system might contain 100 instances of the same one-megabyte (MB) file attachment. If the email platform is backed up or archived, all 100 instances are saved, requiring 100MB storage space. With data deduplication, only one instance of the attachment is actually stored; each subsequent instance is just referenced back to the single saved copy. In this example, a 100MB storage demand can be reduced to only one MB.

Data deduplication offers other benefits. Lower storage space requirements can save money on disk expenditures. The more efficient use of disk space also allows for longer disk-retention periods, which provides better **recovery time objectives (RTO)** for a longer time and reduces the need for tape backups. Data deduplication also reduces the data that must be sent across a WAN for remote backups, replication, and disaster recovery.

Data deduplication uses algorithms to dramatically compress the amount of storage space needed. Many organizations deal with increased scrutiny of electronically stored information because of various regulations; this need to preserve records is driving significant growth in demand for storing large sets of data. Depending on the type of information compressed, deduplication can enable a compression rate of between 3:1 and 10:1, allowing businesses to reduce their need for additional storage equipment and associated tapes and disks. Many businesses are already using the technology. Application efficiency as part of green IT strategy is discussed in Chapter 2.

6. Make Use of Rebates and Incentives

More utility providers offer rebates or other incentives that encourage businesses to update equipment and adopt efficient operational practices that can help reduce peak and total power demands. Companies doing this include Pacific Gas and Electric in San Francisco and Austin Energy in Austin, Texas.

New electric power-generation stations are very expensive, and power companies are more than willing to avoid building new capacity. Thus, the power companies encourage data center efficiency through rebates and other incentives. Also, the organization's facilities team doesn't have to build as much new data center space. The IT organization and engineering groups get new equipment that is smaller, cooler and faster than before—and everyone ends up happy. The roles of government and energy utility rebates and incentives are the subjects of Chapter 4, "The Government's Role—Regulation and EPA Activity," and Chapter 5, "The Magic of 'Incentive'—The Role of Electric Utilities."

What This Book Covers

This book includes the following topics to help you understand green data centers and your potential role in creating and maintaining them:

- The significant role data centers have in the world's consumption of electric energy and carbon footprint.

- How companies are offering services and products to help reduce data center energy use—for example, IBM's Big Green $1 billion annual investment in green data centers.

- How IT employees (for example, corporate CIOs (chief information officers), IT architects, IT specialists, and IT project managers) can help drive the implementation of green data centers.

- Case studies of organizations implementing green data centers.

- Details on the best ways to measure data center energy use and report to your executives. Because "You can't manage what you can't measure," the first step is to start the measurement process and understand the need to continually improve your measurement process. This is necessary to better quantify the savings due to your energy initiatives.

- Study of the different ways to measure server utilization and look at trends. You need to answer the question: How has customer server virtualization increased server CPU utilization?

- Continuing follow-up on the literature on green data centers because technology is progressing at a fast pace. The U.S. EPA is key to following the U.S. government recommendations and incentives for data center energy efficiency.

- Survey of emerging technology for server and storage enhancement to reduce data center energy use. This includes the following:

  - **Information Lifecycle Management** (ILM), overall storage management, tiered storage

  - Server virtualization enhancements such as PowerVM®, VMware enhancements, and such

  - Active energy management

  - Enhanced cooling technology

- Analysis of emerging technology for server and storage enhancement to reduce data center energy use.

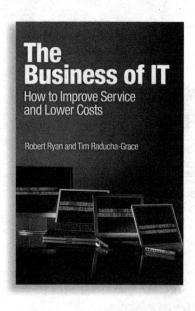

FREE Online Edition

Your purchase of *The Business of IT* includes access to a free online edition for 45 days through the Safari Books Online subscription service. Nearly every IBM Press book is available online through Safari Books Online, along with more than 5,000 other technical books and videos from publishers such as Addison-Wesley Professional, Cisco Press, Exam Cram, O'Reilly, Prentice Hall, Que, and Sams.

SAFARI BOOKS ONLINE allows you to search for a specific answer, cut and paste code, download chapters, and stay current with emerging technologies.

Activate your FREE Online Edition at www.informit.com/safarifree

> **STEP 1:** Enter the coupon code: ATVYWWA.

> **STEP 2:** New Safari users, complete the brief registration form. Safari subscribers, just log in.

If you have difficulty registering on Safari or accessing the online edition, please e-mail customer-service@safaribooksonline.com